7·15

A Little Too Close To God

0   25 miles

0   25 km

Mediterranean Sea

LEBANON

Marjayoun

SYRIA

Kiryat
Shmonah

**Golan
Heights**

*Sea of
Galilee*

Zichron Ya'acov

Naharayim

Jordan River

ISRAEL

Tel Aviv

West Bank

Motza
Beit
Shemesh
Ilit
Jerusalem
Jericho

Ofra

Nitsanim Beach

Bethlehem

Gaza Strip
Gaza

Hebron

*Dead
Sea*

Khan Yunis

JORDAN

EGYPT

Petra

Eilat

Aqaba

A Little Too Close to God

The Thrills and Panic of a Life in Israel

David Horovitz

ALFRED A. KNOPF   NEW YORK   2000

Grateful acknowledgment is made to ACUM Ltd., Israel, for permisssion
to reprint an excerpt from "Count to Ten" by Coby Oz, copyright © 1997
by Coby Oz; and an excerpt from "Song for Peace" by Ya'acov Rotblit,
copyright © 1967 by Ya'acov Rotblit. Reprinted by permission.

ISBN: 0-375-40381-7
LC: 00-102087

For Lisa,
Josh, Adam, and Kayla

Contents

A Little Too Close to God

The Dream and the Reality

Things that were unthinkable yesterday
suddenly, today, they're here.
And what used to be safe and familiar
won't be, tomorrow.
Count to ten
don't get angry
and start from the beginning.
You've got something to say
so don't give up
but choose your words carefully.

—From "Count to Ten," a song by the Israeli pop group
Tea Packs

On the Wednesday, I ate a late lunch with Sharon and Alvin, two colleagues from work, at the Village Green, a vegetarian restaurant on Ben-Yehuda Street. We sat in the shade of a sun umbrella, munching our bean sprouts, gloomily comparing the sizes of our overdrafts.

By Thursday afternoon, the Village Green looked a little different. Its huge plate-glass storefront window had been shattered, its wooden chairs reduced to firewood. A young man in his early twenties, a Palestinian, had strolled along Ben-Yehuda at around three o'clock carrying a traveling bag, conversing easily with two of his friends. He had stopped outside the Village Green; his friends had positioned themselves outside two other shops nearby. Then all three of them had pressed their buttons—three, so that their recruiters could emphasize how many were ready to die for the cause.

For hours afterward, rescue workers were mopping up their blood and scraping bits of their dismembered bodies off the walls and the tables and the chairs at the Village Green, off the fedoras and the trilbies in the display cases at Fuerster's Hat Shop farther up the road, off the bridal gown hanging lopsidedly from the mutilated mannequin in the dress shop next door.

Their blood, and the blood of the five Israelis they had killed.

While hundreds of horrified, ghoulishly curious Jerusalemites were kept behind police barriers all along the street, I walked through the bomb zone with the devastation still fresh. Wonderful thing, a press card. It gets you access to places other folks just can't go near. I looked at a large chunk of a bomber's torso oozing blood from beneath a piece of white plastic sheeting. I heard one of the rescue workers call out from a café, as I scrunched past on the broken glass, "Aaron, there's a foot here." I smelled the faint but unmistakable odor of burned flesh—just like a summer barbecue, made revolting only by the context. And I saw the remains of that green sun umbrella we'd sat under twenty-four hours earlier at the Village Green. The cloth had been ripped away by the force of the blast, but the white metal frame was still there, spattered with blood. Chunks of human flesh were hanging from it, like scraps in a deranged butcher's display.

Almost everybody who has ever been to Israel has walked down Ben-Yehuda Street. My wife, Lisa, when we were at university, used to waitress at the Village Green; her roommate waitressed at the café across the street. Ben-Yehuda is where American seminary students hang out when ducking classes, where tourists shop for souvenirs, where locals grab a cheap felafel or shwarma lunch, where the tarot-card readers and the astrologers drink Turkish coffee during the long waits between gullible customers, where the disciples manning the outreach stand of the late Lubavitcher Rebbe attempt to persuade the secular male pedestrian traffic to don a skullcap, strap on tefillin (phylacteries), and say a prayer. And so, more than with any of the dozen-plus suicide bombings in the past few years, this Ben-Yehuda blast had everybody thinking, That could have been me.

But it really, *really* could have been me—and Sharon and Alvin. All we'd have had to do was eat lunch at the Village Green on Thursday instead of Wednesday.

My wife and I, naturally, discussed at length my closeish brush with death (as compared to the general, ongoing, slightly more distant brushes with death—the blasts in the vegetable markets where we sometimes shop, the late-night shootings on roads we've often used—to which all of us in Israel have tried to become accustomed over the years). But, you'll understand, we did not raise the matter of Daddy's lucky break with our eldest son, Josh, who was only five at the time. Still, the raw details of the bombing did not escape him, nor did we try to shield him from them completely. This is our reality, his reality, and he has to deal with it somehow, while his parents offer reassurance and try to explain the inexplicable. He watched news reports on television, overheard conversations, saw the newspaper photographs. His kindergarten teacher had the kids sit in a circle, their open, innocent faces turned anxiously toward her, to talk about the bomb, their fears, the dead people, the bad guys who had come to Jerusalem to kill.

And three days later, after Josh's five-year-old mind had done its best to grapple with the overload, as his mother and I and his younger brother and his baby sister drove home together from my office in late afternoon, he blurted out from the backseat: "If you both get killed, who's going to make our sandwiches?"

In a way, it is because of that question that I've written this book. Because my generous, sensitive eldest child, whom I've had the arrogance, or the stubbornness, or the blindness, or the faith, to try to bring up in Israel, is so attuned to the wicked violence of the world into which I've pitched him that he has already partly reconciled himself to the loss of either his mummy or his daddy and now is progressing toward preparing for the loss of us both. People are dying everywhere, he was saying, and I don't understand why. I'm scared one of you is going to die too, and that would be terrible. But what am I going to do, what is Adam going to do, what is Kayla going to do, if you *both* get killed? Who's going to wash us and dress us and read to us and hug us? And who's going to make our sandwiches for kindergarten?

I know that putting this down on paper isn't going to alter anything dramatically. It won't stop the bombs or alleviate the hatreds. But it just might open some minds. And it might help me clarify my own thinking about living here: Whether I owe it to my family to keep doing what I came here for in the first place—playing a unique role, however small, in shaping the first Jewish state in two thousand years, completing a circle of history, bringing our modern Jewish family back to the land of its roots, to the city where my ancient royal namesake built his capital three thousand years ago, to be free, a majority, in our own country, to make our own decisions, and then live and die by them. Or whether Lisa and I ought to take the kids somewhere calmer and safer. I have the arrogance to worry about how growing up in a West Bank settlement may impact my sister's children, but what am I doing to my own, exposing them to all the anger and bloodshed? When you have children, you take more care crossing the road, you drive a touch more carefully. And, in my case, you start looking more deeply at how and where you're living, your reasons for being here, and whether they're still valid—whether what was right for a student, or a single man in his twenties, is right for a married man with three kids a decade later.

The theory, the way I absorbed it through years of largely mediocre Jewish education in London, was that this Israel was supposed to be the safe haven for the Jews, the refuge for the persecuted people, the democratic, free, independent homeland, awash in a sea of Arab hostility but holding its own and slowly rolling back the tide of hatred, gradually eliminating the existential threats, making its peace with its neighbors.

But it has not turned out that way—not completely, not yet. We have proved ourselves, gloriously, as a safe haven for Jewish people, a country that, had it existed at the time of the Holocaust, would have saved millions of lives. We have gathered hundreds of thousands of Jews over the decades from the countries of the Middle East, from North Africa, from all over Europe. In the past few years alone we have opened our doors to people from Syria and Yemen and Iran and Iraq, when Jewish life there became unlivable. While the combined might and resources of the Western world struggled to cope with the hundreds of thousands of ethnic Albanians made homeless in 1999 by the conflict in Kosovo, Israel, in the course of the 1990s, took in 800,000 Jews from the former Soviet Union— flew them here, housed them, gave them money to get on their feet, found jobs for them.

At the height of the Kosovo crisis, in May 1999, I flew on a Jewish Agency aid plane to Albania, carrying clothes and school supplies and toiletries, financed by private Israeli and American Jewish donations. We landed at Tirana Airport—a strip of tarmac in the countryside with rows of NATO helicopters lined up on either side—and were bused into the capital, where several thousand Kosovo Albanians were living in tents around the commandeered outdoor public swimming

7

pool. The younger generation assured us that they would be going home soon; their parents and grandparents said far less, more conscious of the uncertainties that lay ahead. All of them were helpless, stranded, their lives in limbo. And then we flew on to Budapest, where 400 Jews from Belgrade were taking refuge in a Jewish-owned hotel while NATO bombed their capital. Most of them, too, assured us that they would be returning in a matter of days, but 30 of them—mainly in their late teens and early twenties—flew back with us to Israel, to try out life in the Jewish state. Another 150 had already made the journey. So while the world dithered about the ethnic Albanians, Israel was sending out its planes to collect the Jews, Jews who had never wanted Israel, who had assumed their country was stable and never dreamed they would need Israel. Israel helped pay for their hotel stay in Hungary. It paid for their flights to Tel Aviv. It lodged them in absorption centers, organized sightseeing tours and Hebrew classes, gave them pocket money, offered them automatic citizenship and every opportunity to stay. Many did. I felt proud to be flying back with them, proud of my country, proud that it was there for them.

But as for rolling back the tide of hatred and making our peace with the neighbors, here our record is less commendable. And while it would be comfortable and comforting to place all the blame for our woes on the other side, the Arabs, we have often been as pigheaded and racist and proprietary as they are, if not more so. For the three years that Benjamin Netanyahu misruled Israel, between 1996 and 1999, we made no real effort to reach peace with Syria, a peace that would also have put a halt to our miniwar with Lebanon. Only with the election of Ehud Barak as prime minister, in 1999, did that quest resume in earnest. Jordan did make peace with us, in 1994, a warm peace that saw the late King Hussein popping over to Israel just to say hello, like any ordinary neighbor.

Netanyahu rewarded him, in the late summer of 1997, by sending a team of Mossad hit men to assassinate one of his citizens, in broad daylight, on the streets of his capital, using the kind of terrifying chemical agent that we are so horrified to see Iraq and Iran developing. Our most awkward enemies, the Palestinians, who unfortunately happen to be living on much of the same land that we covet for ourselves, claimed to have chosen the path of coexistence a full decade ago, embracing the "two-state" solution—each side settling for an equitable share of the territory. When our prime minister of the day, Yitzhak Rabin, attempted to negotiate the formal separation, one of our own people, a purportedly Orthodox Jew, gunned him down.

Of course, it is not all as simple as that. Not much is in these parts. But, to some extent, we've spurned opportunities for peace because we've convinced ourselves that the Arabs are lying, that they are tricking us about their good intentions. Some of us seem to be waiting for every single Palestinian and Jordanian and Syrian to declare their love for us before we reconcile ourselves to them. And some of us, I think, although few Israelis would admit it, have even come to rather like being the big, bad guy on the block, the uncompromising toughie whom everybody would love to bring down but can't. The pre-state desire to build a tough Jewish nation, a self-sufficient people that nobody, not the Nazis, not the Arabs, could ever again render defenseless, has become embedded and sometimes exaggerated in our psyche. The power, our power, has gone to some of our heads.

In a recent Jewish New Year special issue, the Hebrew daily newspaper *Ma'ariv* published a commemorative magazine of photographs, landmark moments in our evolution. And there, in this slim volume of black-and-white images and short paragraphs of text, was encapsulated not only our awe-inspiring rebirth and rise to power, but also our fall from its graceful use. Israel has never been an easy place to live. It was born amid controversy, sanctioned by a world seeking to provide recompense to the Jews for the World War II extermination of their millions, but at no small cost to the hundreds of thousands of Arabs of Palestine. It was formally established, in May 1948, in the midst of hostilities intended by the Arab world to kill it before it could draw breath. And not a decade has since gone by without a major war and dozens of minor confrontations.

But the nature of those conflicts has changed as the years have passed, the relative moralities of the warring parties have shifted. And this matters. Because in the early pages of that *Ma'ariv* commemorative magazine, Israel is a gutsy young nation whose leadership and population cry out for peace but will struggle bravely through the wars imposed on them. Here is David Ben-Gurion, our first prime minister, reading out the "Declaration of Independence" in Tel Aviv in May 1948, with its call to the Arab peoples to make their peace with the new/old Jewish entity in their midst, a call issued even as the fighting gathers intensity. There, eight years later, is an anonymous kibbutz member turned soldier, easy but not arrogant with success at the culmination of the 1956 fighting in the Sinai. Then we see Rabin, the chief of staff in the 1967 Six-Day War caught unawares by the camera as he prepares to make his victory speech on Jerusalem's Mount Scopus, a speech in which he will talk, modestly, of a historic military achievement tinged with sadness for the fallen sons of Israel and the fallen Arab fighters.

Those were difficult days, but, at the risk of romanticizing a period long before my own time here, days apparently colored by generosity of spirit, by a national will for reconciliation; a belief that each war would be the last war or, if not, that it would be *one* of the last wars—that there would, someday soon, be a last war—and that Israel would finally find its quiet place in the region.

But our greatest military victory, that destruction of the Arab air forces at the start of the Six-Day War, the capture of the Sinai desert and the Gaza Strip and the Golan Heights and, especially, Jerusalem's Old City and the land on the West Bank of the Jordan River, turned out to be the start of our corruption. For somewhere in the national mentality, a latent messianism was reignited, an urge to call in an ancient debt: to reassert Jewish rule over all the territory that the God of Abraham and Moses willed us in the pages of the Bible. So now, in the *Ma'ariv* album, the photographs show the divine assurance in the arrogant posture of Rabbi Moshe Levinger, seated on the shoulders of his admiring supporters, defying the 1975 Rabin government by founding a Jewish settlement deep inside the captured West Bank. Flip the page and you face the last moments in the life of Emil Grunzweig, murdered by a right-wing Israeli during a left-wing protest against Israel's reckless invasion of Lebanon in 1982. We see the bitter yet confused features of an Israeli soldier in Gaza in the early days of the Palestinian Intifada in 1987, helmeted and kitted out with rifle and grenade launcher, yet helpless and uncertain in the midst of a milling swarm of Palestinian teenagers armed only with rocks and the frustrated recklessness born of twenty years of Israeli occupation. And finally, in October 1995, the camera immortalizes the venom in the eyes of a group of Jewish demonstrators, brandishing placards that denounce Rabin as a traitor for trying to make peace with the Palestinians, for daring to trade some of that God-given land—stigmatizing him with the perverted charge of treason that, a month later, would lead to his assassination in Tel Aviv.

It was a gradual descent from the moral high ground, so gradual that, even when we hit rock bottom with Rabin's assassination, we refused to acknowledge how low we had sunk. Four days after the prime minister was killed, the rabbinical leaders of the Orthodox community from which his assassin had emerged held a public meeting at Beit Agron, in central Jerusalem, at which one bearded sage after another rose to defend the values that Yigal Amir, the gunman, had absorbed, to argue in the face of all evidence that they bore no blame for the killing and the seething climate in which it had occurred, to castigate more moderate and secular Israelis—the hated "left"—for pointing the finger of blame in their direction. The one brave, foolhardy rabbi, Yoel Bin-Nun, who stood up to ridicule the delusionary effort at self-defense and who alleged that one or more unnamed rabbis had actually sanctioned the assassination, found himself threatened and ostracized by parts of his community.

In the murder of our military hero turned peacemaker, by one of his own Jewish people, we lost the last vestiges of our innocence.

At the end of the millennium, to live in Israel was to alternate between hope and despair, as the progress under Rabin gave way to the fatuous posturing of Netanyahu, replaced, in turn, by Rabin's would-be heir, Barak. Peace seemed close at hand, then receded, then came closer again. Our military superiority was challenged by Iran's drive to nuclear self-sufficiency and by the relentless attacks of the Hamas bombers and the Hizbollah gunmen on our northern border. Intifada violence flared intermittently. The spiritual father of the Hamas suicide bombers, Sheikh Ahmad Yassin, assured his extremist Islamic followers that Israel wouldn't be around much longer. And in the lower ebbs—especially when you read census figures predicting that the 1 million Palestinians of 1978, grown to 3 million today, would become 7.5 million by 2025, while we are 5 million Jews in 1999—it was hard to deride him.

Even more damagingly, we Israelis ourselves were dis-
united and bickering, grappling not only with internal rifts
over the viability of making peace with our neighbors but with
divides between the established Jews of European origin (the
Ashkenazim) and those who came here, in poverty, from the
Middle East and North Africa (the Sephardim), between Jews
who cleave to the most zealous interpretations of God's law
and those who seek a more pluralistic approach to their faith,
and between our Jewish nation here in Israel and our fellow
Jews who live overseas.

Barely fifty and heading into terminal decline? I hope not.
I'd like to think of the late 1990s as our national coming-of-
age, with the customary frustrations and growing pains, our
maturity finally demonstrated in 1999 in our repudiation of
the hate-mongering Netanyahu and our preference for a
leader, Barak, seeking to achieve the near-impossible: leading
us to peace and healing our internal divisions.

I want to believe that half a century from now, my children,
grandchildren, and great-grandchildren will be celebrating
the Israeli centenary and laughing gently at the concerns we
are grappling with today, that we will have long since divided
this land equitably with the Palestinians and the Syrians, and
opened our borders to each other. I want to believe that Israelis up north won't be ducking into bomb shelters because
of rocket fire from Lebanon, nor Israelis in Tel Aviv hiding
underground to evade missiles from Iraq—that people, in
short, won't be dying senseless, premature deaths; that the
awful cycle of violence will have long since been broken.

I want to believe, moreover, that ours will be a Jewish
country in the moral sense—a country admired for its ethical
fiber, a genuine light unto the nations. I hope we will be a
country, for example, ready not only to airlift Ethiopian Jews
out of a life-threatening civil war—as we did in bringing fifteen thousand "home" to Israel on a single weekend in 1991—

13

but to open our doors to other persecuted peoples as well. In the spring of 1999 we hardly excelled on that score: We rapidly repatriated to Egypt a few hundred Bedouin who had crossed the border to join relatives inside Israel and who claimed that a feud with another tribe was placing their lives in danger; and while we welcomed the Jews displaced by the Kosovo crisis, we found room for just two hundred Albanians—plucked arbitrarily from among tens of thousands at a refugee camp on the Macedonian border—bringing the first group in on Holocaust Memorial Day, a coincidence that ought surely to have helped prompt a greater generosity of spirit. Netanyahu, milking their arrival for all it was worth on the tarmac at Ben-Gurion Airport, carelessly described this tiniest of gestures as the fulfillment of a "symbolic obligation"—"symbolic" being the operative word.

Israel, at once a moral Jewish state and a normal state—is it attainable? Well, that is the dream that sustains me here.

All the Jews of modern Israel are engaged in an ongoing experiment. And all of us, by being here, living the kinds of lives we do, and fighting for the causes we believe in, are determining how the experiment turns out. We have had our amazing successes: We have resuscitated a Jewish national entity on the very land where the Jewish people flourished thousands of years ago, its modern-day inhabitants able to gaze at the same golden landscape, climb the same gentle Jerusalem hills, bathe in the same Mediterranean waters. We have taken Hebrew out of the pages of our holy books and transformed it into a living, breathing language—the language my children speak as naturally as the native English of their parents. We have built a first-world economy and are on the cutting edge of science and technology. Rescuing those persecuted Jews from around the world, we have grown tenfold. And if we made a hash of the early absorption efforts in the 1940s and 1950s—brutally severing Sephardim from their traditions and trying to impose a secular, socialist lifestyle—we have tried to do better in the 1980s and 1990s, with some success with the Russians and rather less with the Ethiopians.

But many of the challenges are still ahead of us, and that is why, when things seem to be going backward, it gets so depressing here. Our democracy is not as stable as many of us would like to believe. We have killed one prime minister, and the potential for further political violence is undeniable. Death threats to politicians and judges are now routine. Our leaders move around in cordons of bodyguards.

There are powerful forces here for whom Orthodoxy is a priority and democracy an irritant. At precisely the same time the U.S. chief justice was presiding over the nonremoval of President Clinton from office in February 1999, and praising the robustness of American democracy and the high standard of the Senate hearings, our Supreme Court was coming under attack by our ultra-Orthodox politicians, its president derided by one legislator as a "Jew-hater" for having had the temerity to intervene in issues of birth, marriage, and burial that the ultra-Orthodox regard as their exclusive purview. The state's chief rabbis participated in a demonstration attended by hundreds of thousands of ultra-Orthodox Jews, called by the community's political leaders to challenge the Supreme Court's authority. Police were assigned to surround the Supreme Court complex itself for fear, unfounded this time, that the demonstrators would march on the building as they had two years before. We defenders of democracy were reduced to holding a counterdemonstration in the park below the Court, garnering a far smaller turnout, to chant our support for the embattled judges within. And none of our leading political figures, terrified of alienating ultra-Orthodox voters, chose to attend.

A few months later, when the Jerusalem District Court found Aryeh Deri, leader of the ultra-Orthodox Shas political party, guilty of bribe-taking, and sentenced him to four years in jail, Deri's rabbi simply rejected the court's ruling and declared that "Reb Aryeh is innocent." And again, terrified of the ultra-Orthodox influence at the ballot box, our mainstream political leaders failed to immediately break their ties with Deri, failed even to suspend him from the Knesset (parliament). In the elections of 1999, more than 400,000 Israelis voted for Deri's party, giving it 17 of the 120 Knesset seats; they voted Shas even though the party was led by a convicted criminal, even though his campaign was essentially a rejection of the rule of law here, even though Shas would like to turn Israel into a theocracy. The Shas supporters, mainly working-class Sephardim, backed Deri not because he was challenging our democracy, but because that democracy had failed them— because the state schools in their development towns are run-down and overcrowded, because job opportunities are scarce, because they live in poverty—and because he promised to use his influence to right those wrongs. If the government does not reach out to these people in the next few years, if it does not reallocate its funds to give them better schools, create jobs, and draw them into the mainstream, Shas and the other antidemocratic, ultra-Orthodox political movements, taking their adherents out of the workforce and into dependent, full-time Torah study, will flourish, and Israel will decline.

And yet, to look at the glass half-full, the Supreme Court remains independent, fights antidemocratic legislation, pushes for pluralism. Deri eventually had to resign his Knesset seat. And if his appeal is denied, he will go to jail. He and his supporters may hold his rabbi's word to be law, but the courts, for now, prevail.

We are still trying to find a middle ground on religion, to build a framework in which all our citizens can freely practice their own interpretation of their faith. The Orthodox-secular conflicts are vicious. And yet, in the last few years, small outreach groups have sprung up and flourished, ordinary people from different religious worlds sitting down to talk through their differences. And I have found, even in increasingly ultra-Orthodox Jerusalem, a framework for Judaism that is perfect for my family. I love the fact that my children are living in a Jewish environment, where it is the Hebrew date that gets written on the chalkboard in their classroom in the morning, where they learn about Jewish festivals in their regular curriculum, not at Sunday school, and where they experience those festivals with their entire nation. We can buy Chanukah doughnuts at every bakery in town. We see menorahs lighting tens of thousands of apartment windows. We shop in supermarkets bursting with matzoh every Passover. We put up a sukkah each year, just like our ancient forebears did in the desert, and hear the same hammering all along our street. My blond, blue-eyed Adam, in one of the more innovative casting choices of our age, was dressed up in his kindergarten class last Pentecost in the white headdress and flowing robes of an Ethiopian Jew, to participate in a reenactment of that group's arrival in the Promised Land.

It is at once enchanting and terrifying living an experiment. We take everything to heart, see every shift as potentially decisive. It is profoundly unsettling—a roller-coaster ride. But it's addictive.

The harshest blow, the biggest threat so far to the success of our experiment, was the murder.

For three years and four months, beginning with the nail-biting election day of June 23, 1992, when Yitzhak Rabin just squeezed into power, he gave many of us the delighted sense that Israel was settling into the Middle East. The years of Likud rule, of settlement-building and diplomatic stonewalling, when peace with Egypt had signally failed to yield peace with anybody else, were receding into the haze. Rabin was bringing

Israel and himself full circle, the former army chief relinquishing the Arab territory he had captured, and winning normalized neighborly relations in return.

That glorious delusion was blown apart by three bullets fired at almost point-blank range on the dark night of November 4, 1995. One of the bullets missed its mark and wounded a bodyguard. But the other two found their target—Rabin's unprotected back—and felled him. The assassin was not deranged. He was not poorly educated. He was no one's patsy. Amir was a former combat soldier, in his second year of law school at a Tel Aviv university. And he was a fixture at the university's "Kolel," the Jewish study center where the best and the brightest minds wrestled with the rabbinical arguments over all aspects of man's relationship with his fellow man and with his God, as conducted within the pages of the Mishneh, the Gemara, and other holy texts.

Amir acted alone that night. There was no one with him in the bedroom of his Herzliyya home as he alternately loaded ordinary and hollowed-out bullets (for extra penetration) into the magazine of his pistol, tucked it into the waistband of his trousers, and walked off to catch a bus to the Tel Aviv square where the prime minister was speaking. But as Amir stepped out of the shadows and squeezed his trigger, he knew he was fulfilling the fervent wish of scores, maybe hundreds, of his fellow Israelis, and that thousands more would not be grieving for the soldier-statesman he was cutting down.

I'm not exaggerating. Nice, easygoing, normal Israelis, people I have worked with, had coffee with, played soccer with, told me right after the murder, while our nation was supposedly deep in shock, revulsion, and soul-searching, that, yes, maybe murder was a bit drastic, but Rabin did have to be stopped. "It's a shame it had to end this way," one of my soccer mates said with a kind of helpless shrug—a shrug that intimated that, while he wouldn't actually have loaded his own pistol and gone out stalking Rabin, he wouldn't have stood in Amir's way.

Amir gauged public sentiment shrewdly. As the student organizer of solidarity visits to the settlers of the occupied West Bank, panicked at the prospect of Arafat gaining control of their valleys and hilltops, Amir had heard the anti-Rabin vitriol, the charges that the government, resting as it did on the support of Arab members of Knesset, was "illegitimate," the assertion that the prime minister was abandoning the brave, selfless, pioneering West Bank Jews to be murdered by the vicious Arab masses who encircled them. Politically astute and involved, Amir had attended rallies organized by Netanyahu's right-wing opposition camp; heard the chants of "Rabin is a traitor," "Rabin is the son of a whore," "Rabin is a murderer"; listened as "respectable" politicians vilified the prime minister for leading his country "to the gates of Auschwitz" by making "a pact with the devil"—Arafat.

Amir told the policemen who grabbed him after the fatal shots had been fired that he had expected to die for the sake of his mission. But he survived. And now he sits in solitary confinement in a cell in the desert town of Beersheba, sustained by a flow of admiring letters, by the knowledge that Orthodox teenage girls tape his picture to their bedroom walls, by his mother's unflagging love—and by the confidence that the supporters who gather outside the jail to celebrate his birthdays will, sooner or later, muster the clout to have him released. He will be freed not for good behavior, he knows, nor on compassionate grounds in his frail old age. No, he will be freed as a hero, a savior, the only man in the country, as his sister once put it, who had the guts to demonstrate how deep was his love for his people.

Alongside the achievements of our young nation, the

murder of Rabin—not by an Arab extremist but by one of his own countrymen—exposed our malaise. It underlined our polarizations, our political and religious divides. And if we cannot heal those rifts, they will grow to overshadow our successes. If we let them, our internal disputes, our anger, cynicism, mistrust, and intolerance, will destroy our society, ruin our relationship with Diaspora Jews, return us to our status of international pariah.

Under Rabin's predecessor, Yitzhak Shamir, I had been dismayed at the determination to spend most available resources on settlement expansion—complicating the prospects of an accord with the Palestinians—to the detriment of other pressing needs, notably building homes and creating jobs for the immigrants from the former Soviet Union. But I had somehow assumed that the wrongs would be put right, and Rabin's election appeared to confirm that. By the time Rabin was murdered, I had two children, and that meant my life had become much more deeply intertwined with that of the country. I could no longer afford to assume that the wrongs would be put right. For one thing, I began to doubt that they would; if they were not, I now had a family that was going to suffer—that I was putting at risk by living here. I had two boys who would one day be conscripted. Before Rabin was killed, I honestly never thought twice about whether I had done the right thing in moving here. Since November 4, 1995, not a week has gone by when I haven't agonized about the choice.

My own wider family—some of them Israelis since the start of the experiment, many of them more recent participants, plenty of them overseas—while overwhelmingly warm and tolerant, happens to reflect many of the divisions afflicting our society. I have relatives who live in West Bank settlements and cousins who attend right-wing rallies—and aunts and uncles who won't even visit the country unless it relinquishes every last inch of the territory captured during the 1967 war. Some of my relatives live in ultra-Orthodox neighborhoods of Jerusalem and study Jewish texts from dawn to dusk. Others have married gentiles. None of this is unique. Nor is it unusual that, as a journalist, I have met a lot of politicians and covered some of the more dramatic incidents of recent years here. But it gives me the opportunity to paint what is at once a personal and a wide-ranging picture of Israel, one whose themes and arguments are drawn from my own experiences.

This is not a comprehensive picture of Israel. There is nothing much here about Israeli Arabs, little about the Sephardic community. It is my Israel, my Western immigrant's Israel, my very politicized Israel—with my mistakes, my prejudices.

I apologize in advance to anybody who feels upset by the way they have been depicted in this book. In some cases, I've changed names and personal details. I know some readers will be offended by some of what follows—there are still so many well-intentioned supporters of Israel to whom the very notion of a Jew writing something uncomplimentary about the Jewish state smacks of treachery. I know, too, that politicians do not take kindly to being stripped of their bombast, and that rabbis do not like to be accused of perverting the faith. In my defense, I say only that I cherish the quirk of history that has given me the opportunity to live in the first independent Jewish state for two millennia, and that, rather than sit by apathetically and wonder whether it is about to sink irrevocably into a morass of avoidable hatred and conflict, the least I can do is try to sound the alarm—and argue for a country in which I can be confident and proud to raise my family.

Chapter One

On Being Here

I write this letter in a desperate attempt to find some remnant of my family who perished in the Holocaust. My name is Leo Laufer. I was born in Lodz, Poland. In the course of World War II, I spent close to five years in slave labor and concentration camps, including a year-and-a-half at Auschwitz-Birkenau. . . .

—From a 1981 letter to the newspaper *Ma'ariv*

It was a Russian immigrant who asked me, after I had been living here for about eleven years, Why? He was a thin, high-cheekboned young soldier named Alexander who had the misfortune to be serving with the Israel Defense Forces in Khan Yunis, an overcrowded, impoverished refugee-camp town in the Gaza Strip. As part of my army reservist's service, I had given a lecture at his base, and he approached me at the end. Why? he wondered, genuinely puzzled. Why was I living in Israel?

Because I'm Jewish, I said, and because Israel is the home of the Jews.

Was it difficult being Jewish in England, Alexander wondered, like in the old Soviet Union? Was I denied a place at university, as he had been? Kept out of certain jobs? Forbidden to travel overseas?

No, none of that, I had to admit. There was an undercurrent of anti-Semitism, the odd snide remark in the streets, a fight here and there. But no, there was nothing life-threatening.

So, he persisted, why uproot yourself from such a haven of Western culture and civilization for a conflict-bedeviled strip of desert in the Middle East?

I talked about the rare opportunity to live in a Jewish state, about building a liberal, democratic society, and about spreading the notion of equality through the benighted dictatorships and theocracies of the Middle East.

Alexander had no reaction.

I started speaking faster, about how the Holocaust could never have happened if we'd had a land to call our own, that only an independent, strong Israel could guarantee Jewish safety, and that I wanted to help shape that Israel. I talked about how the remnants of my father-in-law Leo's wider family—his father, mother, and all seven brothers and sisters died in the Holocaust—had been able to build new lives here and to connect with their history. I mentioned that Lisa, my wife, was able to visit the grave of her great-great-grandfather on Jerusalem's Mount of Olives. I described how Leo, having spent more than three and a half decades after the war convinced he was the only member of his father's family to have come out alive, suddenly found, after a distant relative spotted a letter he had written to an Israeli newspaper, that three of his first cousins and their families were living here. I explained that here, Leo had been reunited with his heritage, with the living and the dead, spending lovely summer afternoons reminiscing with his cousins, tending to the grave of his aunt who passed away before he ever learned that she had come to Israel.

Alexander stared back blankly.

Desperate by now, I talked about my children growing up as native-born *sabras*, suntanned, healthy, speaking Hebrew with a proper, rolling *"r-r-r-r-resh."* They were certain, unlike in the Diaspora, to marry into the faith, to keep their Judaism alive.

Nothing. Alexander clearly thought I was insane.

Okay then. Last chance. "The weather," I blurted out. "The weather. I really came because of the weather."

For the first time, he looked interested.

Ten, eleven months of the year, in England, I told him, it rains. Not let's-get-this-downpour-over-with-and-then-the-sun-can-come-back-out rain, but wheezy, whiny, apologetic rain, struggling to reach the ground, leaking in rivulets down the back of your neck and into the tops of your Wellington boots. The day starts off sunny. But you shouldn't be fooled. In ten minutes, it can cloud over and start spitting on you. And, I said, it will do that every day except the one when you remember your extra sweater, your boots, your raincoat, and your umbrella. That day, it will stay sunny right through. The next day, you'll forget your umbrella, and it will piddle on you again.

Aaah, said Alexander, fully comprehending now. The weather. Sure. Makes sense. And off he went, a pale Russian kid in his oversized green Israeli uniform—whistling, puzzle solved—to peel his potatoes, patrol the jails, or do whatever it was he spent his miserable new-immigrant army days doing.

Sometimes, especially when Netanyahu was in power, the weather really was one of the few reasons I could find for staying here. And, truly magnificent though Jerusalem's climate is, the spring-to-fall near-certainty of daily blue skies with fluffy white clouds sailing serenely across them does not quite justify the lifestyle choice. Not when you're bringing up your three children in a country where you bite your lip with fear when they go on a school trip (even though they have armed parents accompanying them) and where people push to get to the front of the lines for buses, and then spend the journey praying they won't get blown up.

I can cite a long list of day-to-day behaviors, both trivial and significant, that drive me crazy in Israel. The attendants at gas stations smoke as they lean over the pump filling up your tank. Clerks in government offices will tell you that you can't possibly spell your name the way your family has been spelling it for generations. When you breathlessly enter the offices of the rabbinate with your beloved to embark on a new life together, the official at the door will inquire, sourly, "Marriage or divorce?" Leo, asked to prove his Jewishness by an officious government bureaucrat, was almost reduced to rolling up his left sleeve and showing his concentration camp number. Nobody ever yields at a road junction, because only a *freier*, a sap, gives way, and there's nothing worse than being a *freier*, not even killing yourself in your car to avoid being one.

And I can cite as many, probably more, redeeming features. An initial, adamant "no" from the person whose assistance you need will almost always give way to a helpful, even extravagant "yes" if you'll only ask nicely and take a bit of personal interest. The pedestrian you've asked for directions, because he or she hasn't actually heard of the road you're looking for, will make something up about straight on, then take the second left—just so as not to disappoint you. The neighbor you hardly know will pay all your bills and keep an eye on the house if you have to go abroad without warning for three months. Thousands of people will turn out at a moment's notice to give blood samples—including a bus driver who, en route, parks outside the testing station—because a mother in your son's kindergarten urgently needs a bone-marrow transplant. When a cast was taken off Leo's same left arm after some medical treatment, the doctor who had hitherto been particularly abrupt with him suddenly went all mellow. When one macho Israeli driver gets carried away and punches another in the fight over who had to yield at that junction, puncher will take punchee to the hospital, begging for forgiveness all the way; and they'll end up best buddies, and it'll turn out that their first cousins grew up together in Czechoslovakia. When two helicopters crash and seventy-three people die, the prime minister doesn't need to announce a national day of mourning, because the whole nation is mourning as one.

But normal people, in normal countries, don't add up on a daily basis the pros and cons of living where they do. When setting out to visit friends, they don't generally have to debate whether it's worth taking the route through hostile territory to save fifteen minutes. That's what Lisa and I do when we go to see my mother and stepfather in Beit Shemesh—fifty minutes from Jerusalem via the safe Jerusalem–Tel Aviv highway, thirty-five minutes if you take the shortcut via two little tunnels into the West Bank and on past the Palestinian village of Husan, from which local youths intermittently lob stones at yellow-registration-plated Israeli vehicles. Normal people in normal countries don't attempt to gauge whether the small risk of their sons' getting hurt on army duty is outweighed by the likelihood that the boys will maintain their family's religious connection. But that is an equation I am effectively contemplating.

But then again, as I told Alexander, normal Jewish people in normal countries like Britain do have their problems too. While Britain is hardly a hotbed of radical anti-Semitism, there is that undertone that, just sometimes, becomes an overtone of dislike for the Jews. Be it the casual anti-Semitic on-field invective you endure when your Jewish day school plays a secular school at soccer; the unpleasantness of the occasional cemetery desecration or swastika-daubing spree; the inevitability that, when a Jew rises to high political office, his or her faith will be highlighted in every newspaper; the fact that there are still "establishment" schools that maintain quotas for Jews.

Many English Jews insist that the spitting is nothing but rain. I once attended a debate at a Jewish educational center where the question being earnestly discussed was whether Britain was an anti-Semitic society, and one speaker was roundly applauded for demonstrating that it was not by citing the fact that St. Paul's public school had just increased its quota for Jews. A well-known London Jewish leader who that night ridiculed the notion of English anti-Semitism was heard just a few days later in his synagogue warning his congregants to keep their wits about them on their journey to and from services, because there had been police warnings about local gangs beating up Jews.

It's spitting all right, not rain. And, if you're honest with yourself and aware of your Jewishness, you grow up in England with a faint sensation of not quite belonging. That is a sensation I have never felt in Israel, not even in the early days when I couldn't speak the language or find my way around town. My generation of Israelis was born in this country and may take it for granted. Hundreds of thousands of ex-Soviet immigrants and other exiles ingathered from "distressed" countries see this as a refuge. Orthodox immigrants come to a land in which the faith that guides their every thought and action is rooted. I share some of that last group's sense of return, but I came here also out of Jewish nationalism. When Robin Cook, the self-important British foreign secretary, or any other puffed-up would-be international statesperson, flies in and tries to tell us what we ought to be doing, spells out "the steps that need to be taken" to resolve our disputes with the neighbors, what a joy it is to be able to laugh that off, to know that, sorry, you may not have noticed, but you don't run this country anymore. I might be treated rudely at the post office or in the bank, my kids might get beaten up at a school soccer game, but it won't be because we're Jewish—after all, the offenders (generally) are too. Our government may be useless, but it is our government. If we have to go to war, well, we Jews are all in it together.

I came here when I was twenty, enthusiastic, optimistic, and naive. I thought I was coming to the heroic land of wars won within a week, of Nazi mass-murderers seized overseas and brought to justice, of daring distant rescue operations like that at Entebbe—not Lebanese invasions, Intifada, and political violence. I believed, pretty much, that the Israelis were the good guys and the Arabs the bad guys; that if only the Arabs wanted peace, we would do everything to make it happen; that Jews couldn't possibly hate other Jews. I knew nothing about the Sephardi-Ashkenazi divide. I knew little about the left-wing–right-wing political hatreds. I didn't quite grasp the fact that, in establishing our nation, the United Nations was taking a large chunk out of land other people had claims to, and that they were understandably angry about it. There was a lot I didn't know then that I know now. Even had I known it, I would have come here. But now that I do know it, I realize that the challenge of making Israel work, shaping a country that Jews here and elsewhere can be drawn to and proud of, is far greater than I'd ever dreamed. I came to live here because I imagined that, from our diverse backgrounds, with our conflicting views and differing expectations, the people of Israel were nevertheless one bickering but solid family, dysfunctional in some ways but fundamentally happy, taking a stand in a bad, bad neighborhood and somehow, most of the time, managing to hold our own. That, and the weather. At least I was right about the weather.

Mine was a relatively unremarkable childhood spent in entirely unremarkable Hendon, northwest London. My parents divorced when I was four; I was too young to pay much attention. My Jewish primary school (as they call elementary school in the U.K.) was a tad too Orthodox for my tastes but still fairly tolerant. The teachers did carry out the occasional "tsitsit" inspection ("tsitsit" are the ritual fringes Orthodox males wear under their shirts) but didn't seem overly put out to find I wasn't wearing them. Most of my observant friends from school graduated from Menorah Primary to Hasmonean Grammar—a ramshackle collection of crumbling Victorian buildings and leaky prefabs. Hasmonean boasted a faculty of venerable rabbis weak on humor but strong on exam results. It was like a conveyor belt, turning out an endless supply of first-class graduates in math, applied math, advanced math, physics, and religious knowledge. I, however, followed my older sister's example and went to the Jews' Free School, a vast institution in distant Camden Town, where the grades were lousy and many of the locals were inborn anti-Semites (as we made the fifteen-minute walk from the Camden Town underground [subway] station to the school, clad in our un-mistakable bright-blue blazers, local toddlers, clasping their mothers' hands, would make V-signs and spit at us).

I had not been looking for it, but Jews' Free School, in contrast to Hasmonean, offered a subtle Zionism. The school imported annual consignments of genuine Israeli Hebrew teachers—who had no idea how to teach but did at least speak Hebrew with a modern rather than Ashkenazi Diaspora pro-nunciation. It also played host to a transient population of ar-rogant Israeli diplomats' kids. And, at age fourteen, it shipped most of us off to Israel for three blissful weeks.

Unless you grew up in England, you may not be able to comprehend the impact on my teenage Jewish psyche of three late-spring weeks in Jerusalem, Tiberias, Tel Aviv, and Eilat. And it's not simply the inexplicable tug on the heartstrings at the first glimpse of the Tel Aviv coastline through the airplane window, a stirring of something fundamental deep inside; nor only the predictable yet breathtaking sight of the Western Wall, with those impossibly large flagstones, rendering this at once a foreign and a familiar country; nor solely the strange sensation of being able to read but barely understand all the signs and newspapers. And it is certainly not just the awful fascination with bad-tempered taxi drivers, overcrowded vegetable markets, and chain-smoking supermarket staff. No, it's all of that, first impressions that somehow combined to make me feel connected to this place, to feel that I was like these people but different from them, to feel that I nearly belonged here and ought to—that this was my world. It was all of that, with one magical added ingredient: sunshine. You see, Alexander, I really was not lying. Getting up day after day after day and seeing the sun riding high in a clear sky, twenty-one straight days of natural heat, was unprecedented for a Londoner—and wonderful. On day one I discarded my coat. Day two, my sweater. By the halfway point, I was resolving never to go home. And by the end of the trip, more pragmatically, I had decided to come back to live in Israel before I was too old to know better.

I scraped through high-school graduation (A-Levels in England), spent a year working in the salaries office of a big department store making absolutely certain that I wasn't cut in my accountant father's image, and signed up for journalism school in Cardiff, Wales. From there, I got a job at the *East London Advertiser*, a local weekly on whose turf the Kray Twins, the East End of London's most notorious 1960s gangland bosses, had carried out many of their most celebrated killings. After less than a year with the *Advertiser*, covering such everyday East London occurrences as dockland stabbings and police-station murders, I decided that the time had come. "I'm going to live in Israel," I announced to my mother one evening, expecting tearful pleadings, emotional embraces, or, at the very least, the flourishing of checkbooks.

"Oh, all right, darling," she murmured mildly, as though I had said I was popping out to the supermarket for a packet of biscuits.

"No, Mum, I mean I'm going to live in Israel, for good," I persisted. "Packing my cases. Giving you back the front-door key."

"Yes, darling," she smiled sympathetically, "I always knew you would."

So I did.

My wife-to-be had arrived about eight months earlier, eighteen years old, to start college. Lisa was following a tradition: Her three older sisters, encouraged by their parents, had also come to Israel for shorter or longer university stints. One sister had already married an Israeli and made a home here.

Israel was an integral part of Laufer family life. Her parents had been visiting since the late 1960s, bringing various kids most summers, and involving themselves in every Israel-related event in Dallas. Lisa knew Hebrew better than most of the kids in her Jewish day school. She had marched in every year's Jewish community Israel Independence Day parade. In 1973, when Israel won the Eurovision Song Contest, Lisa had the T-shirt. At her elementary-school graduation ceremony, she read the prayer for Israel.

In the summer break before her final year in high school, Lisa was a volunteer at Kibbutz Or Haner, near Ashkelon in the south, taking care of the young kibbutz kids, cleaning the communal dining room, working in the rivet factory. Returning the next year for college was natural, inevitable. "I couldn't imagine myself going anywhere else," she says. "I was utterly certain that this was where Jews should be, that anywhere else was second-best." And then, a year after that, she and I got together, and Israel was our common ground.

We met at Hebrew University, where we were both studying international relations. For me, the degree was something

31

of a hobby; I was already working at the *Jerusalem Post*—then a newspaper firmly advocating territorial compromise with the Palestinians, and thus wonderful (as opposed to what it became for a while after I left in 1990—a determinedly right-wing publication, and thus rather less to my taste).

They should not have hired me. I had barely enough Hebrew to seek directions to the nearest bus stop. But David Gross, a kindly, passionate senior editor, took a gamble, sensing somehow that I would get the hang both of the country and of cutting copy and rewriting leads. And so, before I knew it, I was a subeditor, editing news stories on the night desk.

There were three particular highlights—or, in fairness to the readers, lowlights—all stemming from my initial inability to converse in the language of my newly adopted country. The first: editing the work of Jamie Altman, our Spanish-born economics reporter whose grasp of his subject may, for all I knew, have been unparalleled the world over, but whose facility in English was, sadly, not. There we would sit, Jamie and I, night after night, as the deadline approached, conversing in pidgin English, Hebrew, and Spanish, desperately trying to agree on what the governor of the Bank of Israel had said that day, what it meant, and how to convey this to our hapless readers. I truly shudder at the thought of what must have got lost in the translation. The more heinous crimes were invariably exposed the next day by the paper's editor, Erwin Frenkel—the export rises that had become import rises, millions somehow transformed into billions. But what of the errors nobody realized were errors, the howlers left uncorrected? A whole generation of economics aficionados may have been misled daily by the dazzling ineptitude of the Altman-Horovitz combination.

Lowlight two concerned, uh-huh, the weather. The meteorological center would call up every night with the temperatures nationwide and the forecast. The numbers I could deal with. The forecast was another story. Suffice it to say that many weeks would go by with the same sterile message in the forecast column: "No significant change." Looking back, I think the weatherfolk were saying things along the lines of, "Partly cloudy in the morning" and "Brightening up in the Jordan Valley." But this was Israel, I figured, where the sun shone almost every day. Who needed a weather forecaster?

Lowlight number three is the one about which I feel most guilty. It involved my work with Menachem Horowitz, the paper's thoroughly professional, ultrareliable reporter in the north. At ten o'clock every night, Menachem would phone in with his report of the day's doings on and around the border or, farther north, inside Lebanon, where the Israeli army was caught in futile frozen-invasion mode, staving off daily attacks by ever more confident guerrilla forces. Horowitz's articles were accurate, concise, impeccably written. There was only one difficulty: They were dictated in Hebrew. It was the subeditor's job to translate them.

As ten o'clock neared, I would do my best to be elsewhere—consuming the nightly fare of aged hummus in the basement canteen or buried in brown folders at the dim end of the archive. But often, far too often, someone would come and search me out to "take Menachem." I would explain that my Hebrew honestly wasn't up to it. The sweet, trusting fools thought I was being modest, that I protested too much.

So I would be dragged back to my desk to pick up the phone and struggle with Menachem's immaculate prose. I didn't know the Hebrew for "roadside bombs." I didn't know how to say "stretchers," or "warnings," or "alert," or "reinforcements," or "personnel carriers," or "air support." I would ask him to repeat great chunks of copy over and over, in the forlorn hope that, here or there, a phrase would stick, a penny would drop—enough for me to hazard a guess about the whole sentence. But it was a futile task. And for the first few months, while I savaged Horowitz's first-class reporting, I cannot believe that nobody compared notes between "our" Menachem stories and what should have been their identical Hebrew twins—his daily articles in *Ha'aretz*—and had me fired. But nobody did. Menachem, it's a decade and a half late, but I'm sorry. Your diction was always perfect. There was no crackling on the line. It was all my fault.

The *Post* quickly became my new home, a place I never thought I'd leave, not least because it was the only English-language daily in the country. But sometime in 1989 the various Labor party–affiliated companies that owned the paper decided that selling it might help stanch their hemorrhaging debts, and the international media sharks were soon circling. Conrad Black, whose reputed $20 million–plus offer was so high that, it is said, the owners phoned him back to ascertain that he really did mean 20 rather than 2, took us over.

Black was no direct interventionist. But the Canadian newspaper tycoon installed a retired Israeli army officer as the grandly titled president and publisher, and he pulled the newspaper firmly to the political right. Now, had I been working in a factory packing glue (something I once did in England, as a matter of fact), the plant manager's political inclinations wouldn't have mattered much. I dare say, too, that had I been a scribbler on a national daily in the United States or England, I might not have been massively affected by even a radical shift in the newspaper's editorial line—a switch, say, from Democrat to Republican, or from Labour to Conservative. But this is Israel, where your political stance is part of the essence of your being, where the question of how high a price we should pay for peace with the Palestinians or the Syrians is a daily obsession. I proudly carried, in my ideological baggage, the conviction that we Jews ought to set the example, ought to go at least halfway to meet our enemies on the path to peace. So when it became clear where the *Post* was now heading, and when a naive effort to persuade its Canadian owners to change publishers was dismissed, there was nowhere for me, and about thirty others who felt much the same, to go but out.

It was a grand gesture, and it felt good. But I'm not sure I could have allowed myself the luxury if I'd had children to support. As it was, the timing of my departure was almost hilariously awful. Lisa and I were in the process of buying our first apartment and, having been comprehensively outmaneuvered in the haggling (the seller was a psychologist, and her lawyer one of the country's top criminal advocates), were working our way through the mountain of paperwork—immigration certificates, bank statements, salary slips—that accompanies an Israeli mortgage application. For reasons that have never been clear to me, would-be mortgagees have to provide the lending banks with the names of three to five "guarantors." In the civilized world, if you default on a housing loan, the bailiffs come around, chuck you out into the street, and repossess the property. In Israel, with commendable generosity to the defaultee, but rather less to his or her trusted friends, they leave the scoundrel alone in his illegally held home and chase up his "guarantors" for payment. And they don't take no for an answer. (I have a friend who, in a characteristic act of kindness, once agreed to act as a guarantor for an Australian immigrant she didn't know all that well. He disappeared, and for years afterward she was obliged to make monthly payments to the rat's bank.)

So, Lisa and I are about to sign the last few bank forms, and most of our guarantors are colleagues from the *Post*. The day before signature, my guarantors and I leave our jobs in a light shower of publicity. Some of our names are in the next morning's papers. The bankers have only to open to the right page to see that I, until so recently a safe, steady worker, just the kind of guy you would happily lend your assets to, am now an unemployed has-been, and so are the people promising to pay my debts if I welch. Luckily, nobody put two and two

35

together, so I made off with hundreds of thousands of shekels and am now writing to you from a sun-drenched island in the Caribbean.

Bereft of the *Post* (which would in later years, under the same owners, ditch its ex-military president and swing back toward the political center), I freelanced for a while, and then, in early 1990, I landed a job at the about-to-be-launched *Jerusalem Report*, a biweekly magazine that started life in a cramped office on the tenth floor of an apartment block, graduated to the back room of a grocery, and finally moved into far grander accommodations which had previously served as the Jerusalem bureau of the *New York Times* and a brothel—though not, I think, simultaneously.

I am still with the *Report*, reveling in the sedate fortnightly deadlines that enable me to get home to my kids early most evenings, and to enjoy the luxury of thinking twice or even three times about what I'm writing before it gets published.

We have a good life here—at work and at home. Work-wise, the *Report* is taken seriously by Israel's political, economic, and other bigwigs, so the movers and shakers are always available, and each fresh interview is an entrée into a fresh world and an opportunity to open windows for our readers, most of whom live abroad and are fascinated by all things Israeli. It's great to know that, if you put in a request to interview the prime minister, sooner or later he will find the time; to be able to enter the West Bank hot spots at will and write freely about what you have encountered; to trade (generally) good-natured barbs with a mayor of Jerusalem you know has been scrutinizing every word you and your colleagues have been writing about him. A world away, Lisa's work, in real estate, has more satisfactions than frustrations, too—chiefly because her boss is honest and considerate, qualities not normally associated with that profession.

We live in a lovely apartment, on a quiet Jerusalem street, with a small garden and neighbors we'd choose as our friends. Our biggest problem was persuading a cellular-phone company to remove the antenna it had secreted in a false chimney on the roof next door.

We bought the apartment after a long and exhausting search, and after fortunately failing to outbid other purchasers on two old Arab homes in Ein Kerem, an idyllic hillside village on the city's western edge. I say fortunately because, in retrospect, we are relieved not to have bought an Arab property, the most sought-after real estate on the market, with traditional high ceilings and other architectural features absent from modern Israeli buildings. We didn't realize it at the time, but we would have felt thoroughly uncomfortable knowing that we were living in a home built for an Arab family that had chosen or been forced to leave in the past and that, in all likelihood, was still clinging to the front-door key and the dream of returning. I admit that these thoughts only occurred to us belatedly, after Lisa had made the connection between what we would have been doing and Leo's experience in Poland: She had accompanied him on a return trip to Lodz in the mid-1980s, and they found the two-room apartment his family had grown up in before the Holocaust. Warily, the current occupants let them in and showed them around; they still had the Laufers' mirror and dresser in the hall. Lisa once had real-estate clients who told her they would look at any property in a certain neighborhood provided it wasn't a former Arab home. She dutifully told them that Arab homes were the most distinctive, the most likely to accrue in value. But when her clients explained that they wouldn't feel right living in someone else's house, Lisa told them she understood. "Thank you," they said. "You're the first agent who has."

We enjoy the benefits of Israel's unique cultural range—

bookshops filled with *New York Times* best-sellers and Hebrew-language whodunits and Holocaust memoirs; concerts by passing international rock stars and ballet troupes interspersed with appearances by homegrown heroes. We can choose from the latest Hollywood blockbusters and the more resonant local movies at the cinemas, and choose, too, whether to watch *Prince of Egypt* in the original English or the even more original Hebrew. And we're offered a variety of adult and children's theater now increasingly influenced by the deluge of Russian immigrant artistes. Every year, for instance, the Jerusalem theater stages a series of free outdoor performances for children; every year, the Russians make their presence more clearly felt, introducing my own and other open-mouthed kids to jugglers and contortionists and weird puppet shows featuring dancing bugs and disappearing princesses, a magical world away from the Teletubbies, Barney, Ninja Turtles, and the rest of our customary television fare.

We have wonderful family days and weekends away—be it visiting the dolphins at the baking-hot southern resort town of Eilat, or sledding in the sprinkling of snow atop Mount Hermon in the north. There's a safari park at Ramat Gan, outside Tel Aviv, with real if sleepy lions and ostriches that stick their heads in your car window and have been known to bite the hand of your second son that feeds them. You can almost imagine yourself in Africa—if, that is, you narrow your vision enough to exclude the streetlights from the six-lane Tel Aviv–Haifa highway that runs alongside.

We've spent days clambering through underground caverns in central Israel that hid Jewish rebels of millennia past; we've edged our way, hand-in-hand, through a pitch-black, subterranean, crumbly white-walled "flour" cave near the Dead Sea, not far from the pillar popularly believed to be the salty Mrs. Lot; we've searched, in vain, for more Dead Sea Scrolls at Qumran; walked atop Jerusalem's Old City Walls;

gone horseback-riding in the verdant Galilee; bathed in mini-waterfalls in desert oases; walked over ancient aqueducts and around ancient amphitheaters and through ancient synagogues; toured the tombs of prophets and kings; examined purported dinosaur footprints; seen traces of a church on the site where the pregnant Mary is said to have rested en route to give birth in Bethlehem, something uncovered a few hundred yards from home. Whenever we think we've taken in everything this country has to offer, a friend will mention a newly discovered inn on the Sea of Galilee or a tour of museums and artists' houses in Tel Aviv, and off we'll go.

Most important, we have a supportive circle of friends who don't just share many of our values, but also—acting *in loco parentis*, because many of our parents live overseas—provide a practical safety net. We carpool to and from school, share baby beds and clothes, take meals to each other when someone gets sick. When Lisa went to the States for a week and a half not long ago, leaving me to juggle work and the kids, she typed up a seven-page, single-spaced survival list with daily timetables reminding me that Linda was picking up Adam at 7:35 to take him to kindergarten, Tom was driving Josh to school, and I only had to ferry Kayla to child care, leaving me clear for more than seven hours at work before I had to collect Kayla and get home in time for Josh and Adam being brought back, respectively, by Abby and Ellen (except that, as it turned out, Ellen had to take Cindy's kids, because Cindy was sick, so Shelly picked up Adam instead and dropped him off at Linda's . . . you get the picture). The kids could have been on play-dates at three different friends' homes every afternoon. We got five invitations to Friday-night dinner.

Life "in the cocoon," says Lisa, "is wonderful. Shul, school, pool"—as a friend of mine once put it. The shul—the Reform synagogue that most of these friends attend, and where Josh and Adam went to prekindergarten. The school—Tali Bayit

V'Gan, a state-tolerated, part-parent-financed institution that defies its cramped premises to offer a pluralistic, open-minded Jewish education. And the pool—at Kibbutz Ramat Rachel, a grassy oasis at the very edge of Jerusalem, a minute's drive from our home, where we spend lazy summer Saturday afternoons. Life in the cocoon *is* wonderful. It's just not reality.

And reality has a habit of intruding. It intrudes, amusingly, most Fridays, when an end-of-the-week, winding-down afternoon snooze is interrupted by shouted appeals from the street outside for "*alte zakhen*"—the traditional Yiddish phrase for "old stuff"—imported from Europe and now adopted by Israel's scrap collectors, the Arabs; or, slightly less amusingly, when you're startled out of your sleep in the early morning by an impoverished Arab ringing the doorbell or knocking on the window to ask if there's an odd job or two he can do to earn a few shekels. It intrudes at almost every downtown traffic light, where Palestinian ten- and eleven-year-olds who ought to be in school instead spend their days peddling towels, screwdrivers, and cheap cigarette lighters. It intrudes when you go to work the morning after two Hamas gunmen have indulged in a murderous late-night shooting spree along the row of restaurants below the office, and you exchange sad, philosophical smiles with the owners as they sweep up the glass and check the pecan pies for bullets.

It intrudes on even the most solemn day of the year, Yom Kippur, when local kids at the junction around the corner from our house spend hour after hour Arab-baiting. The only cars moving on Yom Kippur are Arab cars, passing our neighborhood en route from Bethlehem to the Old City or Ramallah, farther north. The local teens, though evidently uninterested in attending synagogue services, bareheaded and clearly non-Orthodox, apparently find this Day of Atonement driving unacceptable. They mass at the junction, force the cars to slow down, then spit at the windows, kick the tires, swear at the drivers. Last year, the police deployed patrol cars to escort the Arab vehicles safely through. Three cops were hurt—attacked by the neighborhood kids for daring to arrest one of them.

It intrudes even when we are planning some of those days out: We have made the most of the snow on Mount Hermon because quite soon now, it seems, it will have to be returned to the Syrians, from whom it was captured in 1967; I hesitate to take the kids to Herodion, an extravagant fortress built by King Herod that I visited as a schoolkid, but that now involves a tense journey into the West Bank; and, for the same reason, I have still not visited the Mar Saba monastery nearby—an intriguing-looking complex of towers and domes sprouting from a Judean Desert mountainside, open to men only, named after a hermit who founded a monastic order in the surrounding caves fifteen hundred years ago.

If our new Ehud Barak–led government can rebuild and really stabilize our partnership with the Palestinians, we'll be able to go to those places. Lisa won't adamantly refuse to enter Bethlehem, all of five minutes away inside Yasser Arafat-controlled territory. And I won't find myself accused by some of my friends of endangering my baby's life for having driven five hundred yards past the roadblock at Abu Dis, on the edge of Jerusalem, to go see the intended Palestinian parliament building under construction.

Reality intrudes on our national days of mourning each spring—Holocaust Day and, a week later, Remembrance Day for fallen soldiers—when lists of the dead are read out at official ceremonies and on television, and the talk shows take a respite from politics to let the bereaved tell stories of loss and grief undiluted by the passage of the years. Sirens wail across the land, and most of the country stands to attention, frozen, cars halted on the highway, doors open; figures immobile on the crosswalks, in the shops, silhouetted in office windows.

41

Last year, on Remembrance Day, Leo told me in tears of the elderly woman he saw halt when the siren blared as she crossed Jerusalem's Bethlehem Road, straighten herself, and stand utterly motionless for the full two minutes—her arms the whole time holding two bulky shopping bags she had chosen not to bend over and put down. Most of the country comes to a standstill—but not the Palestinian workers building the apartment blocks on the newly cleared lots at the end of my street where, until last year, the trees of Kibbutz Ramat Rachel dominated the skyline; and not all the members of our ultra-Orthodox community, who regard standing to attention to mark our respect as a Christian custom, alien to their practices, and have insufficient consideration for the rest of us even to humor us by playing along.

Reality can intrude into even the unlikeliest of places—like Josh and Adam's judo class, a twice-weekly session in the hall of our synagogue overseen by Tito, a great bear of a man from Argentina with a bark several thousand times worse than his bite who can pick up Adam by the belt with his little finger. One week, the synagogue was simultaneously hosting a seminar on Jerusalem attended by Ahmed Tibi, an Israeli Arab who at the time was also serving as an adviser to Arafat, and was, as such, regarded as something of a traitor by right-wing Israelis. Lisa arrived with Josh and Adam to see policemen guarding the entrance to the building. As she entered the hall, a man in his early twenties, skullcap on his head, pushed past and began shrieking in Tibi's direction, "Death to the Arabs." As he was dragged away by the police, Lisa, shaking, confronted him and demanded to know why her children should have to suffer his racism. He had no comment. Josh and Adam, meanwhile, puttered off to judo, another unfathomable image seared into their subconscious.

Reality intrudes every three weeks or so when you're walking downtown or you're at the bus station and you suddenly realize that all the cars have been stopped and the police are keeping back pedestrians because a "suspicious object" has been left unattended at a bus stop or under a bench. It almost always proves to be a false alarm—some mislaid shopping or the bag of a soldier who just popped off for a second to buy a newspaper—but, also almost always, only after the sappers have arrived and performed a "controlled explosion," blowing the thing up or shooting it full of bullets. An absentminded friend from England recently came here for a visit and somehow managed to forget a bag full of clothes and documents outside the Government Press Office in central Jerusalem. The police tracked him down and told him the good news: His bag was waiting for him at the police station near the Mahaneh Yehuda vegetable market. He discovered the bad news when he got there: His papers and underpants were now riddled with bullet holes.

And, of course, it intrudes every night at eight, when we watch the television news, the daily diet of friction and violence. I have to watch it, for work. Lisa tries not to. But when, about once every two weeks in hostile periods, a soldier has been killed in Lebanon, she somehow gravitates from the kitchen to the living room, sits on the edge of the sofa, and stares silently at the body being lowered into the freshly dug earth; the father supporting the wailing mother, their red-rimmed eyes turned to heaven in indictment; the comrades-in-arms paying tearful tribute to the soldier whom everybody liked, who never shirked responsibility. And when the footage from the funeral is over and the military affairs analyst steps in to present a reconstruction of what it was that went wrong this time, how it was that another life was lost, Lisa gives me a filthy look and disappears back into the kitchen—the mute equivalent of asking me if I'm *still* sure I want to run this military risk with my son's lives, since she certainly does not.

Because reality bites, many of our Western-immigrant

43

friends have upped and left as the years have passed. Lots fled as soon as we had finished college, heading to jobs in London merchant banks, to master's degrees in Boston, to real-estate careers in Brussels—having decided in the course of three years at Hebrew U. that this country was not for them. Martin, the Amsterdam realtor, did not see the business opportunities here that he found there. Jeremy was sucked back to Scotland by the simple fact that every other member of his family was living there. Raul is now a stand-up comedian in Amsterdam; even if Israelis do have a sense of humor, which is not always entirely obvious, Raul would have had an impossible time tapping into it in a nonnative tongue. All the men who left at that stage, I think, were also scared off to some extent by the prospect of military service—a stint of basic training and then the annual grind of up to a month's reserve duty away from home. A good friend dashed back to America within weeks of his first tour of reserve duty alongside me at an Israeli-run prison in Gaza, partly because he could not cope with the knowledge that he would have to leave his family again for the same month every year, and partly because he was horrified by the nature of our duties (of which more later).

In the years since, more friends and acquaintances have left—especially those who came from the United States, for whom the gulf in living standards in Israel is greater than it is for those from Western Europe. They have gone back, the way they told it, because the pace of life was too frantic; because house prices in Jerusalem and Tel Aviv were so high that they bought farther afield and found they had no friends out in the boondocks, no social life to connect to; because they thought the school system was diabolical—too many kids per class, too much fighting in the corridors, no respect for the teachers, teachers who screamed too much to earn any respect. In many of their cases, too, the army was a factor. It is not easy on a family having Dad away for the best part of a month every year. It's not easy on the dad, and even harder on the mum. For the two brief years that my reserve duty involved that kind of period away, I was in a state of semi-depression for weeks before the call-up date, dreading being apart from Lisa, and I counted the hours in my prison-guard tower in Gaza until I would be going home. Needless to say, it was while I was gone that we got rats in the apartment and Josh fell out of bed and suffered a concussion. My service involved relatively little risk. But for the families of friends where the dad is in a combat unit, missing him—especially during the Intifada years and other subsequent military flare-ups—is the simple part. The hard part is pushing aside the fear that he might not come back.

Many more of my friends still have one foot here and one foot back in the United States or the United Kingdom—one spouse agitating to leave, the other determined to stay, a perpetual domestic battle. But it's the ones who have passed that dithering stage, who have stayed and are a few years older than us, with older kids, who give me the most sleepless nights. My colleague from work Hanan, whose son is currently serving with an infantry unit in the West Bank, gently suggests that, if there is a time to get out, it's now, before the kids get too big, before Josh and Adam get too intoxicated with the idea of military service in a combat unit, before the macho tradition percolates down to them from the older grades. My next-door neighbors, the Sawickis, parents of two boys, now thirteen and ten, tell us that it's already too late for them, that if they leave now their kids will come back without them, the worst of all possible worlds. Archie, an artist who makes beautiful "paper cuts" in a studio one floor below our office, had two sons in elite commando units until recently. "We encouraged them to serve in good units," he says. "We always supported them. We knew they were going to do it. But then it happened. We waved them off at Bakum [the army induction center]. And the reality, the theory becoming practice, was one of sleepless nights and worries about the telephone ringing at odd hours."

The core group of us who remain used to laugh self-deprecatingly at our attachment to this country. We would giggle at our economic plight, comparing notes about younger siblings and school friends back in the United States or England who had gone into banking or law and were now earning ten or one hundred times what we were and worrying about how to invest their savings while we were worrying about how much extra we would have to fork out to trade in our dying secondhand cars for slightly healthier second-hand cars. But then we had kids, and then Rabin was assassinated, and the laughter went hollow. In few places except Israel does your five-year-old know about exploding buses and flag-draped coffins and ask, when it thunders, whether a war has started. In few places except Israel would a young kid muse about not wanting to die, not wanting to be "blown away to God," as a friend's eight-year-old once put it.

Josh, down to whom the macho tradition has evidently not yet percolated, inquired recently whether military service was obligatory in America and, on learning that it was not, announced firmly that "I'd like to live there then." After exchanges like that, Lisa and I tend to look at each other, raise eyebrows, and sigh, wordlessly sharing guilt over exposing our children to a country that imposes such a weight of worldly knowledge on those so young. And hours later, when the kids are asleep, we'll likely have one of our circular discussions, in which we'll agree that Josh has a pretty powerful point, she'll muse about whether we would be happier and safer living near her parents in Dallas, I'll tell her I'd go out of my mind with boredom in Dallas and semiseriously propose Manhattan, she'll counter that you can't bring up children in Manhattan, and I'll attempt to close, for now, by reminding her that Israel did reject Netanyahu fairly rapidly, and that Barak has brought real hope of solving our problems.

The truth is, you see, I can't drag myself away from this country. A few years back, we spent a summer vacation with Lisa's parents, played racquetball with her old school friends, sweated in the health-club sauna, kept the gray cells mildly active with chess matches contested on an inflatable board in the pool of a friend's back garden. It was divine; sheer untroubled bliss. We did not watch the news or read the papers and did not miss them—for about five days. Then I started feeling an indefinable kind of itch. Life was just too serene, too easy. What was the point of it? Was this what I had been put on the planet for? I started reading the papers again, watching CNN international, tuning the radio to the BBC World Service. Absurdly, I even began feeling guilty about being away from Israel, not only missing what was happening, but somehow letting the country down. It was only when the plane touched the tarmac at Ben-Gurion Airport, and I knew I was back amid the strain and tension of the Middle East, that I could relax.

Most journalists would identify with some of that—with the helpless frustration of being away when news is breaking. But with me and Israel, it runs deeper. For all my misgivings, this is the only country to which I feel an emotional connection, a personal stake. This is the only country where I feel personally affected by national events—by election results, by Supreme Court decisions on the status of non-Orthodox Judaism, by a rise in the murder rate, by a spate of horrific cases of family violence, by the turnout at demonstrations. I would never have engaged in sweating, terse conversations with my sister over British politics in the way that I do over our political differences here. I would never have implored friends to change their voting habits the way I have shamelessly done here. I would never have gleefully prolonged lobbying telephone calls from representatives of parties I abhor simply to prevent them from calling other voters who might be more susceptible. I would never have wanted to hug the neighbor's kid for handing out the right kind of political stickers. In no other country would I have felt personal pride in the way we have absorbed hundreds of thousands of ex-Soviet immigrants, or in the smooth functioning of the field hospital our army erected in a day to save refugee lives and help birth refugee babies on the Kosovo-Macedonia border. In no other country would I feel affronted by the weekly death toll on the roads, elated at a local scientific breakthrough, delirious that "my" beauty queen had won the passé Miss World pageant (Liora Avergil, 1999), and that "my" transsexual pop singer had triumphed in the supremely irrelevant Eurovision Song Contest (Dana International, 1998). This is the only country I could ever love like that.

Chapter Two

The Way It Is

Tell them it's tiny, loud and passionate. Tell them, the longer they stay, the more confusing it gets. Tell them it's a madhouse.

—A veteran Israeli tour organizer, advising me on what to tell a group of first-time visitors in an "Introduction to Israel" lecture

What is living in Israel really like?

A lot of it is pretty mundane—cursing the alarm clock, dragging the kids to the breakfast table and school, swearing at whatever you do for a living, arriving home exhausted, microwaving the chicken, checking your son's homework and wondering whether he's actually absorbing anything, half-watching the news while half-fainting at the phone bill. . . .

And a lot of daily life is uniquely, for better or worse, Israeli.

The pace of life is frantic, and people have no patience. There is not much lining up in orderly fashion. There is a lot of pushing and complaining and smoking, and pathetic line-jumping ploys in banks, government offices, and supermarkets—like, "I was here ten minutes ago, I just popped out to . . . ," or, "But I was here yesterday," or, even, "I was here before they put the numbers in the lining-up machine."

When you've been here long enough, even if you grew up in oh-so-well-mannered England, your own ingrained politeness starts to erode. I'm quite often asked by BBC radio to comment on the day's news, and whenever they phone from London they're so polite it makes me want to scream. We're so sorry to call you at home, they tell me. We hope we're not disturbing you. It's not an inconvenient time, is it? How are you? Finally, they get to the point: Would it be at all possible to call you in a couple of hours for a quick interview? Are you sure that's okay? Should we call you just a few minutes in advance to confirm? I once admitted my irritation to a BBC friend, a correspondent based in Jerusalem, who looked down at me from his rarefied six-foot-something altitude and dryly observed, "David, my dear, you've been living in Israel for too long."

The country is incredibly crowded—not as crowded as the Gaza Strip, but crowded enough to have seen hill after hill around Jerusalem lose its trees, turn brown and sprout housing, and the Tel Aviv streets constantly snarl up on weekdays. It is crowded enough for the central garbage dump, outside Tel Aviv, to have been closed down because it grew so high so fast that the mountains of rubbish and the birds they attracted came to constitute a threat to planes taking off and landing at the nearby international airport. It is crowded enough for barbecue-loving Israelis, desperate to find a patch of green for the traditional Independence Day cookout, to resort to setting up their charcoal grills on the grassy divides of major highways.

The simple economics of life simply don't add up. Nine out of ten people will tell you, cheerfully and fatalistically, that they are permanently "over"—overdrawn at the bank. Overdrafts carry staggering interest charges, yet everybody pays them. Prices for essentials compare to those in England and are higher than those in the United States. Three-bedroom apartments start at $100,000 in remote locations and $200,000 in Jerusalem and Tel Aviv. Prices of electrical appliances and cars are swollen by colossal taxes and duties. Yet people earn maybe half the typical English salaries and per-haps a quarter of those in the United States. And still, when a festive family occasion comes around, Israelis will spend vast sums of money on a lavish party. I've been to a bar mitzvah bash in a glitzy Tel Aviv hall, featuring a dozen-strong band and a multi-costume-changing dance troupe, thrown by a family struggling to make ends meet. I've attended a wedding where the impoverished young couple were going to live in a mobile home in the West Bank, yet the bride's parents spent enough on the fete to have rented them an apartment for five years in central Tel Aviv.

To get by, almost every household needs two breadwin-ners, and plenty of folks hold down more than one job. The norm for a young mother is that when the baby is three or four months old, she goes back to work and the kid goes to day care. But, despite that norm, the school day conspires against working moms. Kids, often forty or more to a class, typically study only from about 8 a.m. to around 1 p.m. The adult workday runs either from 7 to 3, 8 to 4, or 9 to 5. Every work-ing Israeli mother is thus destined to juggle her way through innumerable extra lessons, play-dates, and emergency baby-sitters, with all the carpooling and impossible extra expense involved, just to hold down her job. And that's before she begins dealing with the teachers' strikes (once or twice most years), the two-month school break in summer, the two-week school holiday at Passover, the week at Chanukah, the on-and-off school month from the Jewish New Year through Succoth.

School here, incidentally, seems to be out more often than it is in, interrupted not only by the major Jewish holidays you've heard of but by others too minor to rate more than an occasional mention in our holy books. One of these is Lag B'omer—the thirty-third day between Passover and Pente-cost—marked by nationwide bonfire parties, on any and every patch of open land, that run late into the night and so necessitate the following day off from school. To keep the fires burning, kids scavenge the neighborhoods for weeks in advance, making off with everything that is wooden and not bolted down. At the relatively modest, school-organized bonfire that Josh attended last year, a classmate tossed a fetching chest of drawers into the flames. That same night, a bonfire-bound kid was seen making slow progress down our street, dragging an eminently serviceable couch behind him.

To save some cash by beating the taxes, Israelis have been known to take brief trips abroad, not necessarily because they want or can afford a break, but mainly to get access to the duty-free stores at Ben-Gurion Airport. Only in Israel do the regulations allow us to purchase duty-free goods on our way *out* of the country and collect them on our return. Travelers arrive at the airport not two to three hours before their flights, as security regulations demand, but four or even five hours early. And they buy cell phones, watches, tennis rackets, and more basic items like jeans, sweaters, and winter coats—beautifully, mercifully tax-free. The Treasury, anxious to recapture disappearing revenue, has now barred the airport stores from selling some of the electrical appliances—like top-of-the-line televisions and washing machines—that made overseas travel really worthwhile. But the stampede goes on. Because of the fear of aircraft bombings, planes won't take off until all passengers who have baggage in the hold are safely on board. And so, all day at the airport, the announcements boom out for Mr. and Mrs. Ezekiel and Mr. Lebrett and Ms. Wolf, last calls, please, plane about to take off. And you see the sweaty, red-faced, errant travelers reluctantly tearing themselves away from the kettles and the sports-shoe racks and running for the departure gates. The newspapers had a field day with one family who, seated, seatbelted, and in a plane taxiing to the runway, realized they'd forgotten their infant, in her stroller, back at the duty-free.

Israelis, frantic by nature, drive like fools. Every week, about ten die in road accidents; five hundred each year. Just imagine the outrage if that number were killed in Palestinian-inspired violence. In the teeming rain, on a badly lit, slippery, potholed road, when you are doing 80 or even the 90 kilometers-per-hour (50 and 55 miles per hour) limit, cars will come flying past at 120, 130 (75 or 80 miles per hour), overtaking you on the outside, the inside, weaving across. There is a section of road we use every day to leave our neighborhood and join the Hebron Road into central Jerusalem; it narrows to the point where only one car at a time can get through. In a normal nation, if you see a car already entering that bottleneck and coming toward you, you stop and wait for it to pass. That's what we do. But at least half the time, when we're coming through, a driver will insist on trying to squeeze past from the other direction, in defiance of all reason. And we'll all get stuck and start shouting at each other. I'll have my parentage questioned. There will be threats of violence. Traffic will build up in both directions, horns will honk, new participants may get out of their vehicles to join the fray. Lisa is reduced to tears by that stretch of road an average of once a week.

Lisa goes out on the roads, she says, with a daily sense of foreboding—the belief that an accident is waiting, literally, around the corner. She has been rammed twice in the past two years. Almost every journey, to the Tali school or anywhere else, comes with its near-miss—the driver who tried to overtake her when she was turning left, the car that blithely reversed off the sidewalk in front of her, the crash scene she drove past near the Malha mall in which, we later learned, a child, un-seatbelted, had been thrown out of a car window and killed.

A Little Too Close to God

A few months ago, Lisa went with Josh's class on a school trip. Heading back at the end of the day, with dozens of kids on board, the school-bus driver attempted to clear a railway crossing just as a train was approaching. So desperate was he to get across, to avoid the intolerable two-minute wait for the train to pass, that he accelerated even as the automatic crossing barrier was coming down in front of him. He didn't make it. The barrier actually came to rest on the front of the bus, forcing it to halt and reverse. The train passed by just a few feet ahead.

The other day, while I was waiting at a yield sign, a car was coming across in front of me, and the Volvo driver behind me started honking impatiently. What did he want me to do? Drive forward, crash, and die? I put on the handbrake, got out, walked back, and screamed at him; an elderly man, he thought I was going to hit him, and immediately apologized.

I was wrong to go nuts. But I cannot adequately describe the nightmare that is driving in Israel. Everybody, but everybody, routinely ignores the regulations. Ministers and Supreme Court justices frequently get ticketed for hitting 120 km-plus on the 100-km-limit Jerusalem–Tel Aviv highway. Former police ministers and police chiefs have been caught driving with cell phones clamped between shoulder and ear, hardly the ideal motoring stance, and illegal. (Our cell phone obsession is a story in itself: four Israelis in a restaurant, five cell phones on the table. Think your countryfolk are too attached to their cell phones? Have you heard them ring at memorial services, or at a funeral, as the body of the deceased is being lowered solemnly into the ground? I have.)

Perhaps we are maniacs behind the wheel because bad driving habits are ingrained in the army. Maybe it's because life is somehow cheaper here. Even people who have suffered directly from our road rage don't always seem to change. Recently, Lisa narrowly avoided a head-on collision with a car careening the wrong way down the hill that leads to our street. As the offending vehicle squeezed past her, she caught sight of a sticker in the back window that read: BE CAREFUL ON THE ROADS. I LOST A FRIEND IN A CAR CRASH.

We are a nation obsessed with politics, or, specifically, the politics of peace and security—hardly surprising when, in these parts, government decisions genuinely do spell life or death. How many soldiers were spared by the decision to withdraw the army from Gaza in May 1994? How many families were saved the awfulness of having Dad, on reserve duty for a month a year, patrolling the alleyways of the Khan Yunis and Rafah refugee camps? Then again, were the innocent lives lost in the bus bombings and suicide attacks of the past five years a direct consequence of that dubious peace partnership with Yasser Arafat? What price should we be paying for coexistence with the Palestinians, and the Syrians, and the Lebanese? How much land can we safely give up? What becomes of the settlers of Gaza, the West Bank, the Golan Heights? What do you do with East Jerusalem—relinquish it to the Palestinians, slap a Berlin Wall across the city? The dilemmas are endless; the borders aren't off in the theoretical distance but just a few miles off—the West Bank is five minutes from my house, Gaza is a ninety-minute drive away, Lebanon and Syria three hours to the north, Egypt less than three to the south. We all use the buses, serve in the reserves, shop in the bomb-vulnerable fruit markets. The solutions we eventually choose will directly affect us all. The billboards opposite the railway station and outside the high school near my office change every day—accusing the prime minister of being too soft, too tough, a liar; declaring him a hero, a leader with the nation on his side; urging us to spend a Sabbath with the Jews of Hebron, to gather in memory of Rabin—which billboard I see in the morning depends on which interest group was out last with the posters and paste the night before.

A Little Too Close to God

It goes without saying that the first thing Lisa did on leaving the hospital after Adam's birth in 1993, it being an election day, was vote. And that was a city, not a national, election.

Our battle with the Palestinians ebbs and flows, envelops us completely then recedes, obsesses us then bores us. But it never disappears. We relate to it by invoking the full weight of our collective history, discussing it in the context of God's biblical promise to his wandering Children of Israel and in the context of the Holocaust. Does that biblical promise mean that we must liberate and retain every possible inch of our ancient land now, or can we forgo some of it in exchange for saved lives and tranquillity? Would forgoing it save lives and bring tranquillity? Is the lesson of the Holocaust that we must never again be weak, never again trust the non-Jews, never turn the other cheek, never make ourselves vulnerable? Or is it that we Jews must be better, must never oppress another people, never take away their freedoms?

Everyone thirsts for information—newspaper sales are astronomically high; passengers stand up and shout at bus drivers who don't turn up the volume for the on-the-hour radio bulletins; television news is almost universally watched, and the myriad nightly chat shows invariably feature politicians, generals, and current-affairs analysts. Many Israelis have paid a personal price for the hostility in our region. The rest of us know too many colleagues, relatives, and friends who have. We all shudder when planes boom through the sound barrier overhead, initially fearing a bomb. All eyes on the buses check out the faces and the bags of each new passenger, scenting a potential threat. If there is an explosion, we all frantically phone friends and relatives to assure ourselves of their safety, and the cell phone network generally collapses under the strain. When Lisa takes the kids to the center of town, after parking the car she gives them an if-there's-a-blast pep talk. "If you hear a loud noise, a bomb," she reminds them, casually, just to ensure they remember, "you lie down on the ground."

"What about Kayla?" Josh asked the last time they went through the routine.

"Don't worry," Lisa assured him. "I'll lie down on Kayla."

Everyone has a fiercely held opinion, however shallow, and wants to express it. Here is a conversation overheard on a Saturday at Monkey Land, a theme park off the Jerusalem–Tel Aviv highway:

First dad, leading an immaculately dressed, pigtailed eight-year-old girl past the orangutan enclosure: "But they'll never be satisfied, however much we give them. They don't just want the West Bank and East Jerusalem, they want West Jerusalem and Tel Aviv as well."

Second dad, while attempting to prevent a chocolate-stained eight-year-old boy from force-feeding an ice-cream wrapper to an orangutan: "I suppose you're right. We're never going to have peace here. Benjie, would you please stop doing that!"

National habits are directly related to the length of time since the last bomb went off. After the Ben-Yehuda triple-blast, for instance, I steered clear of the Village Green for a few days, and we didn't go to Jerusalem's main indoor shopping mall at Malha. After bus bombings, some of my colleagues come in by taxi rather than risk riding the No. 18—blown up twice on Jerusalem's Jaffa Road in 1996, around the corner from our office. The national mood is utterly volatile, entirely dependent on how secure we're feeling. We sniff frantically at breaking news of violence involving Palestinians, urgently trying to discern whether it is "ordinary" crime (a laborer who has stabbed his boss to death because of a dispute over wages) or what is defined as "nationalist" crime (a laborer who has stabbed his boss to death because the boss is Jewish). The police definition of motive, a thin, wavy line, can determine whether we're panicking or shrugging our shoulders. You can rely on a group of racist hotheads to gather at the scene of every bombing and scream out death threats to the Arabs in general and Yasser Arafat in particular. But even moderate Israelis feel an anger they don't always show, an unwillingness in the first dark hours and days after a blast to draw distinctions between good and bad Palestinians, between Arafat and Hamas. There is a despairing urge just to say, Screw the lot of them, cancel peace. And then, for most of us, common sense takes over. Except that, after each blast, there is another slice of the population that may not make that jump back to pragmatism.

There is no escaping the conflict. When you think the washing machine is getting really noisy, it turns out there is an Israeli army helicopter flying overhead, making reconnaissance runs above Bethlehem. You sit down to watch a rock-music documentary, charting the progress of one of Israel's most influential bands, Caveret, and barely ten minutes into the show you are seeing band members discuss the impact the 1973 war had on their careers and realizing that the song you have been humming for years, "Natati Lah Hayai" ("I Gave Her My Life"), without thinking much about the lyrics, is actually a subtle endorsement of the two-state solution—an early plea for Palestinian independence. You try to book your son's favorite clown, the gravel-voiced Yuval, for a birthday party, and he tells you, Sorry, he can't make it. He is a paratroop officer in the military reserve, and he just got called up for service.

You arrive for a family day at Nitsanim Beach, between Ashdod and Ashkelon on our Mediterranean coast. And as you start the trek from the parking lot to the golden sands, Frisbee and kite in one hand, bucket and shovel in the other, you are reminded of the time you dashed down here with a handful of other reporters in May 1990. The contours of three bodies of dead Palestinians were visible under blankets in the sand dunes, and a perspiring police chief was explaining that the boat carrying the gunmen had been spotted early, and they had been "taken out" as they sped in toward the crowded beach on rubber dinghies stocked with machine guns and hand grenades.

Because of our hot-spot status, we live in a goldfish bowl—almost every local news event, it seems, leads the international network television broadcasts. When Netanyahu sent bulldozers to clear land for a disputed neighborhood on the edge of Jerusalem, the networks broadcast live from the site, interviewing the tractor drivers when they took a coffee break. A minor explosion in a garbage can in Tel Aviv that injured no one relegated Boris Yeltsin's pneumonia to a secondary story on CNN. This place is a dream for foreign journalists—there are few restrictions on coverage, a collapsed censorship system, long-running miniconflicts, guaranteed international fascination because of the religious associations of the Holy Land, easily accessible leaders, and civilians who are passionate, articulate, and speak English.

As my reservist's service, I give lectures to soldiers up and down the country on democracy, the peace process, and the media. Soldiers have often come up after a lecture on the media to complain about what I would call Israel's commendable determination to afford open coverage of the Intifada and of our other conflicts—in contrast, say, to Britain's cynical, controlled news management of the Falklands War, or America's of the 1991 Gulf War. Yes, I have to agree with them, it has cost us dearly in terms of the army's image—Israel's image—abroad. Disproportionately, we often top the world news agendas simply because here, as opposed to, say, Damascus or Teheran, the camera crews can go just about everywhere, anytime—and fresh footage of a West Bank scuffle outweighs a telephoned report of hundreds of people dying in Algeria. But for all the damage that intensive exposure has done internationally, I suggest to the soldiers, it is a price worth paying, because every Israeli understands the realities of day-to-day conflict in southern Lebanon or Gaza, and so every Israeli has the necessary information to make an informed decision when election time comes around. Sometimes, I convince a few of them. Most of the time, though, I can see them thinking, Yeah, well, he's a journalist, he would say that.

On January 17, 1997, the day that 80 percent of Hebron found itself without Israeli occupying troops for the first time in thirty years, I went to the city to see how it would deal with its newfound partial freedom. Predictably enough, those in the four-fifths of the city that was now Israeli-free were jubilant. There was dancing in the streets, the odd burst of joyous gunfire into the air, much hoisting of Arafat placards. And equally predictably, the 20 percent, downtown, where the Israeli army still patrolled—offering two-on-one protection for 52 Jewish families and 150 Torah students—was fairly miffed. There was no dancing in the streets, no joyous gunfire, no hoisting of cardboard Arafats.

A week or so before, a deceptively gentle-looking Israeli soldier named Noam Friedman had opened fire indiscriminately in the town's teeming vegetable market. Although he immediately and explicitly confessed that he had been shooting in a bid to prevent the military pullout, he was subsequently categorized as deranged and therefore unfit to stand trial. Anyway, come January 17, I was talking in that same market with Ahmad, a wiry, mustachioed Palestinian who runs the stall nearest the point where Friedman started shooting, and who'd had the presence of mind to dive out of the way.

Ahmad was in the midst of telling me that the fifteen thousand or so Palestinians left behind in Israeli-controlled

Hebron were feeling particularly peeved with the new
divided-city arrangement when someone nearby expressed a
similar sentiment with slightly more force. This someone,
whom I couldn't see, threw an orange at an Israeli soldier. It
missed. Then he threw a banana. The soldier raced across the
street toward massed ranks of bulletproof-vest-wearing Israeli
men in green deployed for just this sort of eventuality. Half-a-
dozen soldiers waded into the market—the inevitable cue for
more flying fruit. Then things really took a turn for the worse.
The Palestinians started throwing radishes. I know they were
radishes because I saw them flying, and I saw them land. The
Israeli soldiers, jumpy on this first day of the new Hebron
order and intent on avoiding a serious confrontation, began
trying to impose a curfew, shouting at the traders to pack up
their stalls, announcing through loudspeakers that Hebronites
were to return to their homes. The locals were slow to react,
but then the plainclothes agents of Jibril Rajoub's tough West
Bank Palestinian security force appeared out of nowhere
and bustled the people indoors. Rajoub's men, too, were anxious to avoid violence. Within five minutes, the streets were
empty . . . of Palestinians, that is. Neither the yeshivah students nor the Jewish families of Hebron are affected by curfew
orders.

Watching all this unfold from a sheltered vantage point
alongside the walls of a cemetery were perhaps two dozen
journalists from the American networks, the BBC, various
U.S. and European newspapers, and even a crew from Dubai
television. And when I, extricating myself from the core of the
fruit fight, found my way across to the press benches, I ran
into a friend of mine who works for an American TV station.
He was on his cell phone to mission control in the States. He
was assuring them that this was not a fierce clash. No one had
been even slightly hurt; there had been no gunfire, not even
stones thrown—just oranges, bananas, and radishes. But they

61

weren't having it. What they saw was violence and a curfew on the first day after the Hebron pullout—a big, important story. My friend the correspondent swallowed hard and agreed he would do a live interview from the field to the studio. But he had a request: Don't tag the report with the dramatic BREAK-ING NEWS logo. They complied, but for the rest of the day they led their hourly international news broadcasts with our marginal fruit fight.

The passion that politics breeds is incredible, and by no means confined to angry demonstrations. I hosted an evening at a Jerusalem educational institute, Yakar, a place with a commendable dedication to harmonious, genteel discussion, at which the guest of honor was Carmi Gillon, the former head of the Shin Bet security service, reviled among Jewish settlers and others on the political right who perceive him as an ideological enemy. As his talk progressed, Gillon was heckled and jeered increasingly loudly by critics in the audience and ultimately forced to cut short his appearance, while the evening's organizers, recent immigrants from England and South Africa, watched in dismay. I've had phone calls from readers of the *Jerusalem Report*—who must be overall a fairly open-minded group, given the spectrum of viewpoints that appear in our magazine—denouncing this article as dangerously pro-Palestinian, that one as horribly conciliatory to settlers. One Jewish reader phoned to cynically inquire, following our publication of a piece on the threat posed by settler radicals, whether I was a member of Hamas. Another called to cancel her subscription because she deemed a piece on the killing by Palestinians of a West Bank settler to be overly sympathetic to the murdered man's ideology.

Your politics permeates every aspect of daily life. The rumor that the wife of Jerusalem's right-wing mayor, Ehud Olmert, votes for the left-of-center Meretz party is widely discussed because it is unfathomable. What do they talk about over breakfast? How can she live with the man who strongly supported the secretive, late-night opening of an archaeological tunnel in Jerusalem's Old City, in September 1996, a move that led to furious Palestinian protests and the loss of seventy Palestinian and fifteen Israeli lives? One of the best TV documentaries in recent years was made by an army veteran turned filmmaker named Avi Mugrabi, who loathed the then defense minister Ariel Sharon for initiating the Lebanon War, became obsessed by Sharon, started interviewing and filming him before the 1996 elections, and ended up naming his film "How I Learned to Stop Fearing and Love Ariel Sharon." Poignant, funny, and utterly serious, the film also wound up documenting the breakup of the Mugrabis' marriage; it wasn't her husband's obsession with Sharon that his wife couldn't endure, so much as the treasonous softening of his attitude toward the minister.

Lisa and I—and we are not alone in this—even make driving decisions on the basis of political bumper stickers. If the car that wants to change into our lane or pull out ahead of us into the traffic features a FRIEND, WE MISS YOU sticker, in memory of Yitzhak Rabin, or one pronouncing A STRONG NATION MAKES PEACE, whichever one of us is driving is likely to yield. But if, as is more common in right-wing Jerusalem, the back windshield is adorned with something like HEBRON, FROM DAYS OF OLD AND FOREVER, we'll try to freeze out the offending vehicle and honk, angrily, if it gets the better of us. (Yes, we all eventually decline into steering-wheel dementia.) Even the kiddies' toy cars, in some of the most politicized homes, feature right- or left-wing bumper stickers (not ours, I promise, although we do maintain a permanent exhibition of pro-peace stickers on the inside of the front door). Start 'em young: Plenty of people are going to try and indoctrinate your children, a columnist at the *Report* remarked to me once, so the parents might as well get in first.

A Little Too Close to God

In a country where almost everybody watches the evening news, the daily papers are ravenous for fresh morning head-lines—an incentive that renders them brash, sensationalist, and frequently completely wrong. They'll carry headlines confidently asserting that the prime minister has canceled his trip to Washington that are undermined within hours when he confirms his U.S. visit. They'll tell you ministers are resigning who end up holding on to their jobs for years; assure you that the Hashemite kingdom is on the point of collapse; that Jonathan Pollard, the American Jew serving a life sentence for spying for Israel, is to be freed within days. And they'll be wrong, wrong, wrong. The former London correspondent of *Ma'ariv* recounts this story: Six years or so ago, before Israel had nurtured any kind of meaningful relationship with any of the Persian Gulf principalities, there was a trade fair at the Earl's Court exhibition center in London. Qatar had a stand, and a journalist from the competing Israeli newspaper *Yediot Ahronot* sauntered by and casually asked the Qatari official manning it why his country hadn't initiated relations with Israel. "As far as I'm concerned," replied the official nonchalantly, "we could do it next month." Main headline in the following morning's *Yediot*: QATAR TO OPEN DIPLOMATIC TIES WITHIN A MONTH. And just pity my friend from *Ma'ariv*, who got an earful from his editor—for "missing the story."

What is amazing, given the proportion of entirely inaccurate information contained in our newspapers, is that most Israelis continue to regard everything they read there as the gospel truth. The power of the press is truly staggering. When *Ma'ariv* reported on somewhat flimsy evidence that a certain brand of milk might have dangerous silicon in it, Israelis stopped buying it immediately. When the same newspaper, backed up this time by incontrovertible TV news footage, exposed the fact that Israel's blood bank was routinely throwing away blood donated by Ethiopian immigrants because it was too expensive to check whether the donors were carrying the AIDS virus, the normally reticent Ethiopians massed for a stormy demonstration outside the prime minister's office, which police broke up amid clashes not unreminiscent of the Intifada.

Just a few years ago, Israel had six mainstreamish daily Hebrew newspapers. Sadly, three of them had hardly any readers, so now we have only *Ha'aretz*, which likes to think of itself as Israel's *New York Times*, and the aforementioned *New York Post*–style *Yediot* and *Ma'ariv* tabloids. Each of these is effectively controlled by a single family, and that limited concentration of ownership is downright dangerous. In much the same way that Rupert Murdoch and Robert Maxwell used to do battle for the hearts, minds, and wallets of the British public, the Moses family that controls *Yediot* and the Nimrodis of *Ma'ariv* compete for Israeli affections. And when they can't win us over fairly, they cheat.

Yediot, in its advertising campaigns, calls itself "the nation's newspaper," and, since it holds a 70 percent market share, that's a reasonable claim. In 1991, Maxwell bought *Ma'ariv* and tried to make it more competitive, investing in a new color press and paying top salaries for top journalists. It didn't work. After Maxwell fell into the swirling clutches of the Atlantic over the side of the *Lady Ghislaine*, *Ma'ariv* fell into the swirling clutches of the Nimrodi family, whose fortune was reportedly made in arms-dealing. Thenceforth, *Ma'ariv* used less conventional means to close in on *Yediot*. It hired ex–intelligence officers to bug *Yediot* phones, presumably getting the lowdown on *Yediot*'s planned scoops. And when the folks at *Yediot* noticed that *Ma'ariv* was getting sharper, they got together, quite coincidentally, with their own ex–intelligence officers to try and find out where the leaks were coming from. And here's the loveliest twist: In some cases, obviously unbeknownst to each other, *Ma'ariv* and *Yediot* were using the same ex–intelligence officers to check each other out. For a few wonderful months in 1994 when the bugging was at its height, *Yediot* and *Ma'ariv* produced virtually identical newspapers. We'd go down to the corner shop, and it didn't matter a whole lot whether we bought *Yediot* or *Ma'ariv*. They would have the same lead story, same photo, same second lead, same back-page lead—the same story on page eight, for goodness' sake. We all realized something was seriously awry, and a police probe yielded a slew of indictments for illegal wiretapping.

Allegations of corruption have snowballed recently, to drag *Ma'ariv*'s publisher, Ofer Nimrodi, into still murkier waters, to embroil President Ezer Weizman and Netanyahu in investigations over suspected financial misdealings, even to raise questions over the legality of some of the campaign financing that brought Barak to power—badly staining Barak's image of integrity. National figures we would expect to be able to trust are letting us down time after time, breeding a growing public cynicism.

And corruption is not our only grave problem. The crowding, the pace, the tensions, have all combined in recent years to make ours a more violent society—there is violence between new and older immigrants; increasing domestic abuse; violence in the schools; attacks on judges; attacks by ultra-Orthodox gangs on non-Orthodox Jews; attacks on the West Jerusalem apartments rented by Israeli Arab women while they study at university; verbal, egg, and even shooting attacks on politicians. None of this is completely new. It's just intensifying.

We also lead the world in car thefts per capita (one every eleven minutes in our worst year) and are scoring impressively in robberies too—both rare areas of genuine Israeli-Palestinian cooperation. Senior Palestinian officials have been spotted on numerous occasions driving stolen Israeli vehicles.

Only here, you can be sure, would a woman get her car back safely because the Palestinian thieves, instead of delivering the vehicle immediately to the "slaughter houses" outside Hebron in the West Bank (where purloined Israeli vehicles are rapidly resprayed and redistributed or stripped down for parts), were apprehended by police after stopping to burn the "Zionist literature" they had found in the backseat. Our car, like everyone else's, is required by our insurance company to feature not just ordinary door locks but a gearshift lock and an electronic engine "immobilizer" as well—which means it will take the thieves all of twenty seconds longer to drive away with it. The national obsession with cell phones pays one of its few dividends in countering car thefts: On discovering that their cherished automobile has vanished, victims have been known to dial their car phones, converse with the thief in the driver's seat, get approval from their insurance firm, and negotiate a "ransom" for the vehicle's return.

Some of the violence and crime is a product of the occupation, of war after war. But some is a consequence of social inequality—to what should be our shame, we have one of the widest differentials between salaries in the top and bottom ten percentiles of any developed nation. In the last few years, betraying our socialist pioneering heritage, some of Israel's rich have gotten ludicrously rich; those paid the minimum wage are being exploited with quintessential Western capitalist ruthlessness. And the hundreds of thousands of hapless Thais, Romanians, Poles, and other foreigners we have brought in to do our dirty construction and agricultural work (not to mention the few tens of thousands of Palestinians we still allow in), are exploited to a degree that would shame some Far Eastern sweatshops—their passports confiscated, housed in appalling conditions, paid twenty-five dollars for a day's labor, if that, and dumped in a squalid tent camp if they've come in illegally and are about to be deported. We have

A Little Too Close to God

started to see homeless people sleeping in the parks and on roadside benches, and begging for money at traffic lights. And meanwhile, the wealthiest among us live in comfortably large homes, drive gleaming luxury cars, belong to country clubs, take twice-yearly overseas vacations, own dishwashers and exercise bikes, and employ Filipino housekeepers. Demand is heavy at pricey gourmet restaurants. Herzliyya marina is home to four hundred yachts. Health spas at five-star hotels are oversubscribed.

The imported comedies and dramas on cable TV have made a virtue of all things American. And, with impeccable timing, all things American have become available to us—from McDonald's and Pizza Hut to Chryslers and Oldsmobiles to Blockbuster and Tower Records, its racks bursting with releases by Napalm Death, Rancid, Primal Scream, and the Butthole Surfers. But the American dream rubs up hard against the Israeli reality. However Westernized we'd like to think we are, however adeptly we surf the Net, however passionately we follow *Chicago Hope* story lines or David Letterman's tie preferences, our fragile delusions get shattered every time a conscription notice drops into a mailbox, every time a young girl gets stabbed to death near her home in a West Bank settlement. McDonald's drive-ins are an unremarkable feature of our landscape, where you can witness the ultimate fusion of Israeli pioneering and American consumer spirit—a kibbutz farmer, dried earth on his elbows, pulling up in his tractor, collecting his Big Mac and fries, and heading back into the fields. But the Jerusalem branch had its doors torched not long ago by ultra-Orthodox men angry that it stays open on the Sabbath and mixes meat and cheese in its Big Macs, in defiance of Jewish dietary laws. When did that last happen in the Times Square or Piccadilly Circus branches? Where else could you see, on the same billboard in a city center, one poster advertising the latest U2 album and another warning

68

Orthodox Jews that it is forbidden for men and women to swim together in the same pool?

Despite the ongoing efforts of fundamentalist Orthodox Jewish leaders (of which more later), this is not (yet) a Jewish Iran. There are several hundred thousand people—10 percent or more of the population—liable to heed their rabbis' orders over the laws of the land. And the long-term prognosis is deeply ominous, given the phenomenally high birthrate in this ultra-Orthodox community, where birth control is considered sinful and families with ten or twelve kids are unremarkable. But, for now, the theocrats are firmly in the minority. And while, for instance, ultra-Orthodox pressure prompted the banning of a semistrip routine by a dance troupe from the Fiftieth Anniversary of Israel gala concert in 1998, that was also the year Israel sent the transsexual Dana International (the former working-class Yemenite boy Yaron Cohen) to sing for it in the Eurovision Song Contest. (To the intense annoyance of the ultra-Orthodox, Dana, triumphant, described her victory as "proof that God is with me.") For all its problems, inside and out, it is (still) a bubbling democracy. But, the burgers, the Buicks, and cable TV notwithstanding, it is not America.

It is absurdly, uniquely, jaw-droppingly Israel, the only country where the following everyday incidents could have occurred. They could have happened to any Israeli. They happen to have happened to my family and to me.

It may have a population of six million, but it's a mighty small country. . . .

David Lubinski and Co., Israel's Peugeot dealership, used to have its main showroom on King David Street, opposite the renowned King David Hotel. I would pass it on the rare occasions when I'd walk home from work. And for some unaccountable reason, I conceived a profound affection for the

Peugeot 309, an undistinguished low-to-middle-of-the-range family car. Various taxes mean that new cars here cost twice, even three times, what they do in the rest of the free world, but immigrants get to buy their first car tax-free. Having sought counsel from two Peugeot 309 drivers, I was determined that our tax-free car would be a David Lubinski Peugeot 309.

Bad, bad mistake.

To say that the car was a turkey would be to stain the reputation of blameless poultry everywhere. Everything that has ever gone wrong with any car you've ever owned went wrong with this one, plus a whole load of things you've never conceived of. We had to get a new clutch every few months, replace the battery, have the engine "reringed." Felix, the pock-faced mechanic who could have flown to work by private jet on our repair bills, initially assured us that all new cars had the occasional hiccup, but was eventually reduced to suggesting that we were just driving the thing too much. (He once actually told us, and I quote: "It's not really designed for short journeys around town.") The side-mirrors imploded on a weekly basis. The glove compartment collapsed. The map pockets fell off both doors. Blue smoke came out of the air-conditioning vents. The fracturing of a part known in Hebrew as a *shtengl*, which apparently plays a crucial role in linking wheels to axles, saw us marooned in an early evening traffic jam outside the Jerusalem Railway Station. The final straw came in midwinter, when it rained in through the overhead light.

The obvious solution would have been to sell the car. But we couldn't. A characteristically Israeli small-print clause in the tax-free car deal for immigrants stipulates that you must hold on to the vehicle for at least five years. If we sold within that period, we would have to pay the government the tax we had saved. So I opted for letter-writing instead. I penned a note to David Lubinski and Co. arguing that they should continue to pay some of the repair bills—the first year's had been covered by them—because the car was so appallingly fault-prone. And to give them their due, they came through with a few hundred dollars here and there. And when they balked, I wrote directly to Peugeot in France, enclosing an article I had written headlined, IS MINE THE WORST CAR IN THE WORLD?, which I said I planned to send out to car magazines. (My lawyer assured me this wasn't extortion, but it must have come close.) They sent me $1,000. A week later, the clutch went again. Repair bill: $1,100.

While David Lubinski's and Peugeot's patience and pockets were limited, my 309's capacity for problem development clearly was not. So we changed tack and began parking the car, doors unlocked, a good distance away from the house. We live only a short drive from the West Bank car slaughterhouses. Our neighbor's Chrysler Voyager van was pinched in mid-afternoon. A coworker of Lisa's had her Mazda stolen when she left it for ten minutes, just around the corner from us, to run an errand. Other friends three streets away, Mark and Kim, had their twelve-year-old battered Subaru stolen from outside their house a week before they were planning to sell it. But would the crooks come for our Peugeot? Nope. We considered putting a sign on the back window, PLEASE STEAL ME, but figured that might undermine any subsequent insurance claim. So night after night it sat there, an unloved, unsellable, unstealable, forlorn testament to its maker's mechanical ineptitude.

Until finally, in the spring of 1996, our five-year sentence was up. Spirits soaring, we placed an ad in the local weekly. Early on publication day, the phone rang, and shortly thereafter a woman in her early twenties appeared in the doorway. Sensibly, she wanted the car tested by one of the authorized dealers. Off we trooped, she full of optimism at her imminent purchase, Lisa and I wary of the catalogue of flaws the inspection would unquestionably reveal. At the garage, while other vehicles got their okays in five to ten minutes, our Peugeot held center stage for a full half-hour. Teams of blue-overalled mechanics gathered to marvel at its dysfunctional innards. There was much sucking in of cheeks and shaking of heads. Eventually, they summoned our potential buyer to an upstairs office to pass on the grim tidings. She returned, tossed the car keys back at me, and pronounced, "This car's the pits." But miracle of miracles, as my shoulders sagged and I began to nod my head in sorry agreement, she suddenly brightened, snatched the keys back, and chirped, "Just kidding." Ten minutes later, we had agreed on a price. Two days later, we had completed the paperwork. The car was gone. We were free.

I still see it around town occasionally, unmistakable with my Arsenal soccer club stickers in the back windshield. And I do feel the odd pang of guilt. But I tell myself that the price we sold it for wasn't steep, and five-year-old cars are expected to go wrong now and again. And, anyway, maybe it was a personal thing: The car simply didn't like us, and it has stopped misbehaving now that it's in fresh hands.

A couple of months after the happy farewell, now driving a trouble-free secondhand Toyota Corolla, I am asked by the army to give a lecture on Israeli-Palestinian peace efforts for an officers' course at Tel Hashomer, a huge base north of Tel Aviv. The unit's educational officer, short-haired and businesslike, meets me at the main gate to assure the guards that I'm *persona grata*. And she hops into the Toyota for the short journey to the lecture hall. When we park, I take great pains to lock the car, checking that the gearshift padlock is on, that I'm centrally locked, that the "immobilizer" light is twinkling. She laughs gently at my paranoia, remarking that not many car thieves chance their luck inside army bases, and I explain that I'm particularly anxious to hold on to this car, in contrast to its predecessor.

Then I launch into a lengthy tirade about the evils of the Peugeot 309, detailing the innumerable horrors I've endured. She tries to stop me, protesting that "You really shouldn't be telling me this." But I rush on, expressing my bafflement that drivers would keep on buying the bloody model and that the manufacturers would dare put such a lemon on the market. I am so involved in the tale that it takes me a few minutes to notice that my officer escort has now fallen silent and is staring at me, white-faced and seething.

"Oh God, what's the matter?" I ask her, finally realizing that I must have reopened some terrible driving trauma.

"My father," she says, "is David Lubinski."

. . . with a population of fascinating people . . .

Close to one million immigrants have arrived in the past decade, the vast majority from the former Soviet Union. Their reception here has represented much that is best about Israel—we've taken in a full fifth of our population, taught them the language, and found them housing and work—but some of the worst too: Tension between the Russians and veteran Israelis of Moroccan origin has produced at least one murder and innumerable cases of gang violence. And as a consequence of that and other absorption difficulties, the Russians seem to be retreating into their own communities, retaining their language—there are some terrific Russian-singing rock bands emerging from the working-class neighborhoods in southern Israel where many of the immigrants have made their homes—patronizing their own specialty stores and restaurants, voting for Russian candidates in local and national elections.

Although it seems fanciful to talk, as some immigration

officials do, of a wave of Jewish arrivals from the United States sometime down the line, the potential for more immigration is unlimited—dependent only on how many people we want to take in, and how elastic we want to be in determining Jewishness.

In the steamy climate on either side of the Burmese-Indian border, for instance, there are thousands, maybe hundreds of thousands, of people willing to join the Zionist adventure: the Shinlung tribespeople, many of whom believe themselves descended from one of the Ten Lost Tribes, Menasseh. They have a firm faith, unique for their locale, in one God. They still sing ancient folksongs with uncannily Jewish themes, about splitting the sea, getting water from a rock, and traipsing through the desert on the trail of a cloud by day and a pillar of fire by night. When an earthquake or other major natural disaster passes their way, they reportedly rush out and start shouting, "Don't worry, Menasseh, your people are still here," or words to that effect. And a generation ago, one of their elders had so powerful a dream about the imminent "return" to Israel that his most loyal followers took their kids out of school and packed their bags in readiness for the move. This particular elder died a disillusioned man, but about 3,500 Shinlung have kept his vision alive: They've built synagogues, circumcised their malefolk, even learned Hebrew—with the encouragement of a Jerusalem-based rabbi who cites biblical sources in support of their claims to Jewish heritage. Astoundingly, this rabbi, Eliahu Avichayil, who lives in a modest Jerusalem apartment and visits the community periodically, has persuaded the Israeli authorities over the years to allow in several hundred Shinlung. Some of them work as farmers on Jewish settlements in the Gaza Strip; some have been conscripted into the army. Their cousins, and then their cousins' cousins, and then their cousins' cousins' cousins, are ready to follow them as soon as the Interior Ministry gives them the green light, as are other groups in distant African and Asian locales, all claiming descent from the "lost tribes," some of them, like the Lemba in southern Africa, with supporting genetic evidence.

The only one of these groups to have so far cemented this claim, and thus to have come here in large numbers, is the Ethiopian Jews, tens of thousands of whom have arrived in recent years—fifteen thousand within forty-eight hours in May 1991, airlifted out of civil war–riven Addis Ababa, thanks to a $35-million "smooth passage" payment delivered by Israel into the pocket of the tottering Ethiopian president, Haile Mengistu Mariam.

Mengistu imposed just one condition on the "Operation Solomon" airlift: If word of it leaked to the international media, it would be halted. In Jerusalem and Tel Aviv, the government censor's office contacted every reporter, local and foreign, and begged us not to run the story. Yes, it was a very moving tale, Israel bringing home thousands of black Jews from the midst of a war zone. But, please, could it wait? Premature reporting of the airlift, ran the plea, could endanger lives; the would-be immigrants might be stranded in Addis at the height of the civil conflict. Amazingly, the censor's appeal was heeded. The story did leak out—but from Addis Ababa, where the BBC spotted the frenetic activity at the airport. And after a few frantic telephone calls between Israel's fixers and Mengistu's aides, the airlift was allowed to proceed. To reward our uncharacteristic restraint, the coordinating officials invited dozens of reporters to the airport to meet the incoming flights, and it was an unforgettable experience.

Ethiopian Jews from the larger cities had generally immigrated to Israel in the 1970s and 1980s; these arrivals were from the more remote provinces, people who had somehow clung to Jewish traditions and aspired to a home in Zion without knowing much about modern Israel or modern anything else. Packed like sardines into the jumbo jets, which had their seats ripped out—an El Al 747 from that airlift holds a place in *The Guinness Book of Records* for bringing in 1,088 passengers, including two babies born en route—the Ethiopians emerged into the light evening breeze at Ben-Gurion Airport with an evident mixture of delight and trepidation. They came slowly down to Israeli earth, elegant, slender figures dressed in traditional white, to start a life that would be utterly different from everything that had gone before.

One couple appeared at the head of the stairs with a newborn baby. If it wasn't delivered on the plane journey, then it certainly wasn't born long before, and it was clearly several weeks premature. An ambulance pulled up on the tarmac with an incubator ready for the new arrival. Reaching the bottom of the aircraft steps, the young Ethiopian couple—the tall, stick-thin father and his shorter, only slightly rounder wife—looked at each other gravely, nodded mutual assent, and handed their child gingerly over to a nurse, unsure of what was going to become of it, but prepared to place their faith in her hands. It was a tender, noble moment.

Seven years later, I'm driving home from a lecture in the north, and I pick up two hitchhiking soldiers, one of them Ethiopian. We stop at the McDonald's drive-in and get to talking. The Ethiopian, Moshe, had arrived on the Operation Solomon airlift—he had been barely in his teens. He loved it here, believing passionately in Israel and the return to Zion. He had signed on for an extra year's army service, and now he was on his way home on leave from Lebanon. He didn't think about dying. He was doing his duty. When I dropped him and his friend off in Tel Aviv, and he collected his hamburger detritus, he thanked me extravagantly for the ride. Then, utterly unprompted, he leaned in through the passenger window and told me gravely: "This country saved me. And now I'm helping to defend it. I am honored to be an Israeli soldier."

. . . wildly, wildly different people. . .

Names are important here.

Our friend Estelle gave birth on February 25, 1996—the same day that a Hamas suicide bomber blew up a No. 18 bus on Jerusalem's Jaffa Road. While Estelle was in labor in Hadassah Hospital, the doctors there were treating a long line of the dying and the wounded. When her daughter was finally delivered, toward evening, the doctor in the maternity ward told Estelle, gratefully, that she had provided some light at the end of a blighted day. Fittingly, Estelle and her husband Ezra named the child "Lior"—My Light.

Our third child, a girl, was born in the early hours of Monday morning, October 21, 1996. It was a happy day, not only for our household but also for the Netanyahu family. Bibi, our prime minister at the time, turned forty-seven on the very day that Kayla joined the world. Had we had a boy, we were thinking of naming him Benjamin. But that would never have done for a son born on Netanyahu's birthday. People would have got quite the wrong idea.

A few months later, Kayla had to go for a checkup at the health-fund headquarters in central Jerusalem. While she and Lisa were in with the doctor, Josh, Adam, and I played in the waiting area with a lovely girl, a baby boy, and their parents— he, tall and gentle, with a knitted skullcap atop his black curly hair; she, a soft-spoken, attentive woman, modestly dressed with head covered in the style of the modern Orthodox. Then Kayla emerged, and the next patient was called—the baby boy. "Yigalhebron Something," the receptionist read out. I thought I must have misheard. I asked Lisa if she had caught the name. She wasn't sure. So when the family had gone in to see the doctor, I asked the receptionist to look up the boy's first name again. "Yigalhebron," she repeated. Two Hebrew proper nouns had been squashed together—Yigal Hebron—to form a name that can be translated as "He will redeem Hebron." The caring parents had apparently named their baby after Yigal Amir, the prime minister's killer who had sought to halt a peace process that would see Hebron coming under the control of Yasser Arafat. An innocent boy was being forced to carry a murderer's name through his life. Like I said, names are important here.

. . . wildly different people crammed up against each other . . .

Lisa's father, Leo, comes to Israel for a visit, gets sick, is hospitalized at Hadassah.

Noticing numerous soldiers passing to and fro along the corridor outside, he hauls himself out of bed to investigate and discovers, a few rooms farther down the ward, an Arab man in his midtwenties, handcuffed to the bedframe, watched by four gun-toting soldiers. The heavily guarded patient, wounded when captured by the Israeli army in the West Bank outside Jerusalem, is apparently suspected of having orchestrated various attacks on Israeli targets.

Leo shares a room with Walid, a soft-spoken hospital porter who, only in his mid-forties, has suffered a heart attack. Leo and Walid pass the hours regaling each other with tales from their respective childhoods—Walid's as an East Jerusalem Arab, a devout Muslim living first under Jordanian then Israeli rule; Leo's as a rebellious member of a Polish Hassidic family—and musing about what the future holds for the handcuffed Palestinian down the hall.

. . . which can be a little awkward . . .

My stepfather Charlie's theory was that one of the upstairs neighbors spat a pit out the window. Other informed sources suggested a seed gently planted by an unusually intelligent bird. Whatever its origin, the indisputable fact is that, one morning in the summer of 1998, we noticed that a strange round thing was growing in the garden. The passage of a few weeks confirmed that it was a nascent melon. Every day, we would marvel at its roundness and greenness and healthy growth. Every day, Josh would ask us if we could eat it yet. Every day, we would tell him to wait.

Now it was summer vacation and we faced a major dilemma. The melon was big, but it looked like it still had some growing to do. Should we harvest it now and risk unripe disappointment? Or leave it and risk a rotten return? Patience won out. We went to Pompeii—and came home to find . . . that the melon had left us.

Had the farsighted, horticulturally proficient bird returned to claim its matured investment? Or had the melon gone the light-fingered way of Josh's bike, two bikes from Judith and David (neighbors to the left), and one bike from Susan and Tom (neighbors to the right)—all of which had vanished in our absence?

We might never have known were it not for the fact that, a few days later, two more minimelons made their appearance amid the rose bushes. Again, we checked and marveled and waited. Finally, on a morning in late September, one of the two, yellowed and juicy-looking, was deemed fit for the slaughter. It was to be plucked by Josh on his return from school. Except that morning the gardeners came. Not *our* gardeners, you understand. Our overgrown, ill-tended patch of lawn and rosebush is our own inexpertly maintained handiwork. No, it was the gardeners who beautify the flower beds at the front of the building—an Israeli boss, Rami, and his two, inevitably Palestinian, workers.

Lisa takes Josh to school, does some shopping, and comes home to find . . . no melons. Rami is nowhere to be found, so she confronts the Palestinian duo. Yes, they confirm, there was one melon, but it was rotten, so they threw it away. Lisa, distinctly upset that, for a second time, Josh has been deprived of his homegrown fruit, goes to the outdoor garbage bins to get what got dumped—to show Josh that it was inedible. She finds one part-eaten, rotten melon and one healthy melon skin. Confronted again, the Palestinians sheepishly half-admit that, yes, it was they who ate the fruit. "What can I tell you?" asks one of them with a sad shrug, when Lisa brandishes the incriminating peel.

Now, we don't want to get these guys into trouble with Rami. And, for sadly obvious reasons, given the propensity for Israeli-Palestinian disputes to turn unpleasant, we don't want to unduly antagonize them. So there's nothing much we can do except tell Josh that the gardeners ate the melons because, presumably, they were hungry, and, presumably, don't have enough money to buy the food they need themselves. And Josh, home from school and surveying the spot where the melons used to rest, is commendably calm, only muttering, slightly crossly, that, "They should have asked us first."

Lisa, being Lisa, heads off out to the plant nursery at nearby Kibbutz Ramat Rahel. The melon season is over, they tell her, but they give her their last four melon treelets, with one or two teeny melons on them, to plant "just for the fun of it." Next spring, I'm going to ask Rami and his crew to sprinkle some seeds around the rosebushes, and maybe there will be enough melons for all of us.

. . . but can also have its advantages. . . .

Charlie and Evelyn, my mother, are building a house for themselves in Beit Shemesh, a rapidly expanding city midway between Jerusalem and Tel Aviv. Not for them the convenience of living in, say, Jerusalem, close to the grandchildren; nor even the ease, if Beit Shemesh it has to be, of moving into an existing home or even buying one that is going up in a well-organized housing project. No, bless them. They may be both in their sixties. They may speak only halting Hebrew. But that hasn't stopped them from purchasing their own plot of land, hiring their own architect, steering their blueprint through the labyrinthine procedural channels at city hall, and getting to work on their own dream home.

Plain sailing it has not been. What with the unexpected and crippling city taxes, the arguments with the council about knocking down the old hut that stood on the site, the problems with the owner of the land next door, the mounds of incomprehensible bank loan paperwork, the effort to purchase components at bargain prices that, one afternoon, found them driven, in blissful ignorance of the potential danger, to the outskirts of Hebron in the hunt for floor tiles, it is a tribute to their improbable resilience that, as I write, an elegant, three-floor, gleaming shell of a building now stands proudly awaiting its windows, doors, floors, and furniture—a tribute to their resilience, to good-neighborliness, and to good fortune.

The good neighbors are Avraham and Aliza, owners of the home two doors down, a retired couple of Moroccan origin who have become fairy godparents to Mum and Charlie. For no evident reason, other than that they are particularly decent people and that my mother is a sweetheart who is able to converse with them in particularly good French, Avraham and Aliza have essentially adopted them and made it a retirement mission to ensure that they get their house built. To that end, Avraham, formerly an employee of the Bezek communications company, has used his extensive *protektzia*—the personal contacts without which Israeli bureaucracy virtually cannot be negotiated—to get paperwork approved by city hall, to track down pile-driving equipment for the foundations, to find contractors to build the house, to locate concrete and roofing and window and flooring experts, to shout at these suppliers when

81

they are late, and to put them straight when they are over-charging. The relationship has extended to Avraham renting Mum and Charlie a basement apartment in his home until the building is finished, overseeing continued construction when they had to fly to England briefly at short notice, and showing up to meet them at the airport on their return at two in the morning. Since he knows that Evelyn and Charlie observe the Sabbath strictly, avoiding all work, Avraham was also to be found at dawn one Saturday morning, hose in hand, watering the newly poured concrete floors—apparently essential to the proper settling of the construction.

When Charlie was hiring the building contractor, he had dozens of offers from Beit Shemesh builders. But the most reasonable offer came from a West Bank Palestinian, Omar, whom Avraham had tracked down. The overlooked local Jewish contractors were somewhat disgruntled. One of them, David, lives only fifty yards away and for several weeks afterward bestowed dirty looks on Charlie whenever their paths would cross. Another, an Orthodox man, came to the site to remonstrate, pointed to his own and Charlie's skullcaps, and chastised my stepfather for not hiring "a good observant Jew." Retorted Charlie, "I would have hired you, if you'd given me a good observant Jewish price."

Omar has done a good job, when he and his workers have been able to. Building in today's Israel invariably features at least a part-Palestinian workforce—modern Israelis, in contrast to their swamp-draining predecessors of half a century ago, are notoriously reluctant to get dirt under their fingernails—and, therefore, occurs on an intermittent basis. It has tended in recent years to be punctuated by shorter and longer periods of "closure," when Israel "seals off" the West Bank and Gaza, barring Palestinians (even those, like Omar and his team, with bona fide jobs) from entering the country, for fear of, or in response to, suicide bombings or other attacks.

(Quite apart from the dubious morality of punishing three million people for the violent activities of a few, the "closure" is singularly ineffectual and serves only as a kind of psychological crutch for traumatized Israelis. Would-be Palestinian bombers are hardly going to present themselves for inspection at the army roadblocks and crossing points. Only decent Palestinians like Omar go through those proper channels, and so only they are affected by the closure orders. The bombers, by contrast, closure or no closure, can cheerfully cross into Israel undetected via any of thousands of open fields along the miles and miles of unfenced border between Israel and the West Bank. Living as we do, in Arnona on the outskirts of the capital, we only have to drive a few hundred yards down the road to watch the convoys of Palestinian vehicles driving into Israel from Bethlehem, across the open land on either side of the soldiers manning the Israeli roadblock.)

But Omar is not perfect. His interpretations of the architect's drawings often involved the concrete equivalent of poetic license. When Charlie or Avraham spotted especially egregious cutting of corners, they put him right. But they didn't catch everything. Quite by chance one morning, after the second floor had been poured, the spurned contractor David happened to stroll past and noticed that Omar had failed to install a critical support beam, without which the floor would, sooner or later, collapse. And, though David had been slighted, he was good enough to tell Charlie about the omission, which was corrected.

You get the feeling that, apart from Avraham and Aliza and David, someone else is watching over them.

Sometimes we Israelis get on surprisingly well . . .

Most Thursday nights, in a losing battle against mid-thirties spread, I play seven-a-side soccer on an outdoor field at Ramot community center, on the other side of Jerusalem.

The center, in the heart of a densely populated, working-class neighborhood, is heavily in demand. But the locals have somehow got the (mistaken) impression that our raggedy bunch of ex-Brits, South Africans, and Aussies pay for the field and the floodlighting. (We have elected not to put them right.) So, just before 8 p.m., they generally scoot off home for dinner and leave us to play in peace until about 10. Generally.

One Thursday, though, two kids in their late teens insisted on joining the game. We shrugged, put one on each side, and got on with it. It's friendly stuff, our soccer. People play fair but not too hard, no one is frantic to win, no one wants to break a leg. One of the locals was a pretty smart player and slotted in easily. The other couldn't kick to save his life. In a rare moment of potential glory, angling to shoot at goal, he was forced off the ball, a tad roughly, and limped off home. His friend also slunk away. We shrugged again and thought no more about it.

Ten minutes later, back came the pair, smirking, trailing the useless player's Mike Tyson–sized older brother. "Which one of you bastards kicked my brother?" this hulking thug demanded. Not surprisingly, none of us owned up. The apparition grabbed a player at random, by the ear. "Was it you?" he grunted. The player in question, who hadn't been involved in the incident, squealed away in a torrent of denials.

Now Gil, the tallest and hulkiest of our group—a potential match even for Mr. Tyson—came forward. "Listen, no one hurt your brother," said Gil, the voice of reason. "He was tackled, lost the ball, maybe got rapped on the ankle. But there was nothing deliberate, and he didn't get hurt."

Unbelievably—this is the heart of residential Jewish Jerusalem, remember, where parents still let their kids play outside after dark, not a crime-infested American or British inner city or a mixed Arab-Jewish neighborhood close to the border— the guy reached into his back jeans pocket, pulled out a switchblade, flicked it open, and positioned it under Gil's nose. Things were getting serious.

At which point Jonny, our goalie, did something rather brave. He wrapped his arm around Mr. Tyson's substantial shoulders, turned him gently away from Gil, and led him off for a chat, the central theme of which was, "Come on, our lot may be a bunch of Anglo-Saxon immigrants, but all of us— you, me, everybody here—are Israelis. And we shouldn't be fighting each other, should we?"

It took a few minutes, and it was touch-and-go, but it worked. "I guess you're right," our would-be assailant finally agreed with a sigh, flicked the blade shut, clicked his fingers at his brother to fall in behind him, and sloped off homeward.

A few weeks later, the kid brother turns up and asks for a game. Sure, we tell him, no problem. And he plays well. Mind you, nobody was too interested in tackling him.

. . . but there's no shortage of tension . . .

The Malha shopping mall in southwest Jerusalem is said to be the largest in the Middle East, though its operators probably have not been to Dubai, Saudi Arabia, or Kuwait to double-check. Ultrachic and ultramodern, it boasts European fashion boutiques, cutting-edge computer emporiums, and supermarkets stocked with four dozen varieties of soda. It also features, between a gleaming electrical store and a shop offering Indian mirrors, bamboo magazine racks, and soap-stone fruit bowls from Kenya, the local gas-mask distribution center.

A few months ago, we spent a lovely early evening clothes-shopping, keeping the kids happy with a Whopper and fries at Burger King, and having our gas masks checked—making sure we had the appropriate model for each kid, just in case Saddam should come a-Scudding again. They have discontinued the see-through-plastic, baby-in-the-bubble model that they were issuing during the Gulf War in 1991—whenever the alarms sounded, you would pop your toddler into a mini-playpen, complete with ceiling and air filter, a few cookies, and a soft toy —so Kayla will just have to make do with a big plastic hood, complete with a motor to keep the filtered air circling. And Josh and Adam, they are such big boys now, they have graduated to the regulation black design. (Just remember, Mum and Dad, when the sirens wail, put your own masks on first, so that, if it is a chemical attack, you are breathing easily and can help your kids get safely strapped into theirs.)

Malha has an eight-screen movie theater showing the latest American action blockbusters just a few weeks after they open in the Big Apple. In the 1970s and 1980s, our audiences would cheer at the sight of big-screen Israeli heroes, and there were a lot of Israeli movie heroes in those days, routing their devious Arab foes. It was all in good fun, of course. And nobody laughed louder than we did at that scene in *Airplane!* when the control tower barked, "Air Israel, please clear the runway," and we saw a Jewish jumbo jet complete with skullcap, sidelocks, beard, and ritual fringes. The best local laugh in recent years was provided by John Goodman, playing a convert to Judaism and proud of it in *The Big Lebowski*, refusing to ride to his buddy's rescue on a Saturday because, goddammit, he's "Shomer Shabbes"—Sabbath-observant.

Seeing a movie at Malha, though, is not quite as escapist as you would wish. Even when the intelligence assessment is that suicide bombings are improbable, there is fairly stringent security at the entrance doors—guards, with bleeping devices to check for concealed weapons, rummage thoroughly in your bags before admitting you. Unless you have kids in the back, they search your car before letting you into the parking lot, opening the trunk, asking for your name. At times of even relatively high alert, like when we saw that absurd Mel Gibson thriller *Conspiracy Theory*, they won't let the audience out en masse back into the street outside when the film is over—presumably because we might be vulnerable to attack by passing gunmen. (Two soldiers were shot waiting at a bus stop nearby a few years back.) But, that night, they could not let us go out the way we had come in either, because the audience for the next showing was waiting. So we got directed through a side door and back toward the center of the mall via various tiny service corridors never designed for this kind of crowding. Progress was slow; someone tripped; folks started impatiently lighting up their cigarettes. Aaah, moviegoing bliss.

The tensest moviegoing experience at Malha was a more recent one—watching *Saving Private Ryan.* Lisa and I were both exhausted, and we knew the film was about three hours long, but we'd been wanting to see it for weeks and decided that we absolutely had to go that night. If one of us fell asleep in the middle, we agreed, the other would give a postmovie briefing. In the event, of course, neither of us took our eyes off the screen. Nor, for the first and only occasion in my Israeli filmgoing experience, did any member of the audience. There was no talking, no coughing, there were no cell phones ringing. In Jerusalem, anxious to sell Coke and popcorn, the movie theaters still insist on plunking an intermission into every movie—not between reels, just somewhere arbitrary, whenever the mood takes them. When the screen went blank halfway through *Private Ryan,* I looked around to see that while the women in the audience had been shocked into silence, one or two dads were still talking macho—the man behind me, for instance, telling his son about how much more accurate machine guns were today, over how much greater a distance, than in World War II. By the end of the movie, when the lights came on again, even the macho dads had been battered into submission by the casual horror and futility of what they had seen. Never have I been in a cinema audience that left the auditorium without a word, clutching each other's hands and arms, faces paled by a sixty-year-old evocation of something still all too real to young Israeli sons and their terrified parents.

. . . or violence (1) . . .

After the first few Scud attacks in the 1991 war, we Jerusalemites realized that we weren't the ones being targeted. Tel Aviv was bearing the brunt of the attacks; Saddam was evidently trying to hit the Kiriya, the central army complex there. So those Tel Avivans who could afford to fled to Eilat, to the south of the target area; and some even chose to slum it in the capital, although old-fashioned Jerusalem is so looked down upon by many chic Tel Avivans that *The Siren's Song*, a postwar movie involving a young woman who chose to gamble on the Scuds rather than hot-tail it to safety in Jerusalem, resonated widely.

Laughing in the face of danger we could now assume was some distance away, many of us Jerusalemites stopped carrying our gas masks with us by day—defying the home command orders—and chose not to put them on when the sirens blared by night. When Judy, a Tel Aviv–based friend of mine, dashed into Gilly's restaurant downtown on the third day of the sirens, pulled out her gas mask and struggled into it, she looked up, rubber-faced, to see that everyone else in the place had blithely carried on eating, indifferent to what had become only a remote possibility of imminent demise.

But just a few days earlier, at the very start of the "Scud war," it had been a little more hectic, certainly in our household: At 2 a.m. on Friday, January 18, the first-missile-is-imminent siren wails—and it really does wail, with the outraged power of a bullying giant, badly wounded and bent on revenge—and we panic. For weeks, I, the great expert, have been assuring Lisa that this is not going to happen. Now it is happening. As the television and radio broadcast warnings to enter our inner rooms or bomb shelters, we rush toward our designated bedroom. But our friend VeeVee is staying over, with her two cats, because her husband, Sid, is somewhere in Gaza doing three months' army service. And the cats are panicking, too. She bundles them into their carrying cage, but they escape, so she chases them around the apartment. Lisa and I are imploring her to first put on her mask and then hunt down the cats. But no, for VeeVee, heavily pregnant, the cats take precedence. She finally catches them, and we shut ourselves in the bedroom. Lisa soaks a towel in bleach and puts it along the bottom of the door—she has heard somewhere that this affords extra protection from chemical attack. We fumble with our gas masks. There then follows a few seconds of complete, terrifying silence—and more panic. We haven't heard the crash of a landing missile, but our masks are undeniably filling with the smell of something chemical.

Saddam's gas?

Lisa's bleach.

I grab the offending towel, open the sealed room door, chuck it out into the hall, and slam the door again. The phone rings. It's LBC, a London radio station. Sure, I'll give them an interview—journalism conquers all fear. "Yes, it is just slightly scary," I tell the interviewer, in muffled tones through my mask. "I'm sitting here with my wife and a friend, quite helpless, and I don't know whether this is a ridiculous false alarm or the end." VeeVee is gazing at me like I have gone completely insane, doing an interview at a time like this. VeeVee, pregnant VeeVee, who put her cats first. Lisa is commendably and typically unfazed. Forty-five minutes pass, agonizingly. (To this day, Jerusalemites will tell you they sat in the sealed room for hours that first night.) The all-clear sounds. We rip off the masks and breathe freely again.

One of the next alarms interrupted *The Simpsons*. When the all-clear sounded, all over the country, families who had been videotaping the show sat down to watch it, saw the missile warnings come up on the screen to interrupt the program, panicked, forgot that they were watching a tape, thought more Scuds were imminent, headed back to their sealed rooms, and spent an awful night in their gas masks. For the first few days, thousands of new Ethiopian immigrants did the same; the all-clear announcement was not broadcast in Amharic.

I make light of the memory now, but that is because a few years have passed and because, back then, we did not have kids. A friend of ours says that, during the various subsequent flare-ups of Persian Gulf tension, she took out the gas masks, showed them to her kids, and assured them that these were the latest craze, improved Buzz Lightyear helmets. Somehow, I don't think Josh or Adam is going to buy that. In December 1998, when President Clinton bombarded Iraq afresh, and the Patriot missile defense systems got deployed again here, our gas masks stayed right where they are now, on the back of the top shelf of the closet in Kayla's room. Perhaps that sounds irresponsible. But like many other Israeli parents, Lisa and I figured that the likely added level of protection they offered against chemical or biological attack was negligible, and that the trauma of strapping them on our kids could be immense. Still, I don't know what we would have done if the sirens had actually wailed again. I don't know whether we would have got the masks out. I don't know what I would have said to the kids. And I don't want to find out.

or violence (2) . . .

I am the lazybones of the family. Lisa gets up almost every morning with the kids; I sleep in for as many extra minutes or hours as I can grab. And on Fridays (the Israeli work week runs Sunday through Thursday), I have been known to hide beneath the covers until, I whisper it in shame, almost eleven.

So one typical Friday, I stagger out of bed at midmorning, find the house empty, plunk myself down in front of the television, and channel-surf.

Until the 1990s, there was nowhere to turn to, just good old Channel 1, state television, dedicated to boring the pants off you. There would be an hour of news, a deadly documentary, a book program so dull you would reread *Ulysses* to avoid it, topped off with another dollop of news in case you really had nodded off earlier. Some of us, the lucky ones who lived near the tops of hills in Jerusalem, could also pick up Jordan's English-language channel, where the nightly fare revolved around King Hussein shaking hands with an endless tuxedoed crocodile of guests at the Amman Royal Intercontinental or wherever else the munificent monarch had been welcoming notables that day. (And if it was turgid for us, the Lord only knows how awful it must have been for him.) The revolution began in 1990 with the introduction of cable television, hooked into half the country's households within three years. Because our refreshingly informal cable operators evidently take what may be kindly termed a laissez-faire approach to the matter of international broadcasting rights—cheerfully bringing down any unscrambled signal they find wafting above our airspace—we are currently the beneficiaries of stations originating everywhere from India (incomprehensible, melodramatic dramas) to Turkey (violent, incomprehensible, melodramatic dramas), Russia (very bad pop music, very earnest newscasts), Germany (dubbed *Baywatch*), France (nude coupling and arts documentaries), and Italy (seminude talk shows and sunscreen ads). All this in addition to news channels like CNN and the BBC and local cable programming that features Israeli original productions and legitimately acquired U.S. comedy, drama, and soap operas. I am told we once had Television Bophuthatswana, but that disappeared after they threatened to sue us.

91

A Little Too Close to God

So it is late Friday morning, March 21, 1997, and I am flipping slowly from *Gabriella* (an endearingly overacted Spanish soap, subtitled on Channel 3), to an ancient episode of *Mission Impossible* (Star Plus, Channel 18, broadcast out of Hong Kong), when I notice that Israel TV, somewhere in between, has interrupted its routine programming and is screening an unscheduled news bulletin. Inevitably, yes, it's a bomb, at Apropo, a hip café in downtown Tel Aviv. First we get a hysterical correspondent on a mobile phone describing the devastation. Then the cameras and the ambulances arrive, and we hear the screams, see the blood, watch a policewoman search in vain for the mother of a bloodied baby (later to be identified as Shani, whose mother, it turns out, is one of the three fatalities) before handing it gently to an ambulance crew. Now come the eyewitness accounts: the shivering waitress who had been about to take food to one of the tables outside when the bomb exploded; the day manager, in a state of complete, crying shock, recalling the Arab he had seen choose a central table, remembering how the man had set down the bag that must have contained the explosives.

The next voice I hear is that of Maya, a smart young television journalist I know. She had been at the door of the café when the bomb exploded, yards away from death. She sounds amazingly calm, gives a pro's description of the carnage all around her, manages to be reassuring when most of us would have been incoherent. I realize that this is not her first close call. She had been shopping inside Tel Aviv's Dizengoff Center mall in March 1996 when a Hamas bomber tried to get inside, was deterred by security guards at the door, and resorted to self-detonation on the crosswalk outside, taking a dozen Israelis with him. I also realize that I ought to call Maya's folks—better they should hear a straightforward account from me, and know that she's okay, than get panicked by any unclear, perhaps overheard, reports about what has happened.

So I get the message through to Maya's relatives. And then I channel-surf again, less idly now, gathering the latest information as it emerges on the various news reports. And, one by one, the local cable channels close down—cutting off *Gabriella*, the Friday movie, the kids' cartoon channel, and a wildlife documentary. All those programs give way to a printed message of condolence to the victims' families, played over solemn music by Arik Einstein, our marginally less-depressing Leonard Cohen soundalike—all the channels, that is, except Channel 21, the Shopping Channel. There, a pair of slightly sweating salesmen in matching blue ill-fitting blazers are extolling the virtues of a revolutionary car wax. When they are done, we get the hard sell for a set of vegetable-cutting implements and a collection of CD love songs "you just won't find in the stores." An incongruous spark of prerecorded electronic life, this customary vacuous prattling is made not merely surreal but offensive by the context. Only the Shopping Channel is impervious to the bombers of Hamas.

Chapter Three

Fighting for the Country

I'm just glad that Adam's got asthma. Maybe Josh has got flat feet.

—Lisa, contemplating her sons' future army service

The single most agonizing dilemma involved in raising a family here, for me, concerns the army, specifically, my sons' future roles in it.

For the first thirty years of statehood, from the war of independence through the 1956 Sinai campaign, the 1967 Six-Day War and the 1973 Yom Kippur surprise, the army's official name, the "Israel Defense Forces" (IDF), was pretty credible—a military machine fighting to prevent the obliteration of the country. But that changed in the 1980s and 1990s, first when Israel initiated the war in Lebanon in 1982 and then, five years later, when it attempted to use the army to quell the inevitable consequences of a generation's occupation—sending soldiers with no training in handling civilian unrest, and none of the right equipment either, to fire tear gas, rubber bullets, and live ammunition at the stone- and Molotov-cocktail-throwing protesters of the Intifada. With that recent history, compounded by misadventures such as the deportation of political opponents by the hundreds, "Israel Defense Forces" has all too often sounded veritably Orwellian.

In the mid-1990s, the Rabin years, there seemed every reason to believe that, even if conscription was not about to be phased out, our ignoble record of a war each decade was about to be erased—that, having made our peace with Egypt and, latterly Jordan, we were on the way to an accommodation with the Palestinians, the Syrians, and the Lebanese as well. Under Netanyahu, led by a government determined to hold on to as much occupied territory as possible, and thus reducing the prospect of permanent peace with the Palestinians and the Syrians, it became more than legitimate, I think actually my duty, to take stock—to ask myself whether I should be grooming my two beloved boys to fight in this army, for this government, for the people who had elected it. When the people rejected Netanyahu and elected Barak, I relaxed again. Not because conscription is now bound to be scrapped. It is not. Nor are all our conflicts inevitably over. Far from it. But because our people have now chosen someone who will try and make peace, and, therefore, if there is more violence, I will be prepared to believe that it was unavoidable and prepared to contemplate my children being forced to participate in it, to defend their country. That probably sounds utterly heartless—but that's the way I draw the line: Provided that the country is genuinely trying to find peace, I will likely stay here and allow my children to grow up here with the army beckoning. If the Barak era proves a false dawn, if we do slip back into hard-line, uncompromising policies that prompt more violence, well, then I would have to reconsider.

On the day Josh was born, as his mother lay recovering, I accompanied the midwife to the hospital nursery, there to oversee his first swaddling. "Oh, dear," grunted the receiving nurse, with Eeyore-esque gloominess, as she inspected the screaming, purple, male package, "another soldier." I was completely flabbergasted by that comment, but did I ever come to understand it. I told myself over the next few years that there was no way I would let Josh go off to war for the likes of Netanyahu. But, of course, if we are in Israel, off to the army the kids will go—whoever the prime minister is. At ages three and four, when boys are celebrating their birthdays in kindergarten, the other kids parade in front of them in turn and give them a birthday good wish, or "blessing." The most common such "blessing" at parties I attended for Josh and Adam, delivered with innocent solemnity by their classmates, was "You should grow up to be a soldier."

For the *Jerusalem Report* in September 1997, soon after twelve members of an elite commando unit had been ambushed and killed by Hizbollah in a south Lebanon raid, I interviewed a Western-immigrant couple, he English-born, she American, about the traumas they endured as parents with two boys in crack fighting units. The conversation was rackingly emotional for all three of us—mainly for Andrew and Sarah, who were living it, but also, to a lesser extent, for me, because in it I saw my and Lisa's future:

Andrew: We brought up our children to believe that this is our country, the country we have to defend.

Sarah: From late junior high, everything at school was focused on which unit they'd serve in. But until they actually get conscripted, you don't realize the effect it's going to have. . . .

Andrew: When you say good-bye on Sunday mornings, you ask yourself whether you're going to see them again. . . . When the phone rings, I can't tell you how your heart stops still.

Sarah: I talked to my sister-in-law the other day. She said, "How're the boys?" My immediate reaction was, "Why, what's happened?"

Andrew: I try not to listen to the news during the day. I couldn't get any work done. . . . I can't ask them whether what they do scares them. I don't know if that's because it's "not the done thing." But if they said yes, I might totally crack up. *They* might crack up. . . . They went with my total support. But I couldn't have stopped them anyway. There are so many contradictions in what I'm saying. I want my younger boy [serving in a highly sensitive position] with us at home. This week I found myself thinking about what kind of injury he could have that wouldn't leave him permanently hurt, but would keep him out of the unit until the end of his army service. I already have a eulogy in mind.

Sarah: I can't believe you said that.

Andrew: I have something I want to say if, God forbid, I have to stand at his graveside. Absolutely. It's here the whole time.

It wasn't only me and other Western immigrants who were questioning, in the Netanyahu years at least, whether the sacrifices Israel has always demanded of its citizens were still tenable, asking why it was that a nation so advanced in so many other fields was proving incapable of resolving its neighborhood disputes without round after round of bloodshed. Had Netanyahu dragged us into full-scale war, and he seemed to come close on more than one occasion, I would not have been surprised to see plenty of Israelis failing to turn up to fight—with dismal consequences. Many—not all, but many—of our bravest soldiers have traditionally come from the kibbutz movement and the political left, and they may not have been willing to die in a war if they thought it could have been avoided. A few hundred leftist soldiers went to jail for refusing to police the Intifada. Under Netanyahu, that number could have been far higher. As he oversaw the crippling of the peace process in 1996 and 1997, dozens of elite commandos signed a painfully worded letter to him that warned, essentially, that if he got Israel into a war, he shouldn't expect them to fight it. At around the same time, the induction centers were reporting a drop-off in volunteers for elite combat units, and newspapers published the ignominious tale of the unit that called up 340 reservists for duty in the Nablus area and had barely 30 present themselves.

There was a corollary to this disillusionment, in the shape of the growing right-wing-Orthodox influence within the army. The "hesder" program for modern-Orthodox Israelis offers a combination of yeshiva study and military service—a few months of study, followed by a few months on the front line, and so on in rotation. Many of the "hesder" yeshivas are right-wing; many are located in the West Bank. They are producing gung ho soldiers, more and more of whom are making their way up the officers' ladder. But along with their passion for their uniforms is a passion for the West Bank, and a respect for rabbis—some of whom are telling them not to participate in handing over "Jewish land" to non-Jews. Soldiers who have graduated from these yeshivas now have dual loyalties—to the government that gave them their uniforms and to the sages who shaped their minds. I have had skullcap-wearing soldiers discuss their dilemmas with me after army lectures. In some cases, these earnest young men have said they just don't know how they would act if push came to shove; in others, they've said they would follow their rabbis' wishes. "The army has command of my body," one said to me, "but God, through my rabbi, commands my soul." When the really hard compromises are being made with the Palestinians, when the day does come to uproot West Bank settlements, as come it likely will under Prime Minister Barak, whose orders are these soldiers going to follow? The chief of staff's, or their rabbis'?

Because so many Israelis are so conflicted about the role the army has played here lately, how it has been misused by the politicians, and because those politicians, while arrogantly presuming that our regional military preeminence is being maintained, so alienated potentially supportive neighboring regimes in the late 1990s, Israel may be less militarily impregnable than it would like to believe. While our military chiefs are complaining about the budgetary cuts that have left supplies depleted and crack forces underprepared, and while they have had to devote much of their energies in recent years to Intifada policing, the Egyptian armed forces are most of the way through a systematic and costly modernization and have held major war exercises designed for them to face off against an enemy to the northeast. Now who could that be? Syria has its Scuds, their launchers dug in and facing Israel. Iraq has already had the pleasure of demonstrating how a few crude missiles could terrify us. And the Palestinians are more than capable of playing catalyst, not only stockpiling arms of their own—reportedly smuggling in weaponry from Egypt via tunnels and under the nets of fishing boats—but well-placed to unify the Arab world over the single issue all its leaders can be galvanized around: Israel's iniquitous treatment of the Palestinian nation.

Don't get me wrong. I'm not saying that the army would be a walkover. I was in college with paratrooper reservists, rugged, strapping fellows who quite possibly leap small buildings in a single bound. My friend Mark's unit used to perform heroic work extricating plainclothes troops when their cover got blown in the refugee camps of Gaza, and is doubtless capable of highly efficient warfare if pressed into service on other fronts. There are legendary figures like the appropriately named Rocky, a craggy, transplanted Canadian acquaintance from college days, who was sighted ducking and diving outside Rachel's Tomb in Bethlehem when Israeli soldiers and Palestinian policemen were shooting at each other in September 1996, trying single-handedly to achieve a cease-fire.

A Little Too Close to God

But my worries are twofold: that the assumption of moral right, surely a key psychological factor in the successes between 1948 and 1973, has been blown away by the Lebanon War and the Intifada; and that the last of our military "victories," that turnaround from near-defeat in the Yom Kippur War (2,700 Israelis dead in nineteen days of fighting that, at one point, saw the country a last line of tanks from being invaded by Syria, and wound up with Israel controlling the approaches to Cairo and Damascus), came a generation ago. And the years since, especially recent years, contain an alarming amount of evidence that, to put it baldly, our skills at warfare are declining.

Our policy in Lebanon was arrogantly misconceived—proof that our overweening leadership thought it could impose the kind of government and policies it wanted on a sovereign nation next door.

Our military intelligence services failed to predict that the Intifada was about to erupt. Even when it did, our defense establishment, presided over by Yitzhak Rabin, was unable to grasp the scope of the rebellion and truly believed it could be crushed in days or weeks if only enough Palestinian bones were demonstratively broken. Here, too, is an ominous harbinger. The Intifada lasted six years and was never quelled by the IDF. It subsided only amid the initial euphoria of the Oslo peace accords in 1993. For all its disciplined manpower and outrageously superior weaponry, the army was impotent against the stone-throwers. Air strikes and tanks are irrelevant in the alleys of the Nablus Casbah. And it would be close to impotent, too, if it had to fight the Palestinians, now armed, on their own territory again, in the narrow streets of their hometowns and villages. In the 1996 tunnel battles, the worst shoot-out was at Joseph's Tomb in Nablus, a study center purportedly built over the grave of Jacob's dream-interpreting favorite son that had remained under Israeli control when the rest of the city was turned over to the Palestinian Authority. Israeli soldiers protecting the students found themselves beleaguered at the site, trapped inside while Palestinian rioters set fire to the building. The army sent in a rescue squad, inadequately protected, and Palestinian policemen, hitherto ridiculed by Israeli military experts as hapless incompetents who could not hit a barn door at ten paces, killed six of the soldiers.

The decade's major conflict, the Gulf War, also brought no joy, and no experience, to the Israeli military, with the air force denied the opportunity to try and take out Saddam's Scud launchers for fear that Israeli participation would reorient the confrontation into an Arab-Israeli conflict, splintering the coalition ranged against Iraq. What it did bring was another psychological victory for Israel's potential enemies, who saw a country paralyzed by the missile strikes. Was it a passing trauma? Not at all. When the prospect of Israel getting dragged into another round of the conflict flared early in 1998, the nation panicked again—miniriots at gas-mask distribution centers, frenzied mass-purchasing of patently useless plastic sheeting to seal doors and windows for protection from chemical or biological attack.

Our current miniwars offer no sign of any restored prowess. Our very best intelligence-gathering and security measures appear to constitute next to no irritation to the calm, efficient, crazed suicide bombers of Hamas and Islamic Jihad who stroll into our cafes, wander past our shopping malls, and get onto our buses, and then blow them up. Israel does eventually manage to track down and kill the designated "master-bombmaker" of the Hamas military wing every now and again. But, just like on the pop charts, there's always a new number one waiting in the wings. As Yomtov Samia, then the top Israeli officer in Gaza and now the general overseeing the entire Israeli southern command, was honest enough to admit to me in a 1993 interview, Israel will never prevail by taking out the "most wanted" men. In March of that year, for instance, he had 116 Gazans on his wanted list. Three months, sixteen killings, forty-two arrests, thirty-six fleeings abroad and voluntary surrenders later, the original list was down to 22—but 68 new names had been added, to take it up to 90.

And as for the fighting that has flared in south Lebanon ever since the failed invasion, here, too, the enemy has long since gained the upper hand. Though it may sound appallingly callous to present things this way, the fact is that the death-toll ratio has slowly but surely turned against Israel: Hizbollah, inspired, funded, and trained by Iran—with Syrian complicity and widespread Lebanese support—to force Israel out of its so-called "security zone" in south Lebanon, was, until a few years ago, losing three or more times as many men as the IDF. Lately, the ratio has fallen to below two to one— one of the main factors that prompted Barak, late in 1999, to signal his readiness to relinquish the Golan Heights in exchange for peace on the Syrian and Lebanese borders. Hizbollah fighters have become more skilled and more adventurous—acquiring missiles that can pierce tank skins previously thought invincible, outwitting explosives experts by disguising roadside bombs as rocks; their Israeli adversaries, more vulnerable and accident-prone. A 1996 effort to bombard Hizbollah into submission backfired hideously when negligently aimed cannon-fire hit a U.N. base at Kafr Kana and killed more than one hundred Lebanese who had taken refuge there. Attempts at major raids, at seizing leading Hizbollah figures, have also gone awry. A week before the twelve commandos were ambushed and killed in September 1997, five more died in a fire started during a clash with Hizbollah. Most appallingly, in February of that year, seventy-three soldiers were killed when the two helicopters flying them into the security zone collided over the Galilee.

And finally, completing the catalogue of ineptitude, the agencies that are supposed to complement our military forces, the once deservedly renowned Shin Bet domestic- and Mossad external-intelligence services, are also in decline. The Shin Bet compounded its inability to spot the approaching Intifada and to thwart the suicide bombers by failing in what must be considered its most critical task—safeguarding the life of the country's elected leader. This despite the fact that Rabin's killer had boasted widely of his murder plans, and that, having gotten wind of them, one completely credible informant had contacted the security services to alert them to the killer's identity. The Mossad, meanwhile, was at one point recently screwing up on almost a monthly basis—botching an incredibly foolhardy assassination attempt on the Hamas leader Khaled Mashaal in Amman, then getting agents caught in mid-wiretap in the basement of a Swiss apartment building, and finally, shamefacedly, owning up to the fact that one of its most respected operatives, a grizzled veteran named Yehuda Gil, had for years been fabricating intelligence information purportedly showing that Syria was preparing for war—information that conformed to his personal right-wing ideology but was utterly without foundation. On the basis of Gil's "intelligence," in the summer of 1996, Israel very nearly went to war with Syria. At the height of the crisis, Israel even scrambled some of its fighter jets. And it was, reportedly, only when the chief of staff, Amnon Lipkin-Shahak, certain that the Syrians were up to nothing at all, personally promised the prime minister that he would publicly take the blame if he proved mistaken, that Netanyahu reluctantly agreed not to mobilize forces that, had they been called up, would likely have triggered a Syrian countermeasure and escalation into conflict.

Rabin always used to rail against the *"yihyeh b'seder"* mentality—a widespread and dangerous Israeli tendency to assume that "everything will be all right" even if insufficient steps have been taken to ensure as much. That mentality was manifested in Rabin's own death—the assumption, prevalent in the Shin Bet, that no Jew would stoop so low as to attempt to kill a prime minister. It was manifested a quarter of a century ago, when Israeli military intelligence and the political leadership, prisoners of a "conception" that deemed Egypt and Syria would not dare to initiate a war against the mighty Jewish state, refused to read the big, bold, uppercase writing on the wall ahead of the Yom Kippur War. And it was manifested again under Netanyahu, as he emptied the peace process of the mutual trust and partnership that were its essence, apparently disinclined to examine the social, political, and ultimately military implications of deepening the frustration of the Palestinians, themselves supported by every regional Arab regime—at a time when his own military commanders, conscious of the limits of military power in general, and the specifics of the IDF's budgetary constraints, morale problems, and fading qualitative edge, had spelled out to him that the Palestinian problem requires a political, not a military, solution.

If Israel isn't smart enough to avoid another bitter war, I fear that the losses will be far harsher than our leaders are allowing themselves to conceive. In late 1996, after the tunnel-sparked gun battles, the Jerusalem weekly *Kol Ha'Ir* ran a cover story, headlined HERE IT COMES, about looming confrontation with the Palestinians. The cover picture showed row upon row of military graves. The text spoke of preparations for mass burials in Jerusalem's Sacher Park. That article haunts me still.

Amid all this pessimism, I must acknowledge that I have never served in our *real* army, the combat units, the crack commando forces and their ilk. Israeli male conscripts give the

IDF the three years between their eighteenth and twenty-first birthdays, more than one thousand days in which their lives are not their own. (Female conscripts serve slightly under two years.) I have given, over the past few years, including reservist's duties, about two hundred, and the vast majority of those in the Educational Corps. I have been to some of the most secret and inaccessible army bases in Israel—hush-hush missile headquarters accessed along winding roads marked by "no entry" signs; military air bases tucked out of sight all over central and southern Israel; an intelligence unit entered, most improbably, through an anonymous door in an underground parking lot—but only to lecture, not to fight.

As an overage recruit considerably nearer thirty than twenty, I was drafted with other wheezing immigrants almost a decade ago for a program known as "Shlav Bet"—best translated, I think, as "The B Team"—military training so perfunctory that if Israel really needed our services anywhere near the front lines, the existential writing would be on the wall.

The fifty-five assorted military misfits and I who assembled for basic training, at an installation "somewhere in the West Bank," were, variously, overweight, asthmatic, and indolent. We were, all of us, slow learners and heavy sleepers. Most of our group had recently arrived from the splintering republics of the former Soviet Union, where many had seen more than enough army service for a lifetime and were thoroughly disenchanted to be starting over in someone else's ranks. A few were Westerners—some of whom even took basic training seriously and nurtured aspirations to reach combat readiness; and others, like myself, who had never imagined themselves actually holding a gun, found the idea surreal at first but, I confess, got rapidly reconciled to it. And the rest were ultra-Orthodox Israelis who had managed to defer their army training into their late twenties by pursuing years of full-time Talmud study. Prominent among the ultra-Orthodox group were two extraordinary individuals. The first was a noxious character whom we dubbed "Eli Etzba"—"Eli Finger"—because he wielded an exquisitely bandaged right index digit to such devastating effect as to ensure that he was first in the ardently contested line at the shooting range and last in the roster for guard duty, unavailable for our early morning exercises and yet miraculously restored for spare-time basketball. And the second was the egotistical, loud-mouthed, yet strangely lovable Rabbi Daniel, a soldier stunningly inept at the not-terribly-difficult dismantling and reassembly of our rifles, who nevertheless appointed himself our in-house commander and spokesman, and who took it upon himself to re-explain some of the more complicated orders we received, thereby rendering them completely incomprehensible.

Rabbi Daniel forgot his number when we were counting off, stood fourth in line when we were supposed to be parading in threes, fired five bullets when we'd been asked to shoot three at the sorry cardboard targets on the range, but did actually manage to "kill" one of those targets—hitting the wooden stand that propped up our two-dimensional enemy, sending him tottering gently over into the sand to ecstatic victory celebrations from his watching colleagues. This was, I'm delighted to say, the only man we ever gunned down.

Rabbi Daniel, what's more, walked away with the award for the most original attempt at getting home for the weekend—an entirely fictional prize, but one hotly contested at every military outpost in Israel. An ordained spiritual leader, his novel appeal for Sabbath home leave was predicated on his unlikely, though not absolutely impossible, claim to be the sole rabbi of the remote Negev town of Mitzpeh Ramon, a tiny landmark of civilization in the heart of the southern Israeli desert. All Jewish weddings in Israel must be conducted by an officially sanctioned rabbi, and Daniel's contention was that, if he were kept at our base over the weekend, the regular parade of local young studs who, he asserted, wended their way to his door ready to do the right thing by their pregnant girlfriends, would be denied marital salvation. Rabbi Daniel tried his appeal first on Tzahi, one of our more personable commanding officers, who heard him out, laughed in gentle appreciation, but flatly ruled out a weekend pass. With admirable persistence, Rabbi Daniel progressed higher and higher up the chain of command, eventually securing an audience with the biggest cheese in the vicinity, the base commander himself. When he was summoned into the inner sanctum, though, Rabbi Daniel's considerable nerve deserted him, as he later allowed, and he found himself muttering something about wanting permission to get up earlier in the morning for prayers—a request the base commander was delighted to grant.

If Rabbi Daniel was our most colorful character, Isaac was undoubtedly the most unfortunate. He was a nice enough guy, as far as anyone could tell—an Ethiopian, seven years in Israel, married with three children, friendly, and anxious to please. But you could have driven a tank through the gaps in his Hebrew vocabulary. Although our hut was near the middle of a sprawling base, surrounded by barbed-wire fencing, with perimeter guards and spotlights, we were amusingly required to maintain our own nighttime patrols. Just before bedtime on our first night, as enthusiastic as we were ever going to be in our crisp, ill-fitting, new uniforms, we were ordered to stand by the end of our beds to be assigned our night-guard shift, which was to last precisely twenty minutes. Down the hut walked a nineteen-year-old officer, doing his best to hide his embarrassment at having to tell us old-timers what to do, and informed us when we would be expected to report at the front door for our taxing mission in the dark. To double-check that the message had registered, he then ordered us in turn to take a step forward and shout out our assigned starting times. This was when Isaac's linguistic inadequacy first made itself apparent. All went swimmingly until the shouting reached his bed. He stepped forward and announced, with sublime confidence but, alas, woeful inaccuracy, "Quarter to eleven, until two."

The entire hut collapsed into hysterical laughter. We assumed, not unnaturally, that Isaac was having a bit of fun. He was not. "Quarter to eleven, until two," we were to discover, was one of his stock Hebrew phrases. And his was a limited stock.

In contrast to my own first months at the *Jerusalem Post*, where my linguistic limitations could have caused, at worst, financial damage to those who relied on our economic reporting or sartorial inconvenience to those who dressed according to our weather forecasts, Isaac's Hebrew disability made basic training a life-threatening experience. The Israeli army insists on training with live ammunition and, on about day four, after we had been thoroughly schooled in the stripping, cleaning, and, in theory, firing of our M16 rifles, when we headed nervously off toward the gray, squat, hillside barrack from which we were to fire live bullets for the first time at the unarmed cutouts about twenty-five yards away, I had the misfortune to find myself in a party of fifteen that included Isaac. Over and over, our pimply commanders had emphasized the two cardinal rules of behavior on the range: Set the gun to fire single rounds, rather than automatic; and, at all times, keep the barrel within the rectangular metal frame overlooking the range—so that under no circumstances could it swing around and unleash a hail of bullets at the line of soldiers on either side. Isaac would doubtless have recognized the wisdom of these precautions, had he only understood them.

We walked gingerly onto the range and deployed ourselves in a row, facing our designated targets. We nervously loaded our magazines into that aperture whose name I'm sure I knew then but I'm damned if I know now. We checked that the fiddly switch was set for individual bullets, not volleys. We awaited the order to fire. And no sooner had it come, before we had even begun to squeeze our triggers—not to snatch, guys, to *squeeeeeze*—than we heard the unmistakable rapid percussion of automatic gunfire. It was, of course, Isaac.

"Cease fire," shouted the commander, fairly calmly. But we had never heard that order before, and Isaac didn't know what it meant. Seeking guidance, he turned toward the source of the shouting, the barrel of his M16 swinging inexorably in our direction. Thirteen other recruits and I hit the deck in the most alert display of soldiering we were ever to exhibit. The officer leaped on Isaac and wrestled him to the floor, and most of us heaved grateful sighs of relief. Some heaved other stuff. They sent Isaac home the next day. Sometimes it's a strength to know when you're beaten.

There were a few others who fell by the wayside, including an Iranian-born man whose family had apparently suffered greatly during the Iran-Iraq war, and who was thoroughly unnerved by any proximity to gunfire. But, by about day eight, much to our surprise, the rest of us were showing faint signs of military muster. We had mastered the science of the eight-fold blanket, learned not to chew too obviously on parade, hit the odd paper enemy when it wasn't too windy or gray, and even managed to shamble to the parade ground in the mornings at almost the same ungodly hour as the youths doing "proper" training on the base. We were undeniably granted a great deal of slack—smoking breaks, shortened stretcher-carrying hikes, extra, wonderful, sleep. The eighteen-year-olds marching feverishly past gaped in amazement at our impromptu Saturday night singing-while-washing-up routine, which was only curtailed when overenthusiastic percussion led to the demise of some of the crockery. But there was no getting around it. We were becoming soldierly. At the end of basic training, some of us were invited to sign up for further courses that would lead to brave, important duties. And when I wrote a mildly self-deprecating article about our training experiences in the *Report*, two or three of these realish soldiers phoned me up to complain that I had been too mocking, that they took their fighting duties seriously.

They were right. And I am glad, existentially glad, that people do take the army seriously. For the first couple of years after Shlav Bet, I had to take it slightly seriously myself. I spent a month guarding an ammunition dump next to the Egyptian border, listening to the nervous nighttime radio chatter of the electronic eavesdroppers monitoring the movements along the fence, yards away—our peaceful border. Heaven knows how tense it must get after dark along our northern frontiers with Syria and Lebanon. And, for my reserve service the following year, this being before most of the prisons in the occupied territories where we locked up thousands of Palestinians were thankfully relinquished to Yasser Arafat, I was a guard at Ansar II, in the heavy heart of the Gaza Strip.

The Palestinian Authority controls the area now. And when I last went back, I saw that part of the complex had been turned into a Palestinian police barracks, and part had metamorphosed into a landing pad for Arafat's helicopter. The sandy track that led to the main gate was neatly tarred, new multistory apartment blocks gleamed overhead, and a Palestinian heritage center was open to tourists a short walk away—showing the traditions of Arab mud-building, furniture manufacture, cloth-making. The streets were buzzing, the atmosphere tranquil—normal life was being lived, a far cry from the repression and tension of just a few years before. The taxi driver who drove me around happened to mention, as we sped past Ansar II, that he had been incarcerated there at one point. "When?" I asked mildly. "In 1993. What a pit," he spat back. Relieved that he had not been there in my day, I decided it would be prudent not to mention that I'd spent any time there at all.

If anyone had ever needed evidence as to why it was dumb, immoral, and brutalizing for us to be ruling over the Palestinians, they need only have spent a few days at Ansar II when it was an incongruous blot on the surprisingly beautiful Gaza coastline, where Palestinian inmates and their Israeli guards learned to loathe each other with a new intensity hour by slow-passing hour.

Ansar II was a rat-infested hellhole that stank of sewage in the warmish weather and oozed damp in the rain. On first sight, it looked to me exactly how I had imagined a World War II prison camp, except that the watchtowers were olive-green metal, not wood; the perimeter fencing was ultra-modern barbed wire, and the searchlights beamed far brighter than they could have sixty years ago. Technically known as a holding prison, it might more accurately have been described as a dumping ground—a first port of call for any and every Palestinian arrested for any and every "security" offense, from graffiti-spraying to bomb-making, stone-throwing to murder. Several times a day, the two sets of iron gates would be thrown open to admit busloads of new prisoners, passing a sign that really did say WELCOME TO ANSAR II; several times a day, the buses would ship inmates out, to higher-security prisons, to court hearings, sometimes even to freedom. These were the Intifada years, when the Palestinian policemen of tomorrow, our supposed partners, were still the violent activists of today, our enemies. But even back then we kept the relative "moderates" of the pro-Arafat PLO separate from the uncompromising "extremists" of Hamas. The PLO offenders got the concrete buildings; the Hamas prisoners got the leaky tents.

For whatever reason the inmates had initially been brought to Ansar II, one thing was guaranteed: After even a brief stay, the mildest dislike for the Israelis would be inflamed into full-fledged hatred. This was not because of the conditions, and certainly not because of the food, which was reasonable. It was because of the environment. When you lock up hundreds of angry people together and lump in the hard men with the kids and the first offenders, it doesn't take a genius to predict the consequences. The Hamas inmates, bearded and sullen, treated us with such contempt, refusing even to look at us, that we never actually saw how deeply they despised us. But you could watch the PLO prisoners hating us more each day; you could notice a kid in his early teens start to walk more cockily as he realized how exalted was the company he was now keeping, see him learn to ignore the shouted order to "count off" in the morning and at night, and finally have him graduate to gesturing at you in your watchtower up above—drawing an index finger slowly across his throat to signify that, if only he could, he would slit yours in a second and take the utmost pleasure in doing so. I was the one in the elevated tower, the one with the gun and the ammo. But he was the one with the power. Israel claimed that none of the detainees was younger than fourteen, but some of them looked closer to nine or ten, fresh-faced kids caught for throwing stones at Israeli troops.

While I was there, the Rabin government made a spectacularly unsuccessful attempt to smash the Hamas infrastructure responsible for the suicide bombings once and for all, by deporting over four hundred of the movement's purported key ideologues and activists to south Lebanon. It was a misguided and chaotic operation. Late one night, guards at Ansar II and at various other prisons, following hastily drawn-up lists, were suddenly ordered to pull sleeping Palestinians out of their beds. While I stood guard outside one prisoner compound, a series of sleepwalking prisoners were shuffled outside and had their hands tied with the army's patented white plastic, one-time handcuffs, their eyes covered with strips of the cream cloth we used to clean our guns. Then they were packed onto a bus and joined a convoy of fellow prisoners transported up north to be dumped across the border. Presumably, the government believed that from there they would gravitate toward the Palestinian refugee camps of Lebanon, to evaporate as a threat.

But word of the imminent, unprecedented mass exile seeped out, and human-rights groups won an Israeli Supreme Court injunction to suspend the deportation. When it turned out that several dozen of the intended deportees had been tried and were serving sentences, and were thus not "eligible" for deportation (eligible for deportation, now there's a curious legal concept), more lists were drawn up and "replacement" key Hamas activists were rapidly extricated from their jails and transported north. Only those who had not been brought to trial, the court ruled, in its wisdom, could be booted out of the country. By now, the Lebanese authorities had prepared for the Hamas arrivals and, in a masterful public relations stroke, refused to take them, insisting that they were Israel's problem. And so four hundred mostly highly educated and ideologically motivated Islamic activists were left stranded on a hillside for month after month, in the no-man's-land between Israeli-occupied southern Lebanon and the territory controlled by the government in Beirut, there to sharpen their determination to humble the hated Zionists and to give innumerable interviews to the global media from their improvised tent camp. The deportation fiasco achieved what had seemed quite impossible—it gave Hamas, a hitherto internationally reviled, uncompromisingly hardline Islamic movement, good press, its activists portrayed as the hapless, shivering victims of Israeli brutality.

Back at Ansar II, those prisoners who had not been deported spent most of their day playing table tennis on incongruously splendid Red Cross–supplied Ping-Pong tables, huddled in small groups holding animated ideological discussions, or waiting in line for the once-a-week opportunity to grab a few words with a relative through the bars of a tiny booth in the visitors' hut.

That routine sounds mundane. But their stay with us would almost inevitably involve a summons to the interrogation wing—where Shin Bet agents would try to establish just how active they had been behind the scenes or in the foreground of the Intifada, how deep their involvement in any "extremist" group, how detailed their knowledge of any planned attacks on Israeli targets. The Shin Bet agents turned up for work in jackets, ties, and neatly pressed pants carrying small attaché cases, looking like Internal Revenue Service clerks heading for another dull day at the office. Far from it. Those awaiting interrogation were routinely softened up with a day or more of solitary confinement—in a darkened cell no more than twice the size of a shower stall. Their only human contact came with an occasional invitation to empty out their bucket of excrement or when a soldier shoved in or pulled out their food trays at the foot of the door. In many cases, inmates were made to stand for hours outside the interrogation rooms, blindfolded and handcuffed, in sun and rain alike, to await their questioners' pleasure. Reservists like myself did not observe the actual interrogations, but I did sometimes hear the detainees crying softly in their solitary cells, and it is easy to believe the tales of beatings and other torture. Just before my stint at Ansar II, the Israeli human-rights group B'Tselem had issued a report on torture of Palestinian detainees and cited the case of Wa'el Tawfiq Afna, a twenty-eight-year-old from Gaza who, it was said, was beaten on his ears and stomach at Ansar II and had his throat pressed by an interrogator "with such great force that he almost lost consciousness." After eight days of questioning, he was finally hospitalized in a state of "acute hysterical aphasia."

Ironically, given what was happening to some of the inmates, Ansar II, for an Israeli, was just about the safest place in Gaza. It was getting to and from the jail that was my night-mare—the half-hour journey into the Strip from the Erez checkpoint, along roads that, in those days, were shooting galleries for angry Palestinians. Days before my month there began, three reservists were shot dead on the main road running through the northern sector of the Strip. Despite the cold, the awful hours spent in watchtowers overseeing the Palestinian captives, the moral discomfort of being there at all, it was, bizarrely, a relief to arrive safely at the jail.

Hundreds of thousands of Israeli men served in Gaza during the Intifada years. And the vast majority of them saw and did things far more horrible and horrifying than I did—confronting the stones and the Molotov cocktails, picking their way through open sewage in the alleys of the overcrowded refugee camps to wake up the locals in the dead of night to paint over offending graffiti, seeking out the Hamas bombers. It is no surprise that when Rabin promised them an accelerated peace process, holding out the vision of a withdrawal from Gaza, the majority of Israelis backed him. It is no surprise, either, that however impossible the notion of peace-making with the Palestinians has often seemed since, next to nobody has raised the prospect of Israel reinvading the two-thirds of the Gaza Strip given over to Arafat's control in May 1994. That is one war almost all Israelis—a rare near-consensus—do not want to fight again.

There is less of a consensus regarding either the West Bank or the Golan Heights.

If pulling the army out of Gaza, with its massive Palestinian population, its tiny Jewish population (perhaps six thousand settlers), and its relatively minor historical and religious significance for Orthodox Jews, was no great wrench, very different considerations apply to the lands the Bible calls Judea and Samaria. Indeed, a sizable, if falling, proportion of Israelis want to hold on to as much of the West Bank as possible, and are prepared to fight to do so—out of a religious/biblical attachment and/or because they believe that territorial compromise is perceived in the Arab world as weakness and is therefore detrimental to national security. As for the Golan, a hefty proportion of the populace believes that Israel dare not relinquish it, because without the Heights we will be unable to defend ourselves against a hostile Syrian regime.

And yet, despite that mindset, today's Israeli menfolk are most definitely not the mirror image of those who, for the first thirty years of statehood, would if summoned march off to war as a matter of course, of duty, of necessity, many of them genuinely embracing the sentiment of the early Zionist pioneer Joseph Trumpeldor that it was good to die for their country. That kind of spirit flourishes best in a patriotic vacuum—ideally an Iraqi-style dictatorship, but also in a country, as ours was, effectively cut off from the rest of the civilized world and self-perceived as a gutsy little David fending off the brutal attentions of the Arab Goliath. Nowadays, we are not cut off from the democracies; we know that there is a great, big, materialistic, hedonistic West out there, and many of us want to be part of it. Nor do we perceive ourselves as the underdogs of the Middle East; we are thoroughly equipped, technologically advanced, and so ought to be able to outwit the neighbors, not on the battlefield, but in avoiding entering the battle at all. Israelis are prepared to fight, but they'll not troop unthinkingly into battle. A generation ago, training accidents, suicides, and operational failures were ignored by the Israeli media and their tragic consequences suffered in silence by the victims' families. The army was sacred; no one was to dare weaken it, weaken Israel, by exposing it to scrutiny, suggesting that it could be flawed. That is not so today. Every mishap, every death, is explored, investigated. Five soldiers die in 1992 when a missile is fired in error during a Negev operational simulation, and the stench of negligence rises all the way to the chief of staff's office. Those two helicopters collide en route to Lebanon in 1997, and parents publicly demand the resignation of the air force commander. Especially in the wake of the Lebanon invasion, Israelis no longer place blind faith in their military commanders and political leaders. People don't want to die, don't want their children to die, fighting unnecessary wars.

This public shift has not yet extended to the leaders of the Israeli right-wing. It hasn't affected Beni Begin, son of the first Likud prime minister of Israel, Menachem Begin, who remains convinced that all Palestinian talk of peacemaking is dishonest, that Arafat and Hamas work hand in glove, that it is madness for Israel to give up territory won with such loss of life in past wars—and therefore, by extension, that it is incumbent upon us to lose more lives if necessary to hold on to every inch of that territory. The gradual public change of heart failed to sway Netanyahu, who did order the army out of some occupied land but, after signing the October 1998 Wye peace deal brokered by President Clinton for a significant West Bank withdrawal, changed his mind and froze the accord. And it made no impact on Raphael Eitan, who as chief of staff played dutiful Watson to Ariel Sharon's Sherlock Holmes, pardon my sarcasm, during the Lebanon War. Eitan, who found himself deputy prime minister to Netanyahu when he had hung up his army boots and put on his civvies, may have been, when in uniform, a perfectly competent tactician and a fine motivator of men. But he is convinced that every Arab is a bad Arab. He *knows* that no peace treaty signed with an Arab state is worth the paper it's printed on. And he is prepared to prove this, if necessary, by fighting to the last drop of every Israeli's blood—including, it must be stressed in all fairness to his selfless pigheadedness, his own.

In an interview some years ago, I challenged Eitan's unremittingly pessimistic attitude to life in the Middle East. He set forth a worldview that left him arguing against any concessions to Palestinians, Syrians, or Lebanese, describing the peace treaties of history as "meaningless pieces of paper that haven't prevented a single war," and pressing for maximum funding allocations to the military to maintain the ultra-sophisticated fighting force he is totally convinced we will be required to use time and time again.

That's a fairly hopeless outlook, isn't it?, I ventured cautiously. I mean, if you think our destiny here is merely to fight war after war, you must surely accept that lots of us are going to die, and that sooner or later we might actually lose a battle and get wiped out? Surely it must be worth at least attempting to establish neighborly relations?

Already disturbingly ruddy, Eitan's features turned a shade of deepest plum. Where was I from? he demanded.

England, I said.

England, he snorted. You come here from England and you presume to lecture me about the Arabs, what the Arabs want, how the Arabs think. . . .

Eitan is probably best known overseas as the man who, praising a planned expansion of West Bank settlement, is said to have remarked that it would leave the Palestinians "scurrying around like drugged roaches in a bottle." On the basis of my meeting with him, I'd say it's a safe bet he wasn't misquoted.

Significantly, the 1999 elections saw the moderated Israeli mindset spell the demise of all three of these hard-liners. Netanyahu was booted out of office. Begin, a man of unusual integrity, resigned from politics when his party won only four seats in parliament. "I am quitting public life," he noted dryly, "because I no longer have a public." And Eitan, too, was consigned to history, his party winning no seats at all. The elections did not represent the death of the Israeli right-wing, the "Greater Land of Israel" constituency that wants permanent rule over all the land between the Mediterranean and the Jordan River, but the hard-liners are now weaker than they have been in a generation.

Happily, too, Eitan's successors as chief of staff have all been more pragmatic, more worldly, and none more than Lipkin-Shahak, who held the post between 1995 and 1998. A ramrod-straight, sad-eyed, compassionate-looking man who has beaten cancer, Lipkin-Shahak played a leading role in negotiating the security aspects of the Oslo accords under Rabin and reportedly contemplated resigning soon after Netanyahu came to power in May 1996.

Later that year, after the September violence, an Israeli academic named Ze'ev Maoz began speculating about the possibility of a coup in Israel. Never mind the breakdown in trust between Netanyahu and Yasser Arafat; Maoz warned of the breakdown in trust between the prime minister and security chiefs like Lipkin-Shahak, who were angry and frustrated that their warnings about the danger in opening the tunnel had been ignored. They felt that Netanyahu was routinely ignoring their recommendations because he considered them to be too closely associated with the previous Labor governments he so reviled. And they were concerned that his intemperate decisions were destroying Israel's relations with the Arab world and hastening the advent of entirely avoidable, full-scale Middle East conflict. In such circumstances, posited Maoz, a professor known to have close ties with the top-ranking officers of the Israeli defense establishment, a military coup was not merely possible but almost logical—army officers, convinced they know better than the democratically elected leadership, taking over the running of the country until a more sensible civilian government could be installed. Netanyahu's aides naturally ridiculed Maoz's contentions. And, of course, they proved wide of the mark, albeit not necessarily without some foundation. Many defense chiefs were indeed, as Maoz suggested, privately despondent at what they regarded as Netanyahu's clumsy fracturing of sensitive regional ties—especially his determined assault on the partnership with Arafat—and fearful it would lead to unnecessary violence. But the army knows its place in the democratic hierarchy. Even Lipkin-Shahak, who had enjoyed a virtual son-to-father relationship with Rabin and clearly endorsed the peace effort with Arafat, confined his criticisms of Netanyahu to vague, cryptic comments that were susceptible of innocent interpretation.

Personally, I must confess, the idea of General Lipkin-Shahak rolling his tank up to the Knesset and marching Netanyahu off to jail for crimes against the Israeli people did hold a certain, albeit most undemocratic, appeal. On reflection, though, I concluded, as Lipkin-Shahak evidently did himself, that it would be preferable for him and for us that he not pound his tank across the Knesset compound, but attempt instead to take the democratic route to the prime minister's office. When he left the army and did just that in 1999, however, the hardened soldier proved too mild a personality, too lacking in political ruthlessness, to sustain a challenge. It was his predecessor as chief of staff, Ehud Barak, who would put a democratic end to Netanyahu's rule.

Chapter Four

Remembering Rabin

The purest prayer will not bring back him whose candle was snuffed
out and was buried in the dust . . .
Nobody will return us from the dead dark pit . . .
So sing only a song for peace.

—From "Song for Peace," the 1960s peace movement anthem
by A. Y. Rotblit and C. Y. Rosenblum, which Yitzhak Rabin sang
haltingly in Tel Aviv on November 4, 1995, minutes before he
was murdered

Lisa and I didn't go to the rally. Lisa hadn't heard about it. I
kind of knew it was happening but didn't register it. Though
it's uncomfortable for me to admit this now, I was also,
not completely, but a little, apathetic. I was horrified by the
vicious anti-Rabin protests but assumed they would dissipate.
In my mind, I knew that murder was in the air, but in my gut,
like Rabin, I didn't really believe it. So we were at home,
watching TV, the Kenneth Branagh–Emma Thompson movie
Dead Again.

The phone rang—a friend, to tell us that Rabin had been
shot. I knew, somehow, right away, that he was going to die,
that the doctors would not save him.

Ever since then, I've had a recurring thought. I know it is
pointless and dumb and won't change anything, but it still
pops into my mind:

A Little Too Close to God

If only I had gone to the rally, maybe things would have turned out differently. I would probably have pushed my way toward the front, flashed my press card to get near the stage, and, right at the end, tried to shake hands with Rabin, to tell him how stirringly he had spoken, how deeply we supported him. And maybe that would have been enough to alter what happened, to change fate. It would have been a few seconds later that he shook hands with Shlomo "Chich" Lahat, the former mayor of Tel Aviv who had organized the event, to thank him; a few seconds more before he walked to the back staircase and down the twenty-six stairs to his Cadillac. Maybe Leah, his wife, would have been closer to him. Maybe that bodyguard who turned back to look for her would have been where he should have been, protecting Rabin from behind. Maybe somebody would have spotted Amir.

Since that night, I have met quite a few Israelis who have had exactly the same thoughts, people who regret that they weren't at the rally and wonder, pointlessly, whether, if they had been, events would have unfolded differently. Amir had tried and failed twice before to kill Rabin. Maybe he would have failed again—and given up or been apprehended.

I did not idolize Yitzhak Rabin—not before he was dead. I had voted for him, but I knew he had been a weak prime minister in his first term, in the mid-1970s. I knew that, as defense minister in 1987, he had completely missed the significance of the Intifada, which had caught him on a trip abroad, and which he assumed would be quickly repressed by the army. When that didn't happen, I felt that he had compounded his failure, and shamed his army and his country, by demanding the indefensible, that soldiers break the bones of the Palestinian protesters, that the "iron fist" be employed to quell the riots. We had all seen how misguided his Hamas deportation idea had proven. And, though my admiration for Rabin—for

122

the personal bravery, the shift in mindset, the vision—through the Oslo peace process was unbounded, I had my doubts about the details of the accords he had signed.

I had written a story for the *Jerusalem Report* on the Oslo B accord (the transfer of major West Bank cities to Arafat's control) in October 1995, published just three weeks before the assassination, for which I had interviewed many of the people who had worked closely with Rabin through the Oslo process, and I came away feeling that a great deal was being left to chance and to unproven good intentions, and that, scandalously, even some of the most senior Israeli politicians and officials had not completely registered the significance of some of the steps they were taking. The article was entitled "Trusting Arafat" and raised questions about whether the Palestinians, at this stage in the process, could be relied upon to provide "the extraordinary degree of cooperation crucial to its implementation." It also noted that, under the accord, limited autonomy was being granted to the entire Palestinian population of the West Bank, and that it would therefore be hard, in subsequent negotiations, for Israel to annex any West Bank territory, to force Palestinians, now granted partial independence from Israeli control, to take a step backward and submit anew to Israeli sovereignty. I had tried to discuss this issue with very senior Rabin aides and left their offices with the disturbing impression that I was telling them something they had not previously considered.

Because my sister, Miriam, and her family live in the West Bank, I also knew how deep was the sense among settlers that Rabin was blithely abandoning them, that he regarded many of the settlements as liabilities and did not understand or care about the settlers' religious attachment to the land. "While people speak about the anti-Rabin incitement at the demonstrations," says Natan, my brother-in-law, incensed to this day, "no one speaks about the incitement by Rabin himself. A prime minister of my country, even if I didn't vote for him or agree with him, is my prime minister. But when the prime minister says to people like me who don't agree with him on an issue that causes real pain—and I am not talking about raising taxes, but about the very future and destiny of the State of Israel—that 'you're parasites,' 'you're crybabies,' 'you can spin like propellers,' 'you're enemies of peace,' then he alienates that segment of the population.

"It would have been different," Natan continues, "if Rabin had come to Ofra," the West Bank settlement where Miriam and Natan live (and which was founded by Rabin's own Labor party), "and said that, 'I know this is causing you pain, but I believe in my heart that this will bring peace.' If he had promised us that he would do everything that he could to ensure our safety; if he had promised to keep the channels of communication open. If he had said that, the feeling among the settlers would have been entirely different. But he didn't. He just name-called."

To be honest, though, I felt more critical of Rabin for the flaws I saw in the peace deal than for the apparent contempt he was displaying toward the settlers. While I sympathized with my sister and brother-in-law and prayed that no harm would ever come to them, I believed that what Rabin was doing was for the greater benefit of us all, that he should be forgiven for not making a greater effort to win over the settlers and the right, and that, if they were having a hard time out there, and facing an uncertain future, it had been their choice to move there in the first place, and the sooner they moved back to safer, sovereign Israel, the better.

After the assassination, I felt even less inclined to sympathize with the settlers and the right, and no inclination to find fault with Rabin. The bullets ended my apathy. Since the killing, I'll admit, I have come to mythologize Rabin—to use him, or his image, as my own shorthand for the Israel I longed and long to live in, his murder as the puncturing of the dream. It is my obsession. It shows no sign of passing with time.

I didn't know Rabin remotely well, but like dozens of other journalists, I had interviewed him and come away liking him, respecting his straightforwardness, and conscious that here was a man who believed he was fulfilling his destiny—that he had been singled out to lead his country carefully to peace with its neighbors, that he and only he could do it. I don't know how much he believed in God. But I think he believed that God, whoever or whatever that was for him, had brought him to that job at that moment. If he was right, which I like to think he was, what kind of divine plan provided for what happened next?

The first time I met him was on April 16, 1992. A few weeks before, he had defeated Shimon Peres to take over the leadership of the Labor party. Now he was preparing to challenge the Likud's Yitzhak Shamir for the prime ministership. He was sitting in his office in Labor party headquarters in Tel Aviv wearing a white shirt with his top button undone and his tie hanging down, a picture of his mentor Yigal Allon on the wall behind him, and a cigarette burning in the ashtray on his desk.

Prime Minister Shamir, a Polish-born Jew who had seen his mother and one sister killed by the Nazis, his father and second sister betrayed and murdered by the villagers with whom they had grown up, was peddling what he saw as prudence and caution, but which most others, supporters and critics, regarded as stubbornness and intransigence. Terrified of making any move that might render Israel vulnerable, of going down in history as the man who weakened Israel, Shamir's policy was to make no moves at all. It was an honest approach, the one Shamir genuinely believed best served his beloved country's interests, the one he felt confident he could sustain. But it presupposed that the status quo—including the Intifada that was raging in the occupied territories and the wider hostility to Israel that was fueling an arms buildup throughout the Middle East—was preferable to painful land-for-peace compromises with the Palestinians, the Jordanians, the Lebanese, and the Syrians.

Shamir believed that time was on Israel's side. Rabin reasoned that it was not.

In our interview, as in the countless others he gave at that time, Rabin argued that the Intifada could not be halted with tear gas and rubber bullets. This, remember, from the man who, as defense minister five years earlier, had formulated precisely such a tear-gas and rubber-bullet response. A political solution, Rabin now said, was the only way to end the violence, a solution that respected the Palestinian right to self-determination.

Did that mean he now acknowledged the Palestinians' right to a state of their own?

Rabin did not deny it. But he didn't commit electoral suicide by affirming it either. He waved the question away with an irritated shake of the fingers. And it was clear there was nothing to be gained by pursuing the issue. Three and a half years later, in interviews in October 1995, the month before he was killed, he would use the same impatient gesture to wave away questions about his personal safety, about the threats of violence against him. It was a gesture that said, "Don't waste my time with that." So nobody did.

For evidence that the status quo was working against Israel, Rabin pointed to the gradual revolution in the territories—the hemorrhaging of support for Yasser Arafat, the surging popularity of Hamas. He didn't like or trust Arafat. If it was possible to make peace with PLO leaders inside the occupied territories, rather than with Arafat, then in Tunis, so much the better. But Arafat and the PLO were professing a readiness to coexist with Israel, to live alongside the Jewish state, in peace. The perverted Islamists of Hamas were offering holy war until the last Zionist was pushed into the sea. And Hamas was gaining ground among ordinary Gazans and West Bankers.

Rabin knew he was going to win the election. His every gesture underlined his confidence. On the campaign trail, he didn't *ask* for the support of the people, he *told* them why they should vote for him, illustrated the hopelessness of the Shamir path, explained that, for the first time, the opportunity was there to move gradually to a mutually acceptable peace with the Palestinians. He castigated Shamir's waste of billions of dollars of taxpayers' money on settlements in remote corners of the West Bank. He showed how the demise of the Soviet Union and the weakening of Saddam Hussein had combined to create the unprecedented prospect of regional peace.

And many people believed him. If ex–army chief Rabin, the man who had orchestrated the Six-Day War—who enabled Israel to triple the territory it controlled in just one week of fighting—thought it was safe to trade some of that hard-won land for peace, thought Israel's security would actually be enhanced by the deal, who were ordinary Israelis to doubt him?

Rabin offered one more priceless quality: integrity. As with Shamir, but with no other major political leader here since, we knew exactly where we stood with Rabin, that he was telling us what he genuinely believed—with no gloss, no political spin. Until Netanyahu seduced the Israeli majority with American-style politics, slick sloganeering, packaging over content, Israelis had always preferred their leaders tough, gruff, and straight. And Rabin was the toughest, gruffest, and straightest—the legendarily irritable, chain-smoking, no-nonsense ex-general.

The bluntness, the direct manner, the refusal to suffer

fools or detractors, became a liability only after he had been elected, after he had set out on the arduous path to peace with Arafat—when biblical land was being relinquished, and when brainwashed Islamic bombers started blowing up our buses. That was when it became evident that Rabin had never made the transition from soldiering to politicking. It showed up in his insistence on visiting every bomb scene, ignoring the political damage this did him—the perception of an unpopular leader, jeered by right-wing rabble, and rendered impotent by extremist violence—because perhaps he might learn something that would prevent a future attack. It manifested itself in his disinterest in even trying to win over the doubters, publicly mollify the settler hard-liners. These were the traits of a military leader, not a prime minister, a commander who had set his course, led unflinchingly from the front, and paid no heed to the grumbling in the ranks. He was certain that what he was doing was right, that those who doubted him would fall into line sooner or later.

But of course they didn't fall into line. Championed by the freaks on the margins of Israeli society, the racist dinosaurs urging the "transfer" of the Palestinians to other Arab lands, opposition leader Netanyahu led a self-designated "nationalist camp" that targeted incredible vitriol on Rabin. He whipped up the rightist masses at demonstrations that sought to delegitimize the prime minister. He branded Rabin "the man who can't say no to Arafat," derided him as the master of "capitulation." His supporters bayed for Rabin's blood, and brandished placards showing the prime minister's features overlaid with the sights of a rifle. Several times I stood in the heart of those crowds, notebook and pen hidden firmly out of sight in jeans pocket, and I felt as if I were among wild animals, vicious, angry predators craving flesh and scenting blood. There was elation in the anger, elation bred of the certainty of eventual success. The faces were pulled into grimaces of hatred as they screamed their insults, but, between slogans, they were smiling faces. Smiling with the rush that Rabin-baiting provided.

That opposition became murderous when religion was stirred into the mix—when mainstream rabbis began debating whether Rabin's policies were, for want of a better word, kosher; when some of these sanctimonious sages wondered whether the thoroughly secular Rabin, merely the elected prime minister of the democratic state of Israel, had the right to give up territory promised to the Jews by the Almighty, whose policies and preferences only they, standing so close to God, were authorized to interpret and relay. Although after the murder, Leah Rabin reserved most of her anger for Netanyahu, it was these rabbis who supplied Yigal Amir with his pretext, who invoked the talmudic arguments that led the assassin to believe that their god would approve of his actions—that he would be sanctified as the man who saved the Jews from the iniquitous, ungodly capitulations of Rabin, Rabin the unbeliever. To the zealots, Amir was the holy redeemer, successor to the doctor-turned-killer Baruch Goldstein, battered to death as he pumped bullets into the backs of Palestinians on their knees in prayer at Hebron's Cave of the Patriarchs in February 1994, who was sanctified and eulogized by several rabbis, his grave turned into a shrine, a pilgrimage site, for the racist perverters of Judaism.

Only after Rabin was dead did those Israelis who cared—those of us for whom he had represented hope and whose death meant that hope was shattered—come to understand how deeply the vicious taunts of his countryfolk had pained him. Only after Rabin was dead did we realize how lonely he had felt, how exposed. Only when his closest friends revealed that he hadn't wanted to come to that last rally—because he feared he would be made to look a fool, that there would be only a handful of pathetic stragglers in the square to hear him—did we understand how isolated he had become, how unsure of his people. How appallingly ironic that his elation at seeing a quarter of a million people turn out and cheer him as he declared "to the multitudes in the Arab lands . . . that the nation of Israel wants peace" should be followed, immediately, by his death.

Only after he was dead, too, did we learn about the other side of Rabin—the father who never missed his children's school plays and sports days; the gentle grandfather of long, silent armchair hugs; the workaholic who didn't take a holiday in the three years of his murderously curtailed prime minister-ship, and scoffed at his aides' efforts to sneak rest days into his schedule or to budget into his overseas trips spare time to recover from jet lag; the smokeaholic so addicted to his ciga-rettes that his staff secretly installed a smoke-absorbing device behind a plant near his office entrance but who never again lit up in his car from the day that his long-serving driver re-turned to work after heart surgery; the publicly impassive prime minister for whom the bus bombings were so painful that his closest colleagues dreaded bringing him the news of each fresh Hamas atrocity; the stony-faced leader who built up private friendships with families who had lost relatives in the terrorist attacks, telephoned them personally to check on their well-being, dropped in on them for a cup of tea and a heart-to-heart when he had a few minutes to spare. Learning, belatedly, about that other, private side of the man made the loss even keener.

In retrospect, I like to think that I sensed some of that hid-den warmth in my brief contacts with him. But, in truth, the picture that I have in my head, of the prime minister with that gentle, shy, almost bashful smile, is an image that has only become ubiquitous since his assassination. In life, Rabin pro-jected honesty, hardheadedness, and strength. Only with his death did I recognize his compassion.

I look back over my 1992 interview now, and I see that
Rabin, that day in April, spoke of aspiring to go down in history as a military leader turned peacemaker, one who had
grasped the opportunities provided by "a unique period in the
history of the world, the Middle East, Israel and the Jewish
people." He anticipated leaving Syria until last and focusing
initial peace efforts on a five-year interim deal with the Palestinians that would create "new understanding, new realities."
And he expected "no problem with Jordan" once a prelimi-
nary accommodation had been reached with the Palestinians.
If all that, today, sounds banal and predictable, remember that
Prime Minister Shamir, in the very week of the interview, was
castigating Israeli diplomatic officials for daring to hold an
unsanctioned meeting with the devilish Arafat in Cairo.

Rabin said something else prophetic that day: "I doubt that
in my lifetime we will achieve an overall peace," he remarked.
"The problem is not only to dream, but how to materialize
this dream. To fulfill this dream will, unfortunately, take
longer than I wish." Rabin, on the threshold of his election
victory, recognized that he might become a modern-day
Moses, taking his people to the brink of a new golden era only
to fall before his vision could be fully realized. But never—
not then, and not even in the turbulent days that preceded his
death—did he conceive that the dream might be shattered
from the inside, that the enemy to defeat him finally would
rise up from within his own people.

On the day after the murder, Rabin's body was driven from Tel
Aviv to Jerusalem and placed on a bier in the Knesset compound so that, before the state funeral the next day, mourners
could file past and pay their respects. The first to bow their
heads, place a candle by the coffin, and shake hands with Leah
Rabin and her family, were the Knesset members themselves,

the chief rabbis, Supreme Court justices, and other notables. Then came ordinary Israelis, in their hundreds of thousands, to throw a solitary flower, place a photograph, or leave a poem by the dead man's side.

In midafternoon, when Lisa and I first attempted to reach the Knesset compound, the crowds were so huge that we couldn't get within half a mile of the parliament building. So we resolved to try again, much later. At 2 a.m. on this still November night, we woke up Josh and Adam, got into the car, and drove as close to the Knesset as the police would let us— which was at the bottom of a hill a little more than half a mile away. We put Adam, who was still an infant, into the stroller; I carried Josh; and we began the uphill walk. All the pedestrian traffic was moving in the same direction, toward the Knesset; no one, it seemed, was coming back. Along the way, we over-took or, more often, were overtaken by several friends, eyes red from crying. No conversation was necessary. There was nothing to say. If you made that pilgrimage that night, you were grieving for the loss of a figure who embodied your hope for a better future, and you were grieving for the loss of your nation's innocence. If those were not your feelings, you stayed home.

Rounding the hill, moving toward various government offices, the crowds started to thicken. People were walking in the road. The sidewalks were taken up with mourning candles, arranged into Star of David patterns, or into letters spelling out YITZHAK and WHY? Here and there, small groups of teenagers were clustered around a guitarist on the grass, singing the mournful Hebrew songs that had played on the radio after the bus bombings. In front of the Knesset itself, the crowds were so heavy that, after perhaps twenty minutes of waiting almost immobile, it became clear that we were never going to get near the coffin. Adam slept blissfully through all of this. But Josh, who was three and a half, took it all in, saw his mother and his father crying, asked us questions about the man in the box and the man who had killed him. We managed to get to the Knesset gates, from where we could look into the compound, and just stood there for a while, like thousands and thousands of people around us, in silence. And then we walked slowly back down the hill, past the flickering candles, to the car.

Compounding the killing, in the years after the shots rang out, was the evidence, all around me, that Israeli society had failed to learn from it—failed to eliminate political murder from the register of acceptable tools for prevailing in argument. Natan, my brother-in-law, is adamant that the leftist Israeli media, on the basis of "three people clapping in Ariel" (one of the largest West Bank settlements), has created a false picture of settler satisfaction at the killing and sympathy for Amir, when the truth is that "only an extreme minority" condoned it and would condone further political violence. "I remember there was an interview on army radio with [settler leader] Pinhas Wallerstein the day after the assassination," says Natan, "and the first question was, 'So, was there a celebration at Ofra last night?' I couldn't believe that someone would think that we would be dancing because of the murder of the prime minister. We may have had intense political, philosophical differences with him, but murder? It says in the Torah, 'Thou shalt not murder.' It doesn't say, 'Thou shalt not murder but' or 'unless. . . .' You don't kill a fellow human being, a Jew, or a prime minister because you don't agree with him. And the majority of people feel that way, certainly in Ofra.

"Following the murders committed by Baruch Goldstein," Natan recalls, "Rabbi Geiser, the rabbi of Ofra, got up in front of the congregation and said that murder is murder and is absolutely forbidden. One person in the congregation protested.

And another rabbi, Yoel Bin-Nun [the same rabbi who would later accuse unnamed colleagues of sanctioning the Rabin assassination], got up and said, 'Anyone who doesn't want to hear the words of the wise, can wait outside.' And people started to clap. And when Rabbi Geiser finished his remarks, there was an extremely loud 'Amen.'"

Nevertheless, extremists prepared to applaud Amir and the resort to violence were undeniably out there, and they are out there still—associated, in almost every instance, with the political right. At the first hint of a peace breakthrough, back they come—telephoning their anonymous death threats to politicians, sending bullets to one or two of them, pasting vicious posters on the billboards of Jerusalem, scrawling graffiti on the walls downtown. In October 1998, shortly before the third anniversary of the assassination, the left-wing Knesset member Ran Cohen had his car torched outside his home near Jerusalem. The attack came in punishment for Cohen's courageous and ultimately successful struggle to have the army dismantle the shrine at the West Bank settlement of Kiryat Arba for the Hebron mass-murderer Goldstein. Three years after Rabin's death, one might have hoped that bodyguards would no longer be necessary for public figures in Israel. Now Cohen has a bodyguard too. No sooner had Ehud Barak been elected, in May 1999, and pledged to revive Rabin's policies and set Israel back on the road to peace, than he too was being threatened by the extremists. The very day after his victory, a military policeman was taken into custody, alleged to have been planning to attack him.

Ever since the Rabin killing, I have been looking for signs that rifts are healing but finding too much evidence that they are not. Instead of acknowledging at least partial responsibility for the campaign of incitement against Rabin, many on the far right are deluding themselves and attempting to delude others by circulating baseless conspiracy theories that go so far as to claim Shin Bet complicity in the killing, and even to suggest that Shimon Peres, anxious for the top job, conspired to get Rabin out of the way.

There are questions that trouble me about the killing. For all the reporting that has been done, I have found no entirely convincing explanation as to why Amir or someone close to him, according to several eyewitnesses, shouted, "It's all right, they're blanks" when the shots were fired. And there is plenty that is discomfiting in the figure of Avishai Raviv, a longtime activist in the racist Kach right-wing movement and close friend of Amir, who was allegedly advocating the killing of Rabin at the same time as he was working as a Shin Bet agent. But these gray areas don't impinge on the simple, stark truth that Amir planned and carried out the assassination, was seen and even filmed doing so, and recounted all aspects of the murder to his interrogators and in court.

Rather than seeking refuge in conspiracy theories and counterattacks on leftist morality, the Israeli far right, and especially the Israeli modern-Orthodox far right, needs to re-examine its own ideology, to ask itself whether Judaism really ranks divinely promised land above divinely bestowed life. I personally have little doubt that Amir would not have dared pull his trigger without the specific support of a specific rabbi. Just prior to the third anniversary of Rabin's death, reports circled that another Shin Bet plant, in addition to Raviv, was well connected to the extreme right-wing circle from which Amir emerged and could have provided the courts with information as to whether one or more rabbis gave Amir an explicit sanction to kill. But the Shin Bet, according to these reports, was not prepared to "blow" this agent by having him testify. And so no rabbi has ever been charged with giving such approval. What has been established is how widespread was the theoretical rabbinical debate as to whether, halachically—under Jewish law—Rabin should be punished by death. And yet, to this day, the fifteen prominent Orthodox rabbis who felt it was important enough for them to jointly issue a halachic ruling forbidding Orthodox soldiers to participate in the dismantling of West Bank military bases and settlements have not banded together to issue a similar edict reminding their disciples of the sacredness of human life. And when one of them, Rabbi Chaim Druckman, was asked by one of my colleagues about this omission, he replied that no such joint edict was necessary because, after all, everybody knew about the sanctity of life. But no, Rabbi Druckman, not everybody knows.

Only three and a half years after the assassination could we begin to hope that Rabin's death had not been entirely in vain. Netanyahu came close but did not entirely rupture our relations with the Palestinians. And then Barak was voted into power, promising to revive peace talks with Syria and Lebanon, and promising to reembrace the Palestinians in a joint search for reasonable terms of separation, not haggle with them Netanyahu-style, as deceitful irritants, and delay every grudging "concession."

Barak's election was an incredible joy, a vindication. Three years earlier, I had been certain that Netanyahu would win and watched television through the night after the polling booths closed as the pollsters' prediction of a victory for Rabin's successor, Shimon Peres, was disproved. This time, although a close colleague at the *Report*, Peter Hirschberg, had spent the weeks before election day out and about with Barak's activists and was being assured by them that Netanyahu was heading for a humiliating defeat, and even though the pollsters were predicting a huge Barak victory, I did not dare let myself believe it was going to happen. Only after voting was over, and the television exit polls indicated a massive swing to Barak, did I start to feel a sense of relief. And even then Peter and I sat up until four the next morning, just to make sure the opinion surveys were not off the mark again, just to make sure that my countryfolk really had seen through Netanyahu's empty posturing. Tens of thousands of Israelis flooded into Rabin Square, renamed in his memory after the assassination there, in a hugely symbolic act of celebration. They sang and danced and held aloft portraits of Rabin and Barak and banners proclaiming that Israel had "returned to sanity." A circle had been closed, Leah Rabin declared there that night. "For three years we were walking in the fog," she rejoiced, "but now the skies have cleared." Let us hope so.

To a great extent, to my mind, responsibility for the three lost years lies with Shimon Peres almost as much as it does with Benjamin Netanyahu.

I once translated (from the Hebrew) and edited a speech for Peres. He was delivering it in Philadelphia, at a ceremony in late 1996 where he and King Hussein were being awarded a "Liberty" medal. The king, battling cancer and evidently feeling he had little to celebrate following the assassination and Peres's defeat by Netanyahu in that summer's elections, opted not to attend the event. But not Peres. He was not about to pass up a day of international adulation. He agonized over that speech. He made changes to the first version, faxed me entire new sections, then telephoned me to debate the nuances of this and that phrase. I am not complaining about Peres being a tough boss. On the contrary, I had nothing but respect for the effort, the time, the quest for perfection he manifested. I just wish he had demonstrated similar qualities in fighting that 1996 election.

Peres failed Rabin after the assassination by not immediately calling a general election, at a time when most Israelis, horrified by the killing, wanted to distance themselves from the extreme right from which the murderer had sprung, at a time when the Likud was contemplating ditching the tainted,

Rabin-bashing Netanyahu, at a time when opinion polls had Peres beating Netanyahu by two to one.

And when he did belatedly name his date, May 29, Peres mounted an unconscionably lackluster campaign. Yes, he was badly undermined by the four Hamas and Islamic Jihad suicide bombings of February and March 1996 that left fifty-eight Israelis dead, smashed many Israelis' confidence in Arafat, relegitimized opposition to the peace accords, and rehabilitated Netanyahu. But he also contributed mightily to his own failure, by alienating Orthodox Jews through the closeness of his alliance with the left-wing Meretz party; losing tens of thousands of Israeli Arab votes by launching the bombardment of south Lebanon that led to the deaths of the one hundred refugees; and barely trying to win over Russian-immigrant voters. And intolerably, and for this I will never forgive him, he deliberately played down the assassination in party electoral broadcasts—apparently because he was intent on campaigning solely on his own merits, not those of his murdered predecessor.

Worst of all, there was a tiredness about his entire effort, a sense that he had somehow resigned himself to failure long before the voting had begun. Perhaps this was the consequence of four previous failures, as Labor leader, to win an election outright. Deep in his subconscious, it seemed, Peres had told himself that if the people of Israel could not tell where their interests lay in a contest between himself and an arrogant, hollow pretender like Netanyahu, he was not going to bust his gut convincing them otherwise. If they could so much as contemplate choosing an ex–furniture salesman over a statesman, they would be the ones who would have to live with the consequences of their stupidity.

Although the peace process he had pioneered was at stake, along with the legacy of the rival-turned-partner who had died trying to implement it, Peres did not fight with heart and soul for four more critical years in power—not the way Barak fought, professionally, dedicatedly, *successfully*, three years later. While Netanyahu was marching purposefully through the packed Mahaneh Yehuda vegetable market in Jerusalem, pressing the flesh, Peres was making a great show of being prime-ministerial, meeting with local councillors and obscure visiting ministers. While Netanyahu was eating up the miles on a bus tour around Israel, making stops at every village and settlement big enough to merit a polling station, and giving the voters those extra two seconds of full-on, ultra-sincere eye contact to lock up their support, Peres was relaxing with the latest rose-tinted polling figures, refusing to entertain the possibility of defeat, but inexplicably reluctant to expend the energy necessary to prevent it.

And then there was the "great debate" shortly before polling day. Netanyahu had spent the previous forty-eight hours holed up in a suite at the King David Hotel, rehearsing word-for-word answers, and he came across as bright and focused. Peres looked like a gray, elderly communist dictator, dragged out into the podium sunlight for one last May Day wave to the parading troops. It was Clinton versus Dole, except that in our case it was the incumbent who was the old guy nobody could quite believe was running, and the challenger who was the young, energetic, good-looking fellow confidently sailing to victory.

But whatever I, or others in the legions of Peres's critics, feel about him, it was nothing to the anguish felt by Rabin's bereaved family, the horror of the assassination compounded by the failure even to hold a majority of Israelis to Rabin's vision.

Dalia, Rabin's daughter, has come closest to taking up his legacy, abandoning her career as a labor lawyer to enter the Knesset in the 1999 elections. Yuval, his son, briefly pushed himself into the spotlight as head of a mainly young, secular protest movement bearing the cumbersome and somewhat exaggerated title of "An Entire Generation Seeks Peace." And Leah has primarily been active on the world stage, accepting posthumous doctorates and awards in distant, sympathetic capitals.

I interviewed Yuval and Leah in the aftermath of the assassination and Labor's subsequent election defeat, and found both of them, of course, enveloped in sadness, with Yuval, reticent by nature, sunk far deeper in grief. Asking him questions, mild, sympathetic questions over coffee in a Tel Aviv café with screaming gold and mirrored decor, felt like a dreadful intrusion. A large, thickset man in his forties, dressed in black—black T-shirt tucked into black jeans—as much, I think, in an effort to be unobtrusive as an ongoing sign of mourning, he expressed bafflement rather than rage at the direction of Israel under Netanyahu, and it was only when it came to the subject of Peres and the Labor party, and their inability to maintain the support of a majority of Israelis, that any anger showed through. Even here, he bridled at the suggestion that Peres had "betrayed" his father, settling instead for "let down." Mostly, though, he was neither resentful nor angry. Just sad. Yuval, a quiet, self-contained computer software engineer, had stood in the crowd at that final rally and gone home in blissful, uplifted ignorance. He had turned on the television and heard about the gunshots. And he bade farewell to his father, the prime minister, on an operating room table at Ichilov Hospital.

The *Hartsufim*, a wildly popular Israeli satirical puppet show, did a sketch a few months after the murder showing Rabin in heaven, holding typically grumpy conversations with the angels and smoking as merrily as ever, even tapping out his cigarette ash on a passing cloud. I thought it was lovely. That is precisely how I like to envisage him, his usual irritable self, rendered eternal by the assassin's bullets. But Yuval said he found it in dreadfully bad taste. Did he think his father was "up there" somewhere, though, watching? The son was unwilling to respond. Would he despair to see all the painstaking peace-work coming undone? He paused interminably. "I try not to speak for my father," he said, toying with his empty bottle of mineral water. "But I hope he is being spared this."

Leah Rabin has none of her son's reserve, none of his hesitancy. I interviewed her in the spring of 1997 in her office on the fifteenth floor of a glassily modern block in the Tel Aviv suburb of Ramat Gan. She sat with impeccably upright posture, dressed in simple elegance, thin but defiantly strong. The walls were crowded with mementos of her husband—the young Yitzhak in a montage from his army days; a *Ma'ariv* front page from the day he recaptured the Labor leadership in February 1992; photographs of that initial, hesitant 1993 White House handshake with Arafat, and of the following year's warmer first public meeting with King Hussein. And another framed photograph, on the wall directly behind her, of Yitzhak and Leah together at home, he perched on the side of her chair, his arm around her, protecting her. Now, Leah Rabin's protection was supplied by the crop-haired bodyguard who manned the office door and hovered in constant close attendance.

Leah was bitter about those she perceived as having profited from the murder of her husband, and chiefly Netanyahu, but fundamentally still optimistic—most notably about Arafat's viability as a peace partner and Ehud Barak's ability to lead Israel to peace. She could barely bring herself to utter the name "Netanyahu," and when she did it was only to wonder, angrily, why, after suicide bombings such as the then fresh Hamas attack on Tel Aviv's Café Apropo, there had been no protests branding Netanyahu responsible for the deaths of three young women, none of the invective routinely thrown at Rabin. "Whenever there were explosions like this during

Yitzhak's government, there were demonstrations in the streets, accusing him personally of being a traitor, a murderer. Now, there are no more demonstrations. Only one person is accused: Yasser Arafat. There is no traitor. There is no murderer. No one is taking the blame."

This was, after all, the woman who, every Friday afternoon for months, had to endure dozens of protesters standing opposite her apartment, castigating her and her husband, comparing them to the executed Ceausescus and threatening, toward the end, to string him and her up in the square like Mussolini and his mistress. Who could blame her for wondering, angrily, where those protesters were now?

When I asked her whether she was utterly convinced of Arafat's commitment to a nonviolent partnership, she was adamant: Arafat "genuinely wants peace," she insisted, and wanted to suppress the murderous extremists among his own people. He was, she said, "devastated" when Rabin was murdered. "He cried his heart out." And she was unswerving in her belief that the phased Oslo peace process was the only reasonable option for Israel and the Palestinians, the step-by-step approach, building confidence "between the people."

She was echoing her late husband now, using almost identical language. And I got the unmistakable impression that, when Shimon Peres and other Labor moderates were slowly wooing Rabin around to the notion of rehabilitating Arafat, the enemy he was reluctant to legitimize, Leah may have played a significant role in winning him over, so fervent was her defense of Arafat now, so unshakable her confidence in the viability of the Oslo process.

A final thought: Did Rabin know who killed him? Probably not. The amateur film of the murder shows the prime minister, as he collapses, turn, bewildered, toward the gunfire, but not far enough to see his assailant. In his Cadillac, as his driver, Menahem Damti, frantically negotiated his way toward Ichilov Hospital through streets teeming with the happy thousands homeward bound from the rally, Rabin was sufficiently alert to groan that he had been hit, and remark typically that it wasn't "too bad," before he lapsed into unconsciousness. But Damti could hardly have told him who fired the shots; in the chaos at the darkened parking lot where the crime was committed, he would not have paused to pick out the murderer. And once at the hospital, the doctors later recorded, the prime minister never regained consciousness.

It is not much, but it is a small comfort to think that Rabin, who was always aware of the Arab extremist threat but refused to consider that one of his own people might try to harm him, went to his death with that optimistic illusion intact. We learned how false the optimism was. But to echo Yuval, I want to believe that he, at least, was spared that shattering knowledge.

Chapter Five

Surviving Netanyahu

Who was that strange being, who destroyed our Israeli lives, fed his poison into them, ruined everything he touched, and then disappeared as suddenly as he had come? Israel awoke this morning from Netanyahu as though awaking from a nightmare. . . . Netanyahu wasn't merely beaten, wasn't merely defeated. He didn't just lose. . . . We vomited him out.

—Doron Rosenblum, writing on the front page of *Ha'aretz*, May 18, 1999, the morning after Benjamin Netanyahu was unseated as prime minister

Lisa got up on Saturday, May 15, 1999, two days before the elections, and decided we had to go and see Yitzhak Mordechai. Right now. At his house.

Yitzhak Mordechai had been Netanyahu's minister of defense, but there had been a falling-out. Mordechai, another of our generals-turned-politician, feared that the Netanyahu government was leading us toward a war with the Palestinians, tried to steer the prime minister toward compromise, failed, publicly contemplated resignation, and was then fired. Now heading a new centrist party, Mordechai was the third candidate in the battle with Netanyahu and Barak for the prime-ministership. But his campaign had fizzled. As one of our neighbors, who grew up with him in Kurdistan, remarked of Mordechai, "He's a good man, an honest man, but he really doesn't have what it takes to be prime minister." That lack of fiery conviction had manifested itself in the final weeks of the election battle, when it became clear that Mordechai's bid for the top job was a lost cause. And yet, for some unaccountable reason, perhaps his personal pride, he was refusing to drop out of the race. He had promised his supporters he would battle to the end, he recited almost every day, and that was what he was going to do.

If we had a normal electoral system, Mordechai's failing candidacy would have been an irrelevance. But we don't, and so it wasn't. Under our rules for electing a prime minister, the winning candidate must get 50 percent of the votes cast nationwide. The opinion polls were telling us that Barak was going to beat Netanyahu, but he wasn't going to clear the 50-percent hurdle. Barak might get 47 percent of the vote, the surveys were predicting, Netanyahu about 37 percent, and Mordechai and two other fringe candidates the rest. And that would mean a runoff two weeks later between the top two, Barak and Netanyahu, two crucial weeks in which Netanyahu might be able to claw at Barak's lead and get himself reelected. If Mordechai dropped out, however, the other two minor candidates would follow, only Barak and Netanyahu would remain, and our man would likely win.

And so, Lisa decided on this Saturday morning, it was incumbent on us, the Horovitzes, to try to get to Mordechai, to persuade him to withdraw his candidacy. Into the car we piled—the kids, Lisa, her parents, and I—and off we went to Motza Illit, the exclusive neighborhood where he lives outside Jerusalem. I had thought we might find a small crowd of like-minded good citizens spending their Saturday demonstrating outside his front door in the hope that he would see sense. But no, there was no one about except for a female Shin Bet security guard in a little cubicle by the front door. We parked at his next-door neighbor's house—a Barak supporter, it was amusing and gratifying to see, with Barak election stickers all over his Volvo—and walked back to the Shin Bet woman to ask if Mordechai was receiving visitors. No, he was not, she replied. He was spending a quiet day at home, alone with his family and his thoughts. Could we try to influence those thoughts, Lisa asked, perhaps by writing him a note. Sure, she said. So Lisa did—a brief plea to spare us two more weeks of electioneering, to deny Netanyahu time to mount a comeback. "Withdraw your candidacy," she wrote, "for the sake of our children, your children, the country." And Josh handed the note to the woman in the cubicle, and she promised she would give it to Mordechai.

The following morning, twenty-four hours before the elections, Mordechai calls a press conference. Yes, he tells the assembled journalists, he did promise not to drop out of the race. But circumstances have changed. He doesn't want to be responsible for putting us all through another two weeks of vicious campaigning. And so he's pulling out.

The other two candidates withdrew as well. And the next day, May 17, Barak decisively ousted Netanyahu in a one-on-one battle for the prime ministership. Half an hour after the polls closed, Netanyahu conceded defeat and resigned the leadership of the Likud party. The malevolent genie was gone in a puff of smoke. Evaporated. Three years of hell wiped out in an instant.

Now, true enough, Mordechai did not actually specify that he was withdrawing from the prime ministerial race because of the heartfelt note he had received from one Lisa Horovitz of Jerusalem. But he did say that he reached the decision that Saturday, when he was thinking it over at home. . . .

When I was studying international relations at Hebrew University a decade and a half ago, I was taught that individuals don't much matter in international politics and diplomacy, that the currents of history are too strong. Rubbish. Perhaps it doesn't much matter, in the existential scheme of things, whether America chooses a Bush or a Clinton, a Gore or a Bush, but it sure matters here. One man, yes, one man, in hardly any time at all, turned back the course of Israeli history—shut down the bridge-building with the Palestinians, froze the warming relations with the moderate Arab world, left Jordan and Egypt embarrassed about having made peace with us, got Syria gearing up for war.

Within Israel, he fomented hatreds, by stirring up one ethnic group against another, right-wingers against left-wingers, anyone he could against the media. At an election rally in early 1999, he made a great show of defying the Shin Bet's security instructions by removing the bulletproof vest they'd had him wear. "You're all Likud members here, aren't you," he told the gathering—attempting, in complete contradiction of reality, of course, to imply that only leftists would resort to political violence. Later in the campaign, a well-placed reporter's microphone caught him whispering into a supporter's ear during a walkabout in a Tel Aviv market that Barak and the left "hate the Sephardim, hate the Russians . . . Ethiopians . . . everybody." Hate. Hate. Hate. That was Netanyahu all over.

His supporters shouted death threats to rival candidates on political walkabouts and commandeered seats in studios to drown them out during their TV appearances. Gangs of thieves, never tracked down or formally linked to Netanyahu, staged a series of preelection break-ins at the offices of Barak's American advisers in Washington and his strategists in Tel Aviv. Netanyahu condemned all such thuggery in much the same way he sometimes alleged Arafat condemned terrorism—with a wink and a nudge to undermine the purported distaste.

He was lucky to escape indictment himself—over a conspiracy to appoint a Likud party hack as Israel's attorney general, supposedly the country's top independent legal adviser—and his colleagues continually undermined the police and the courts. His own chief of staff, an ex–nightclub bouncer named Avigdor Lieberman who has had a series of brushes with the law, went into politics and with like-minded candidates won four seats in the 1999 elections, on a platform centered on a demand for the police and the judiciary to be "controlled" by a supervisory panel—presumably composed of people like him.

It must be pointed out that, during the Netanyahu years, the Hamas bombers fell not entirely, but relatively, quiet— a development for which the prime minister, true to form, claimed full responsibility, going so far as to broadcast bloody footage from the bombings in the Rabin years as part of his desperate television reelection propaganda. A cynical explanation for the merciful drop in violence is that the vicious Islamic rejectionists had no need to blast away the peace process, since Netanyahu was destroying it all by himself. A more optimistic assessment is that Yasser Arafat belatedly woke up to the damage the bombers were doing to the Israeli psyche, to the fact that he was losing all credibility in Israel and that support for an accommodation with him was declining with each bang, and got serious about thwarting the Hamas militants. For all I know, members of a Hamas cell may be preparing a bomb in a garage in Bethlehem as I write. They have certainly held demonstrations there, parading in green masks, waving axes and guns, cheering as they set fire to cardboard models of the kind of red-roofed settlement where my sister lives. Now that Barak is talking peace again, maybe they will be spurred into action. Heaven forbid.

On a personal level, because of Netanyahu, Lisa and I started arguing heatedly for the first time about whether we wanted to live here. He stretched my faith in this country and its people, weakened my personal attachment to it and my confidence in their judgment, to the point where I was reluctantly prepared to consider living somewhere else. Josh's boyish talk now of wanting to live in America is, I'm sure, a direct consequence of that weakening commitment he felt in me and in his mother.

I was even less inclined than before to visit my sister in the West Bank during Netanyahu's years in power—more resentful of her for living there, resentful of a government that was encouraging thousands more Israelis to live there, complicating the options for separation and peace with the Palestinians. I had always wanted to live in Jerusalem, but, especially in the Netanyahu years, I felt the city was slipping away from me—becoming increasingly right-wing and Orthodox—and we left it more often than we had ever done before, to go to Tel Aviv for the day or abroad for vacations that felt like coming up from the deep for air.

Professionally, for me, the assassination and the early Netanyahu era were far from dull. I had masses of work; nonstop calls for interviews from radio and television stations around the world; a sense that our magazine was critical in keeping alive some sense of pragmatism and common sense and respect for our neighbors. I would gladly have forgone it all. Professionally, for Lisa and her colleagues, Netanyahu was a disaster. Real-estate prices sank through the floor; who would spend a fortune to live in Netanyahu's unstable, unloved Israel? As foreign investors backed away from us, and unemployment rose, it wasn't only real estate that suffered. We saw store after store closed down in the furniture mall near my office. Coffee shops and exotic bakeries and kids' clothes stores opened with much fanfare in our neighborhood, then quietly shut a few months later.

Midway through his tenure, Lisa wrote down a list of her

reasons for contemplating relocation. "No hope for peace," it began.

> *Bombs.*
> *Too much ultra-Orthodox power.*
> *Army service for the kids.*
> *Too many traffic accidents.*
> *People too rude.*
> *Everything too expensive.*
> *Too many teachers' strikes.*
> *Not enough sleep.*

(The last entry, she is now prepared to acknowledge, may not have been entirely Netanyahu's fault.)

Now that he's gone, now that I feel that we're getting our country back, I'm half-tempted to argue that Netanyahu did Israel—moderate, farsighted Israel—a service. By nitpicking over whether the Palestinian leadership had or had not renounced its virulently anti-Israel guiding covenant, he initiated President Clinton's landmark trip to Gaza in December 1998, a visit that effectively paved the way to Palestinian statehood, with guaranteed American backing—ironically, the very last thing he wanted to achieve. He pretty much destroyed his once proud right-wing Likud party. And he showed much of the Israeli electorate that there was no such thing as a "moderate" right-wing government, no such thing as hard-line peacemaking, but only the stark choice between occupation and reconciliation.

But then I think of the time he wasted, the goodwill that evaporated, the economic and diplomatic price we paid for life under Netanyahu, the way he weakened our friendship with the United States and left us abandoned at the United Nations with only Micronesia by our side. I think of the lives lost and blighted, the new hatreds formed. And, since he has told us only that he is taking a "time out," I cannot rid myself of the horrifying prospect of his returning a few years from now, our dictatorial, self-proclaimed "strong leader for a strong nation," to again win over our volatile electorate—so easily influenced in 1996 by the one-two combination of bus bombings by Hamas and his blisteringly vicious attacks on the conniving Palestinians, the capitulating leftists, and the irresponsible media.

I feel this extraordinary bitterness toward Netanyahu. Bitterness because, if I have come to mythologize Rabin as the embodiment of my Israel dream, then Netanyahu, demagogic, divisive, destructive, has come to symbolize the nightmare. I am bitter that he profited, politically, from Rabin's death. When Leah Rabin charged that Netanyahu had helped create the climate that had prompted her husband's assassination, Netanyahu's aides rushed to his defense. How dare she say that! Netanyahu had been a political adversary, nothing more. They'd had their differences, but their arguments had always been civil. Netanyahu had the greatest respect for Yitzhak Rabin's lifelong commitment to Israel, his contributions as prime minister. In late 1998, in an interview that happened to take place on the night that some 200,000 Israelis gathered in Tel Aviv for a third-anniversary memorial rally for Rabin, Netanyahu told me that, even in hindsight, there was nothing he regretted about his behavior as leader of the Knesset opposition to Rabin, nothing he would have done differently. "I don't think I have anything to apologize for," he stated. "I personally stand by every word that I said." But whatever he may claim now, as opposition leader he had the authority and the obligation to restrain the hysteria and set limits for the extremists in his camp. He failed to use it. It was Netanyahu, after all, who stirred up the crowds at a 1995 anti–peace process demonstraton in Jerusalem, vilifying the Oslo accords from a balcony on Ben-Yehuda Street festooned with a banner that read "Death to Arafat." The same Netanyahu who had led a protest march in Ra'anana at which, a few rows behind him (though he claimed to be unaware of it), fellow demonstrators shouldered a black coffin bearing the slogan "Rabin is murdering Zionism."

I am bitter because his stubbornness cost us years of potential peacemaking. I am bitter, as every Israeli should be bitter, because Netanyahu as prime minister was primarily concerned not with advancing his concept of the national interest, but with his own political survival—ready, at one surreal stage of his periodic coalition struggles, to have his hard-line wing believe that he was abandoning the Wye peace accords while indicating to his moderate flank that he would be pushing ahead with them. This was the man who, to quote Dan Meridor, his former justice minister, "made lying routine."

Fighting the losing battle for his reelection, he was willing to flout the law on Election Day itself, giving live radio interviews in flagrant breach of the restrictions on voting-day propaganda. His Likud party even attempted to brand Barak's party as virtual murderers, claiming that a Labor activist had played a part in the death of a Likud supporter—who happened to collapse after a purely verbal disagreement, and whose family silenced the mudslingers only by threatening to sue anyone who made political capital out of the death.

As a person, Netanyahu was no sort of role model. He cheated on his first wife, his childhood sweetheart. He only married his third (current) wife when she was pregnant with his son. And he cheated on her too. He is widely reported to have had a problem paying his bills. He smoked tens of thousands of dollars' worth of cigars at the public's expense. His second wife converted to Judaism through the Conservative movement, yet as prime minister there were times when he backed legislation to bar Conservative conversions in Israel, and to exclude Conservative representatives from local religious councils.

I suppose the personal flaws are none of my business, but I feel it stains us all that this man was voted in as our prime minister. And in that position, I think he tainted us, whipped up our divisions, deepened the hatreds with attacks that I had to take personally—his attacks on the left, on journalists, on Israelis who believe in what I believe in. I suppose much of what I feel about him parallels what Natan, my brother-in-law, says he felt about Rabin. But Rabin was working steadfastly toward a goal for the country. Netanyahu, purportedly dedicated to improving Israelis' security, was prepared to sacrifice even that, in the final days, risking another round of violence by trying to close down the Palestinians' political headquarters in Jerusalem, the Orient House, in his desperation to hold on to power. Only the Supreme Court's intervention stopped that.

And how could you not be infuriated by a man whose basic lack of consideration and common sense led to innocent people, his own people, getting killed? I am referring, specifically, to September 1996. On the face of it, there was no reason not to smash open a new exit at that ancient Hasmonean water tunnel alongside the Temple Mount. It would ease the tourist congestion. Netanyahu's Labor predecessors had no problem with the idea. But they didn't do it, because sparing tunnel tourists the inconvenience of retracing their steps after they'd walked the route was hardly critical, especially given the acute sensitivities at the site. They knew that rumors abounded among the Palestinians that the route actually ran right under the Temple Mount itself, and that, if there was digging down there, it was the Israelis out to destabilize the foundations of the two mosques up on top. Get those mosques out of the way, and the path is clear to the building of the Third Jewish Temple in their stead. These Palestinian fears were groundless. But Rabin and Peres took those fears seriously. Netanyahu did not.

Rabin and Peres kept postponing the opening of the new exit because they were waiting for the right moment—the moment when they could tie the move to some compensatory gesture to the Palestinians: the military pullout from Hebron, say, or the granting of permission for the Palestinians to pray in the new mosque they had surreptitiously constructed on the Temple Mount, in an area known as Solomon's Stables.

But Netanyahu ignored the sensitivities, ignored the warnings from his security chiefs about the likely consequences, and allowed that new exit to be opened late one night because no one was going to tell him what to do, or when to do it, in Jerusalem. To hell with Palestinian sensitivities. And to hell with the consequences—the days of gun-battles, with dozens of fatalities, signaling the collapse of the peace process in the field, among the uniformed men on both sides who were supposed to be implementing it.

At the height of the fighting, I went down the tunnel, to try and understand what all the fuss was about. Although it was arguably the most incendiary spot on the planet at the time, there was no security to speak of at the entrance; a middle-aged doorman-type waved me graciously in. The guide was a sweetheart, slender and serene in her late teens, floating on the divinity of it all, leading us where only Hasmonean water, archaeologists, and a lot of modern zealots had gone before. She was slightly taken aback when I asked her about the secret passages archaeologists in decades past are reputed to have begun digging under the mount; she appeared never to have noticed a blocked-up archway just a few yards in that looked like the entrance to one such dig; and she conducted the tour, indeed, as though, now underground, we had quite lost touch with the real world outside, where Israelis and Palestinians were shooting at each other—in a confrontation sparked by this quiet, harmless, underground walkway.

Netanyahu could have brought a camera crew down here or, better still, Yasser Arafat himself, and pointed out the ordinariness of it all. He could have shown the world the streams of urine running down the walls from the Palestinian homes up above. ("Where's that water coming from?" asked a bald, unshaven man in my group. "That's holy water," breathed an elderly Yemenite matron, drinking liberally.) And he could have reiterated his calming assurance about the route at no point going within 275 yards of a mosque. (Our guide said 60, by the way, but what did she know?) But he did not. He could have thought more deeply about what he was doing, and thereby saved himself the humiliation of having to cut short a "goodwill trip" to Europe when the fighting broke out. If he had coordinated with the Palestinians, he might even have been able to strengthen the partnership rather than destroy it. But he didn't do that either. Because, even though he was the prime minister who claimed sovereignty throughout Jerusalem and was thus committed to ensuring religious tranquillity in the city, he wasn't prepared to address Palestinian concerns regarding the Old City.

During the first few months of Netanyahu's premiership, I convinced myself that he would prove a swiftly passing phase, a short-term impediment. That was the period when I abandoned my customary practice of taping the two main newscasts on Friday nights, the week's most important television news night. In fact, I tended to turn off the television when his features appeared—not smart for a journalist. I scanned quickly through the acres of political coverage in the newspapers rather than reading everything painstakingly, as I had in the past. I snorted at the very utterance of the phrase "Prime Minister Benjamin Netanyahu." I was in Netanyahu denial.

A Little Too Close to God

But it was no use. He marveled at himself, in one of the newspaper interviews that I did happen to read, that his survival defied conventional arithmetic. And he was right. He maintained an impossible tightrope act, holding together a disparate rabble of moderate and hard-line, secular and Orthodox coalition factions, because those politicians were too concerned for their own futures to bring him down, but also because he was so talented a public performer, so quick on his feet, so skilled in defending even the manifestly indefensible. I have met with groups of American Reform rabbis who went into meetings with Netanyahu determined to castigate him for refusing to grant Reform Judaism any real status in the Israeli religious establishment and emerged brainwashed, murmuring platitudes about his remarkable grasp of the issue's complexities and his genuine concern for their cause. I know that some of his own detractors within the Likud party preferred not to meet with him, because they were well aware that they would come out neutered, persuaded that what they always knew to be black was actually white, and what they thought was white was purple. And if King Hussein and Hosni Mubarak initially marveled at him, hell, so did I when I first saw him in action.

At the launch of his successful 1993 bid to succeed Shamir as Likud party leader, when he was a virtual unknown, he did what he was to do again so successfully in 1996: chartered a bus and went off vote-hunting. His entourage included three people who would later become ministers in his cabinet—the talkative Limor Livnat (minister of communications), the sunken-eyed Yehoshua Matsa (health), and the shifty Tsachi Hanegbi (justice, what else?). During the part of the trip when I was on the bus, the "Bibimobile," Netanyahu traveled through the north. Just a few days earlier, he had turned up at the studios of Israel Television, having telephoned earlier demanding to be interviewed. Live on the evening news, he had revealed to a dumbstruck nation that he'd been having an extramarital affair (with the Likud's "image consultant" Ruth Bar), and claimed that one of his unscrupulous political rivals was behind a blackmail attempt against him—a threat to publicize a videocassette of him in action unless he dropped out of the leadership battle. It was a scandal, Netanyahu stormed. Now, as he strode imperiously through the main streets of Safed, an ancient Hasidic town packed with ornate synagogues, he was accosted by an ultra-Orthodox Jew who told him that some rabbis were ordering their congregants not to vote for a philanderer. "There are plenty of rabbis," Netanyahu shot back, not in the least discomfited. One couldn't help but be impressed by his resilience. Here he was, having just told the whole country he'd cheated on his wife, having been temporarily booted out of his marital home, his personal life in complete ruins. And yet he sailed through the Likud leadership campaign with his confidence intact, serene and self-possessed. "I've won every battle I've ever contested," he often said. Perfect indeed was the confidence of the man who had never tasted defeat.

He toured all the way up to Kiryat Shmonah—the border town frequently peppered with Katyushas from south Lebanon—where he was halfheartedly welcomed by the Sephardi mayor, Prosper Azran, a supporter of the Likud leadership challenger David Levy but one canny enough not to alienate the rising Netanyahu. The deputy mayor stormed out of the city hall boardroom when Netanyahu arrived, shouting angrily at Azran, "You're going to sit down with *him*?" Azran shrugged his shoulders, offered drinks and cookies, but made no effort to conceal his disdainful merriment as Netanyahu thanked him for the "mint tea" when he had in fact been drinking tea with *louisa* (verbena), a favored herb among some Sephardim; the mistake underlined how out of touch Netanyahu could be with his own country after many years studying and working in America. In the shopping arcade outside, Netanyahu stopped at almost every store, thrusting out a paw and a greeting; when a felafel salesman insisted on preparing a snack for him, Netanyahu accepted it with extravagant gratitude and faithfully promised the vendor, as the group moved on, that he would eat it. He didn't.

The bus was plastered with huge pictures of Netanyahu, and the message WE'RE CHOOSING A WINNING LEADERSHIP. As we'd barrel past, pedestrians would look first at the face, then at the slogan, and then back at the face again—as though the idea of Netanyahu as Likud leader and perhaps prime minister had never occurred to them. But when the Likud voters cast their ballots, it was Bibi the unknown they went for. The extrasincere eye contact had worked.

Those were the days of Bibi at his most focused, energetic, and youthful-looking. The last of these disappeared as his prime ministership lingered. Burdened with responsibility, he aged and lost some of his charisma. His hair was being combed ever more painstakingly over the top of his thinning dome, parted ever closer to his left ear. He began to look increasingly like Syria's square-headed President Assad. He also lost some of his sure touch with the media: The man who charmed the Arab press corps at the Madrid peace conference in 1991 made enemies of many journalists, chiding reporters for their perceived distortions, lecturing them on ethics and morals, and invariably keeping them waiting. Prior to a 1996 trip to Spain, Portugal, and Ireland, for instance, we were asked to assemble two hours before a midday press conference in Tel Aviv to allow time for security checks. Fair enough, but Netanyahu arrived more than an hour late—which meant we had been hanging around for three hours—gave a brief and superficial address, answered just a handful of questions, and disappeared again—a performance unlikely to generate sympathetic coverage.

(Security paranoia, the kind that saw Netanyahu ringed by bodyguards even inside the Knesset, is a legacy of the Rabin assassination. Things weren't always that way. When Yitzhak Shamir was prime minister in the early 1990s, Lisa came along with me one evening to Tel Aviv's Florentine neighborhood to see him open a museum dedicated to his pre-state Stern Group, the radical fighters who murdered Britain's resident minister in the Middle East, Lord Moyne. The museum was sited in the building where Yair Stern, the leader, was tracked down and killed by the British in 1942. Because Lisa doesn't have a press card and we thought it might be hard to get in, we took advantage of the fact that we had arrived at the same time as Shamir himself and followed close on his heels into the building. There were no bodyguards, no security at all, just the prime minister and the two of us. He strode down the entrance hallway; we followed, figuring he knew where he was going. He didn't. The corridor led to the toilet. We all looked at each other, embarrassed. There was a pause. And then Shamir strode back down the corridor and up the main stairs, where dozens of dignitaries, wondering where he had disappeared to, were anxiously awaiting him.)

Netanyahu got away with his political zigzagging, his little deceptions, his broken promises, for as long as he did, because his rivals were so inept. At a time when the Israeli public was crying out for a unifying figure, a credible leader to work with the Palestinians and heal the social and religious divides, we cast around for such a figure and ended up empty-handed. That large numbers of Israelis in late 1998, myself included—having mistakenly assumed that the stiff, uncharismatic Barak would never be capable of unseating Netanyahu—were looking to Lipkin-Shahak for salvation, when we knew almost nothing about his worldview or his political abilities, underlined our desperation.

The most common, and perhaps the most accurate, parallel employed by Netanyahu's local critics was with Richard Nixon, a fundamentally flawed president whose endless maneuvering could not, ultimately, prevent his downfall. And yet, boosted by an inept opposition, and by the demographics of this country—and especially the rapid population growth among the large families of the ultra-Orthodox bloc that were his most enthusiastic supporters—Netanyahu managed to escape from Nixon's shadow and cling to power. No matter how poor Netanyahu's performance, there is a vast proportion of the electorate that, as a fellow in working-class Netivot memorably put it, regards supporting a right-wing prime minister and his allies in much the same way as supporting a football or a baseball team: Sometimes the team pleases you, sometimes it lets you down. But it is always *your* team. And you would never, ever, abandon it.

On May 17, 1999, 44 percent of Netanyahu's supporters did keep the faith with him. Thank goodness that the other 56 percent of the Israeli public went off to cheer for the opposition.

Chapter Six

Shades of Gray

The Palestinian side does not seek today, and will not seek tomorrow, to enter into any military struggle. . . . There can be no alternative to resolving the disputed issues between the two sides except through negotiations.

—Yasser Arafat, Stockholm, December 5, 1998

Our rifles are ready, and we are ready to raise them again, if anyone tries to prevent us from praying in holy Jerusalem.

—Yasser Arafat, Ramallah, three weeks earlier

Early in the morning of Friday, February 25, 1994, Israel Radio began carrying patchy reports of a horrific massacre inside Hebron's Cave of the Patriarchs, a hulking twelfth-century shrine that is said to encase the tombs of Abraham and Sarah, Isaac and Rebecca, Jacob and Leah, and is thus of tremendous religious significance to both Jews and Muslims. Typically, the first accounts of the incident were confused and contradictory: One, two, even three Jewish men had opened fire on hundreds of Palestinians kneeling in prayer. The gunman or -men were described variously as soldiers and as settlers. The death toll ranged from a handful to dozens.

Sarah Helm, then the correspondent of the British newspaper the *Independent*, picked me up in her battered Fiat, and we set off for Hebron and one of the most terrible days in recent Israeli-Arab history. The main road out of Jerusalem was closed off by the army, so we circumvented the roadblock via a mud track and made it as far as Bethlehem. There again, the army was deployed in force, trying to impose a curfew on Palestinians, also hearing first reports of the shooting, who had taken to the streets to throw stones and burn tires. We zoomed up an alley just ahead of the army position downtown and found ourselves outside Bethlehem University, where students, ordered home by the Israeli authorities, were throwing stones at troops and dodging the tear-gas volleys coming back at them. Unfamiliar with the back routes that might lead us to Hebron without encountering further roadblocks, we stopped by a doorway occupied by a teenage Palestinian who, to our surprise, offered to escort us. Thanks to his local knowledge, we eventually made our circuitous way to Hebron ahead of most other journalists, finally being forced by near-hysterical Israeli soldiers to abandon the car on the western outskirts of the city.

That was just as well. After the rioting near the Cave of the Patriarchs and the local hospital, during which several more Palestinians were killed, Israel had forced all the townsfolk off the streets. But their fury was manifested in the rocks strewn all across the roads and by their continuing presence on the flat roofs above us. Several times as we traversed the eerily deserted streets, picking our way across a carpet of hundreds of thousands of stones hurled in anger, stern faces would peer down from the rooftops, and we would see arms raised, poised to throw more boulders down on us. "*Sahafi*," we'd yell repeatedly, "journalists." And our Palestinian guide—who walked slowly, with a limp, as a result of an injury he preferred not to discuss—would offer enough of a fluent Arabic explanation to stay the stoning. For most of the long walk through the town, there was a sullen silence—a silence I had felt only once before, when I walked around the streets of Jerusalem's Old City, more than three years earlier, on the day seventeen Palestinians had been shot by panicked, unprepared Israeli policemen in a riot atop the Temple Mount.

Rounding the corner just a few hundred yards from the Cave, we were stopped by a short blond soldier, who gazed at Sarah, myself, and our limping Palestinian friend in disbelief. "What are you doing here?" he asked. "Are you tourists? Are you insane?"

When we explained that yes, we were insane, we were reporters, he assured us that we really, really did not want to go to the Cave just now, but he made no effort to stop us. So we finally got to the minihill that leads up to the holy shrine. And here, in contrast to the deathly quiet elsewhere in the city, there was hubbub. Here, the locals were refusing to go indoors. And the Israeli troops had seen too much blood for one day to make them. Palestinian men and women cornered each arriving journalist and forced him or her to listen to their account of the massacre they all claimed to have witnessed and narrowly escaped.

Sarah and I were quickly surrounded by a cluster of agitated Palestinian women, each trying to outshout the other, each giving a slightly different account of events. But as we sorted through the various testimonies, a thread emerged: One man, later to be identified as Baruch Goldstein, an American-born doctor who lived at the nearby Jewish settlement of Kiryat Arba, had put on his reservist's uniform, slipped into the Cave during morning prayers, and, without provocation, sprayed round after round of automatic gunfire into the backs of kneeling Palestinians. Some of the eyewitnesses claimed to have seen one or more Israeli soldiers firing too. One woman, hair hidden in a pale gray silk scarf, told me more calmly that she had tried to flee from the shrine, but that the open doors to which she and the other terrified women were running were suddenly, inexplicably, slammed shut from the outside by soldiers, and that they had all endured many more hellish seconds until Goldstein, having killed twenty-nine people, was finally overpowered by the worshippers and beaten to death with a fire extinguisher.

Behind this small knot of eyewitnesses as they screamed their gruesome tale were the steps leading from the main entrance to the shrine. And all the way down this gently sloping staircase ran streams of blood, still bright red and fresh from the massacre, picking up dust and grit as they wended their way slowly toward the street at the bottom of the hill. No one was being allowed inside the building; the scene was apparently too awful, and the army was engaged in a feverish cleanup. Low iron barriers and small prayer mats were brought out intermittently to dry in the morning sunshine; all bore splatterings of blood that the hurrying cleaners had failed to wipe away.

And behind the eyewitnesses to the right milled a handful of teenage Jewish boys, students at the nearby yeshiva, emboldened by the guns that they carried slung over their shoulders to jeer at the tales of horror. From time to time, one or two of these boys, who spent their days studying holy texts, called out comments in praise of the killer and the massacre he had wrought, lamenting that he hadn't blown away enough Arabs, and shouting that those who had belatedly managed to silence his gun were the day's only murderers. Later, Goldstein's widow would appeal to the Supreme Court, in vain, for her husband's killers to be hunted down and put on trial. A Goldstein memorabilia industry would sell many thousands of key chains and T-shirts bearing his bearded, spaniel-eyed image. He would be buried in the center of a park in Kiryat Arba, his tombstone proclaiming him a holy man, and many Israelis who admired his actions would come there to pray (some of the very same Israelis who would complain about the

Palestinians' immortalization of their suicide bombers). A work colleague whom I otherwise respect would place a photograph of the "righteous" Dr. Goldstein in his sukkah (the temporary hut in which Orthodox Jews eat and sleep during the Succoth festival). He would explain that the Arabs of Hebron had stockpiled weapons in the Cave of the Patriarchs and threatened for days to murder the Jews, and that Goldstein was a "modern Jewish hero" who had saved his people. Later still, in preparing to murder Yitzhak Rabin, Yigal Amir would refer for inspiration to a book mythologizing Goldstein.

The story that I had to report from Hebron was truly horrible—a Jew, a doctor, gunning down innocent people at prayer in a house of worship. And it grew more horrible—as Palestinian outrage at the killing triggered violence throughout the West Bank and Gaza and clashes with Israeli troops that left many dozens more dead, and as it became clear that those smirking Jewish students weren't the only Israelis disinclined to condemn Goldstein. There were only a few dozen voices, on the extreme political right, hailing him as a righteous man, a good Jew. But that was enough to dizzy my naive mind.

Amid all the horror, I was irritated, that day, by a single, relatively minor detail in the eyewitness accounts I had collected: that gray-scarfed Palestinian woman's talk of the troops slamming shut the doors on her as she and other worshippers tried to escape. The image of that scene wouldn't leave me, and I wrestled over whether to report it or ignore it, to give it credibility or cast it aside.

On the face of it, it seemed unlikely. Why would Israeli soldiers willfully trap hundreds of defenseless Palestinians in what had become a shooting gallery? I didn't want to believe that they could have done such a thing. It seemed as unlikely an assertion as, say, the claim by Arafat, early in 1997, that

Israel was somehow responsible for a pair of unsuccessful suicide bombings in the Gaza Strip, when two Palestinians blew
themselves up on the same morning close to Jewish settlements, a few minutes before school buses carrying settler children were due to pass by. The Palestinian Authority insisted
that Israeli agents were to blame and even produced a hapless
Palestinian man who said he had been hired by the Shin Bet
security service to recruit the bombers and give them the
explosive devices that were to kill them. Israel's official response was predictably dismissive. Few objective observers
believed the Palestinian version.

But something about the way the Palestinian woman had
told her story made an impression on me. Her account of the
shooting was so sober and precise that I doubted she would
have thrown in extraneous, false elements. The tragedy hardly
needed enhancement. And so, I did report claims that Israeli
soldiers had closed one of the doors to the Cave while the
shooting was in progress, albeit carefully attributing the assertion to the woman with whom I had spoken. And for months
afterward, I wondered whether I had been right to do so.
Until, later that year, a judicial inquiry into the Hebron massacre confirmed that Israeli soldiers guarding one of the exits,
fearful that they were about to be stampeded by panicked
Palestinians, had themselves panicked and indeed closed the
doors.

I have some journalistic colleagues who probably would not
have doubted the Palestinian woman for a moment, and others who would have instinctively rejected her account. This is
so not because they are good or bad at their jobs, but because,
no matter how hard you strive, you cannot escape your preconceptions. And preconceptions are dangerous out here,
where nothing much is black and white. Certainties can let
you down. Gray is the color.

Take that Palestinian assertion of Israeli responsibility for the Gaza suicide bombings. It may sound unlikely, but I have come across rumors about Israel having intercepted supplies of explosives en route to Islamic extremist groups in Gaza. And it is not completely beyond the realm of possibility to wonder whether Israel might have somehow managed to sabotage certain explosive devices used by Hamas and Islamic Jihad so that they blow up prematurely, kill only the bombers, and undermine even the most indoctrinated extremist's willingness to participate in future bombings.

Another example: the four suicide bombings in eight days, late in February and early in March 1996. The bomb blasts came in pairs: On February 25, a Sunday, passenger bus 18, crammed with passengers on their way to work and soldiers en route to their bases after a weekend break, was blown up on Jerusalem's main Jaffa Road. That same day, there was another bombing at a bus stop outside the southern city of Ashkelon. A week later, again on Sunday morning, again on bus 18, again on Jaffa Road, there was another bus bombing. And the next day, the fourth and final bomber, having tried to get into the Dizengoff Center shopping mall but been deterred by security guards at the doors, blew himself up at the pedestrian crosswalk outside.

Who was to blame? The easy, conventional answer: the Hamas Islamic Resistance movement, which publicly took responsibility for the blasts.

The more complex, less comfortable answer: Israel, at least in part, since it effectively created Hamas in the first place. Over past decades, Israel's military administration in Gaza and the West Bank provided tacit and direct assistance to the forerunner of Hamas, the Moslem Brotherhood, in the hope that it would grow to undermine the power of Arafat's then reviled Palestine Liberation Organization. Unfortunately, the monster turned on its maker, growing into a movement that, while

167

opposed to Arafat, was also fanatically unwilling to tolerate Israel, and sprang military tentacles that recruited and brainwashed willing martyrs convinced they would enter paradise if they could rid the world of a few more Jews.

If that kind of argument is too unpalatable, too much of a historical view, then let's bring in the focus and rephrase the question.

Why did Hamas choose to carry out four attacks on Israeli targets in the spring of 1996?

The easy, conventional answer, offered unfailingly by Israel's political and military leaders: Hamas needs no particular reason to strike. It is constantly seeking to attack Israeli targets and will do so whenever it has the opportunity.

The slightly more complex, distinctly less comfortable answer: The four Hamas attacks were to avenge the death of the chief Hamas bombmaker, Yihya "The Engineer" Ayash, in Gaza two months earlier (just as previous suicide bombings came to avenge Goldstein's Hebron massacre).

Israel never acknowledged that it killed Ayash. But neither did it issue a denial. And Ayash had his head blown off by a bomb hidden in the portable telephone on which he was speaking to his father. And Ya'acov Peri, a previous Shin Bet security chief, had taken over not long before as the head of Cellcom, the Israeli cell-phone company.

But surely Israel's intelligence agencies had a moral imperative to track down Ayash, who had made many of the explosive devices used in the suicide bombings and was training legions of bomb-building disciples?

Track down, yes. But why was he killed rather than captured alive?

Perhaps because Carmi Gillon, the Shin Bet chief who had so ignominiously failed to protect Yitzhak Rabin from the assassin's bullets, and had tendered his resignation, was just about to step down from his post. And perhaps he wanted to bequeath his demoralized organization, shell-shocked by its deficiencies, a spark of success, a headline-making, flawlessly executed assassination, to catalyze the rehabilitation process, and to wipe out some of the stain on his own reputation; hence, perhaps, the decision to wipe out Ayash.

Now, the preceding arguments are not the only explanations that might be brought for those four bombings. Some of my arguments may be plain wrong. Some of them may be crucial. And there were, doubtless, innumerable other factors. But these few insights, right or wrong, complete or not, exemplify how impossibly complex is almost every aspect of our conflict with the Palestinians, and how casually irresponsible it is to speak in certainties. There is always more to the scene than a first impression would suggest.

All the complexities, the contradictions, the hidden motivations—all the grays—are combined in the character of the greatest enigma of them all: our friend, our enemy, our neighbor, our nemesis, Yasser Arafat.

The Palestinians whom I know through work—the politicians, the academics, the military men, the journalists, the ex–"freedom fighters" (they tend to prefer that to "terrorists")—and those I have met in the course of our normal/abnormal half-interwoven daily lives are, for the most part, people I would be comfortable living alongside.

I am certain that the West Bank Palestinian builders who worked on our apartment, the perfectionist Halil and his good-natured, if rather bumbling floor- and bathroom-tiling sidekick Naim (who so painstakingly installed the elegant flower-motif tiles in our shower upside-down), want nothing more than the opportunity to earn a decent living and provide food and warmth for their (seven and five, respectively) children. And if they could work in their own country rather than be subject to the demeaning daily border-crossing checks in order to enter and earn peanuts in mine, they would be happier still.

I know that the Palestinian teachers and students and engineers and tour guides whom I joined for two days of discussion in Gaza in the spring of 1999 are committed to breaking the cycle of violence, to building a normal neighborly relationship. We had gathered ostensibly to examine the ways in which formal and informal education can be used to break stereotypes and breed cooperation, but the real value of the event was in the warmth of the contacts, the heart-to-hearts over dinner in a Gaza City restaurant as intermittent power failures turned the lights off and on. It was there that I met Subhi, a Gaza teacher who said he was teaching his high-school classes about the peace process, even though the Palestinian Authority had issued no new syllabus relating to Israel, even though the official textbooks used in all the schools had remained unchanged since Egypt ruled Gaza before 1967, and even though all the maps used by the school showed Israel, the West Bank, and Gaza as a single territorial unit named Palestine. One of his colleagues, who taught at the only Gaza institution that offered Hebrew classes, argued that "you can't teach about the peace process until there is a final accord with Israel. How can you teach peace when the reality is still so grim, when Israel is still demolishing houses, when soldiers still shoot at our children, when we're stuck in Gaza, the biggest prison in the world, surrounded by a barbed wire and electric fences?" A Palestinian Education Ministry official agreed, declaring that he was not going "to lie to the children, and tell them that everything is fine, that all the problems have been solved." Subhi, black mustache bristling, got up to retort that, "of course we need to start teaching peace now. Not to lie and pretend that all the problems have been solved. But to tell the kids that some people are making an effort. If you wait for everything to be solved before you start trying to change attitudes, we may never get to the end."

I just do not believe that Arafat's chief of affairs in Jerusalem, Faisal Husseini, whom I have interviewed half a dozen times, nurses a secret plan to eliminate the state of Israel—even though his great-uncle, Hajj Muhammad Amin al-Husseini, the former mufti of Jerusalem, led anti-Jewish violence in Palestine, sought to limit immigration, praised Hitler's attempts to get rid of the Jews, and called for a holy war against Israel in 1948. I think the mufti's composed great-nephew wants shared rights for his people in Jerusalem and independence for them in the West Bank and Gaza Strip. I am certain that Sari Nusseibeh, a soft-spoken academic from another notable Palestinian family, has not a violent bone in his body.

I was even pleasantly surprised, on a recent trip to Gaza, by Fuzy Nimer, whose nondescript business card, identifying him as the general manager of the Zahrat Al Madaen beach-front hotel, gives no hint of one of the more unusual lives of our times. Now a sedate, somewhat slow-moving, shy-smiling sixty-four-year-old, with an aura of authority that ensures half-salutes and hurried acquiescence to his every wish by his hotel staff, Nimer grew up in Acre, a predominantly Arab coastal city in northern Israel. In what would these days be considered a rare liaison, but in the 1960s was revolutionary, he fell in love with and married a Jewish woman, Simona Pinto, from nearby Nahariya; fathered two children; and lived an apparently unremarkable life as a truck driver and delivery man. Unbeknownst to Simona, however, Fuzy led a second existence as a PLO bomber—organizing a series of bombings in homes in the Haifa area, killing three Israelis, injuring dozens. When the Israeli authorities finally caught up with him, tried him, and sentenced him to life imprisonment,

Simona, not surprisingly, obtained an immediate divorce, and Fuzy has never seen her since; he presumes she has remarried but claims not even to know her new last name. His son, who sees himself as an Arab, recently married a distant cousin from a village outside Acre and comes to visit Fuzy regularly in Gaza. His daughter, with whom he exchanged letters throughout the fourteen years he spent in jail, has now severed ties with him and lives as an ultra-Orthodox Jew, married with four children, in Bat Yam, south of Tel Aviv.

On his unexpected release, in a 1985 prisoner exchange, Fuzy was deported, went to Tunis, and became part of Arafat's Palestinian leadership. He came back in October 1994, on the very day Israel was signing its peace treaty with Jordan—timing that he insists was coincidental but that may explain why Israeli border authorities, preoccupied with the peace festivities to their south, negligently waved him in through the Jordan-Jericho crossing. They caught up with him again in Acre, where he had visited his father's grave and his mother's home; dispatched him to Gaza; caught him again on a subsequent home visit; and, he says, agreed not to jail him only if he gave up his Israeli citizenship—which he did. So now Fuzy lives in Gaza, running the Palestinian Authority–owned hotel in which I happened to be staying, and building a new life. Fuzy being Fuzy, however, there is nothing ordinary about his second relationship either. Wife number two is Fatma Barnawi, notorious in Israel as the woman who blew up Jerusalem's Zion Cinema in one of the first acts of violent Palestinian protest against Israel after the Six-Day War.

Fuzy told me some of this in the course of a three-hour conversation that began on the seafront at the hotel and continued in his sumptuously furnished apartment a five-minute drive away. And, yes, it did feel somewhat surreal to be driven by an ex–PLO bomber through the streets of Gaza City in the middle of the night, just a minute or two away from the base where I had guarded Palestinian prisoners a few years before, while he nattered to the Israeli mutual friend who had introduced us about the dental treatment Fatma was currently undergoing in Cairo and the difficulties they were having in selling their apartment there. On arrival at his home, we dutifully admired the inlaid mother-of-pearl armchairs, the grandfather clock, the sculpted ivory tusk, and the glass trinkets Fatma has been collecting from around the world. We took in his collection of photographs showing Arafat and Fatma, Arafat and his son, Arafat and his nephew. . . . ("So this is the terrorist's house," he declared, half-proud, half–self-deprecating as he showed us around the treasures in his living room.) Then we sipped outstanding coffee in his kitchen and, after he had told us of the troubles he was having with his (male) cleaner ("You have to stand over him all the time, or he just doesn't know what to do"), heard about the Association of Neighborliness he had just set up—an effort to organize older- and younger-generation "freedom fighters," people his age along with the Intifada leadership, to work to strengthen relations with Israel. The Palestinians had been stupid for fifty years, he said. They should not have listened to the Arab world and rejected the 1947 plan for the partition of Palestine. "We had no guns, and no brains," he said in his slow, deliberate way. "Now, finally, we got brains. Arafat got smart. We broke away from the Arab world, and went alone. And now we will have our country."

"Now, finally, you have brains *and* guns," I reminded him. And that was Israel's concern—the fear of a strong Palestine turning on Israel. "Wouldn't you like to be controlling Acre, your hometown?"

"I'd like to be able to *go* to Acre," he said, grinning. "But, no, you have your state, we will have ours. The West Bank is empty. The Negev is empty. There is room for us all here. You were walking around Gaza City earlier tonight, and you saw that there is nothing to fear. You have nothing to fear from us."

"Couldn't we have come this far without the violence, without your bombings?" I asked him. He had once told an Israeli newspaper reporter that he had not intended to kill anyone, that he regretted the deaths, and that he had simply wanted to awaken the world to the rights of the Palestinians. With me, though, he just shook his head. "There was no other way," he insisted.

I believe that Fuzy Nimer may be a changed man—tired, but also changed.

For three years in the late 1980s, I was in contact with Bassam Abu Sharif, the mastermind behind several airline hijackings and other acts of violence three decades ago, who at the time was floating trial peace balloons on Arafat's behalf. And I am certain that he too, a man who lost fingers and an eye when a Mossad parcel-bomb exploded in his face, is genuinely committed to a permanent peace with us.

But Arafat, impossible, contradictory Arafat, of him I know nothing at all for certain. As a nation, often, we comfort ourselves by ridiculing him. It is no coincidence that in *Hartsufim*, the prime-time puppet show, the rubber Yasser is the most hapless, inept, and lovable of all the characters. He is depicted sitting forlornly by the telephone, waiting in vain for the Israelis to invite him back to the peace talks. He infuriates his wife by moping unhappily around the house. He speaks in a wistful, singsong tone—a melodic contrast to the harsh voices imposed by the offscreen impersonators on his rubber Israeli political counterparts. And the caricatured exaggeration of his features, which makes the lips even thicker and the eyes even sadder, only adds to his pitiful appeal.

The chief writer of *Hartsufim*, the veteran satirist Ephraim Sidon, told me that his program "holds up a mirror to Israeli society"—distorting things here and there, maybe, exaggerating characteristics and trends, but always trying to root itself in reality. And yet, with Arafat, the reality is a world away from that naive, put-upon puppet. Our ex–Soviet prisoner of Zion turned politician Natan Sharansky said it best, I think, when he observed that, in pitting our negotiating wits against Arafat's, Israel was playing checkers while the Palestinian chairman was playing chess. And Sharansky, who spent nine years in a gulag playing mental chess with himself, should know what he is talking about.

When you look back across the decades, Arafat seems like Gary Kasparov to our Anatoly Karpov, or, better yet, like Deep Blue to our Kasparov—smarter, calmer, and several moves ahead. His most extraordinary achievement is that he has survived—survived our attempts to kill him, Jordanian attempts, internal Palestinian attempts, and who knows how many other people's attempts. But he hasn't merely survived. He has thrived as the leader of the Palestinian struggle for independent statehood, moving ever closer to achieving his goal. He displaced Jordan's King Hussein as the inheritor-in-waiting of the West Bank, East Jerusalem, and the Gaza Strip, and then persuaded the international community and almost all sectors of the Israeli public and political leadership of the virtue of his cause. And if you doubt that this is true, remember that *Netanyahu* relinquished West Bank land to Arafat—Netanyahu, a hard-line prime minister personally dedicated to Jewish settlement throughout the West Bank, heading a party that had always argued that Arafat was a terrorist and that there could be no new, distinct entity between sovereign Israel and the Jordan River.

After decades spent hunting Arafat down, and more than half a decade in fragile alliance with him, we still haven't come to terms with him, his intentions, and his character. We know that he is wily, deceptively smart, impossible to pin down. But we don't know, not for sure, whether he genuinely wants to live in peace alongside us, whether his ultimate game plan is to destroy us, or whether he would settle for the former but happily press for the latter if the opportunity presented itself. Is the real Arafat the bareheaded hesitant mourner who paid a tearful condolence call on Leah Rabin days after her husband was assassinated, or the fiery, fist-waving populist who eulogized the mass-murdering bombmaker Ayash as a holy martyr and warned us in November 1998 that his rifle was ready to battle for Jerusalem? Is he the diffident, betrayed peacemaker who welcomed delegations of Israeli leftists to his Gaza offices and pleaded for their assistance in restoring a dialogue with the hard-hearted Netanyahu, or a vicious, calculating manipulator who is said by some on the Israeli right to be building underground bunkers and arms factories in preparation for the eventual full-scale attack on us and to hold secretive late-night meetings with Islamic extremists at which he indicates that he might not be averse to an anti-Israeli bombing or two?

What do you make of a man who, after eight months of intensive negotiations have finally yielded a deal on the Israeli pullout from Gaza and Jericho, decides *during the signing ceremony itself,* in May 1994, a festive event held in Cairo on Hosni Mubarak's birthday before an international television audience in the tens of millions that, sorry, he is not prepared to put his name to the deal after all? Is it enough of an explanation to say that he has his own domestic public relations to worry about, that he has to prove to his people that he is holding out for the best possible terms?

What do you make of a man who does absolutely nothing when the Israeli chief of staff appeals to him in person to take on Hamas after the first two suicide bombs in the spring of 1996 and only goes into action after the third and fourth bombings have been carried out? Is it credible when he argues that he, too, was betrayed by Hamas, that they had assured him that there would be "only" two bombings to avenge

Ayash's death? How can you trust a man who, reportedly, holds secret talks with Ayash's successor Mohammad Dif but tells the Israeli chief of staff days later that he doesn't know who Dif is?

Why does he persist in comparing his various peace accords with Israel to the Khudaibiya agreement between the Prophet Muhammad and the Arabian tribe of Koreish, and to the treaty between the twelfth-century Muslim warrior Saladin and Richard the Lionhearted—both deals subsequently broken after the Islamic forces had used the respite to strengthen themselves for battle and victory?

Our intelligence chiefs, the supposedly independent analysts, offer no guidance at all. We know that the head of the Shin Bet security service, Ami Ayalon, regularly briefs the cabinet to the effect that Arafat is doing his utmost to thwart Islamic bombings, that his heart is truly set on peace. But we also know that military intelligence officers take a different view, and that army chiefs have told Knesset committees of secret deals hammered out by Arafat and Hamas, under which bombings are suspended for various periods, to advance Arafat's perception of the Palestinian interest, and under which bombing orchestrators are told to ensure that any tracks lead back to West Bank areas still under Israeli control, so that Israel cannot blame the Palestinian leadership for failing to intercept the attackers.

For Yossi Klein Halevi, one of my colleagues at the *Jerusalem Report*, there are no dilemmas here. The answers are easy. The evidence is everywhere. Yossi sees Arafat as a stubbly Marlon Brando. "Arafat is like a Mafia boss," he remarked to me once. "He orders a hit and then says, 'Let's have a meeting.'" That keffiyeh on his bald head doesn't just happen, by chance, to fall down his shoulder in the shape of the full map of Palestine.

Just look at the way Arafat runs his regime, Yossi urges.

He's like every other brutal Arab dictator—arresting one journalist for having the temerity to broadcast the proceedings of the supposedly open and democratic Palestinian parliament, and another for daring to relegate a report of the chairman's triumphant return to Bethlehem to page 7 of a West Bank newspaper; ensuring that human-rights activists disappear into dark cells until they have learned the virtues of silence; quietly arranging the torture and murder of Palestinian land dealers whose "crime" is to have brokered property and land sales to Jews; approving executions by firing squad after summary trials.

For Yossi, reconciliation with the Palestinians, if it is to come, will not come during the Arafat era, under the leadership of a man who alienated his monetary backers in the Persian Gulf and brought financial ruin to his own PLO because he simply could not conceal his admiration for Saddam Hussein; a man for whom terrorism is just another political tool—and a pretty effective one at that; a man who wore his military fatigues to the *Nobel Peace Prize award ceremony*.

Israel has had enough of wars, of demonstrating its military might, Yossi argues. We don't need to prove our Jewish manhood anymore. Just witness the failed effort by some ex–army top brass to mark the fiftieth anniversary of Israeli independence in 1998 with a huge military parade. Yossi resents the claims occasionally raised by Western analysts that both sides have forgotten why they need to make peace and require another major round of bloodshed to remind them. *We* don't need more bloodshed, says Yossi. *We* do condemn our murderers. *We* do see our extremists as beyond the pale. *We* don't think they advance our cause, and even if they did, we would still rather do without them. But the Palestinians, he says, haven't got violence out of their systems yet—they are at an earlier stage of their national evolution. It's convenient for us to try and force our psyche on them. We are so exhausted that we refuse to read the other side accurately. Even if we went back to the 1967 borders, he believes, there would be so many grudges outstanding that, sooner or later, the Palestinians would force us into another war and drag the Arab world with them, so the less land we give them now the better. After that war, says Yossi, the pistol-toting Arafat will be replaced by a new leader who won't use terrorism as a weapon, someone with whom we might be able to make peace. For the "fake Oslo peace," Yossi is not prepared to be generous. For real peace, when the Palestinians are ready, he says, he would be prepared to make "almost any compromise."

Well, I think Yossi is wrong about Arafat, and not because I deludedly regard Arafat as some kind of Palestinian Nelson Mandela. I wish he were. But he is the man the Palestinians rally around, so we have to deal with him. Never mind what *his* true ambitions are, it is in *our* interest to work with him, rather than waiting another few bloody years for somebody more tasteful to supplant him. Arafat, with his lower lip trembling, struggling to hold a pen and put his name to the Wye peace deal, may not be with us much longer. And then what? Maybe moderate, elegantly tailored Abu Mazen. Maybe not. There is no other Mr. Palestine, and without Arafat, there is every prospect of Palestinian anarchy, or of a greater turn to the certainties of radical Islam, to Sheikh Yassin's uncompromising, bus-bombing hostility. We'll long for Arafat after he's gone, and ask ourselves why we didn't move faster with him, why we didn't embrace him more fully, even if we doubted his commitment—why we didn't encourage what may only have been a superficial readiness for moderation and force it to take root among the Palestinian people.

My brother-in-law, Natan, argues vehemently that we must never sever our links with Judea and Samaria, with biblical Jewish landmarks like Beit El, Shiloh, and Hebron. "If we say that these places aren't important to us," he says, "that

179

they don't belong to us, if we're willing to give them away, then the Palestinian Arabs will come along and say, 'What right do you have to be here? Go back to where you came from.' Herzliyya, Tel Aviv, Netanya [coastal towns inside sovereign Israel] are modern creations. Where I live is the historical heartland of the Jewish people.

"Look what happened with Jerusalem," Natan goes on. "Probably the stupidest thing that anybody has ever done. Moshe Dayan, shortly after capturing the holiest spot in Judaism [the Temple Mount], gave it back to the Arabs. [Although Israel annexed the Old City, the Temple Mount plaza is administered by a Muslim trust.] He should have taken down the mosques [the Al-Aqsa mosque and the Dome of the Rock that sit atop the mount], because they don't belong there. No nation in the world would have done what he did, captured their holiest spot, the spot that is the heart and soul of their existence, and given it back, after having been denied access to it for so many years. When the Jordanians captured Old Jerusalem in 1948, the first thing they did was destroy the Jewish Quarter, expel the Jews and blow up all the synagogues. It became *'Judenrein.'* "

Historically speaking, argues Natan, Jerusalem was never considered important to the Arabs. "It was always a backwater. There's no mention of Jerusalem in the Koran. Al-Aqsa is mentioned, as the place from which Muhammad, in a dream, ascended to heaven on his winged horse. But it's only relatively recently that Arab scholars have placed Al-Aqsa in Jerusalem. Many Arab scholars, historically, did not claim that that was so. It was criminal for us not to have held on to the Temple Mount. Because now our claim to Jerusalem is weakened. And more religious friction is going to be created because of what goes on at the Temple Mount than would have happened if, in the first two days after conquering it, we had destroyed the mosques, then and there. Of course, destroying the mosques now is impossible, and would certainly lead to terrible violence."

Natan invokes even relatively recent history to "underline" that our right to the West Bank supersedes that of the Palestinians: "In the 1800s," he notes, "Palestine was a desolate country. Read Mark Twain's *The Innocents Abroad* [in which the author says he "never saw a human being" during a journey in these parts, and notes that "even the olive and the cactus, those fast friends of a worthless soil, had almost deserted the country"]. There were Arabs who had been living here for generations, but the population was very small. The Arab claim that they all have been here since time immemorial is rubbish. The Palestinians at the beginning of this century onward were basically the Jews. There are quotes from various Arab leaders saying that there is no such thing as a Palestinian people. In 1956, the founding head of the PLO, Ahmed Shukeiri, Saudi ambassador to the United Nations at the time, told the General Assembly that, 'It's common knowledge that Palestine is nothing but southern Syria.' Two decades earlier, a local Arab spokesman, Auni Bey Abdul Hadi, had told Britain's Peel Commission that, 'There is no such country as Palestine. Palestine is a term the Zionists invented. Palestine is alien to us. It is the Zionists who introduced it.' The Arabs, if I'm not mistaken, at one time even made their provincial capital in Ramle. Only when the Jews began to return in large numbers did the Arabs begin to make an issue out of Jerusalem. Now, that's history."

But even without getting into an argument over history, I do not for a minute accept the assertion that our right to be here is being fatally weakened by territorial compromise in the West Bank. It is a shame, but we cannot reasonably realize the biblical claim to the entire Land of Israel at the moment; that does not mean we don't have a very strong right, a post-Holocaust, U.N.-endorsed, Egyptian-, Jordanian-, even

Palestinian-recognized, full, morally defensible right to the part of it that is today our sovereign land. So why not finalize the divorce from the ever more numerous Palestinians as soon as we can, separate our peoples, and enjoy the pleasures of a solitary lifestyle—and trust our military and intelligence networks to frustrate any devious plans Arafat might be hatching to expand his empire?

Under Rabin, we were transferring control over land in a spirit of friendship, however shallow or fragile, with the promise of permanent peace at the end—a separation for a few generations, in which the hatreds and suspicions might recede, to be followed by a near-normal kind of neighborly relationship. Under Netanyahu, we grudgingly relinquished territory, in an atmosphere of mutual dislike, with the promise only of more demands, more pressure, and no respite. We let the Palestinians open their airport, at Dahaniya in Gaza in 1998, but we boycotted its festive inauguration and delayed its control-tower equipment in customs. Instead of a positive step forward together, the impression was of an angry Israel, under pressure from the United States, allowing the Palestinians another small step forward in the worst possible spirit. We watched President Clinton helicopter into Gaza International a couple of weeks later and saw him applaud the very public Palestinian renunciation of the PLO Covenant, with its more than two dozen clauses elaborating the need for "armed struggle" to "liberate" Palestine and "eliminate the Zionist presence." But was Netanyahu up on stage alongside Clinton to welcome the move? Was he there to shake Arafat's hand in appreciation? No, he was in Jerusalem, sour-facedly allowing that a significant development had occurred but promptly issuing a further series of ruler's demands for his hated subjects' compliance. If we do it open-armed, or if we are dragged kicking and screaming to each concession, both processes must lead eventually to the same result on the map—the establishment of an independent Palestinian state in almost all of Gaza and the West Bank. But while the first approach offers the prospect of true coexistence, the second will see us reluctantly divested of our bargaining chips, having failed to win the cooperation and harmony for which we were saving them. Giving up the land, in other words, but not getting the peace—the worst of all worlds. In Gaza in December 1998, we saw the Palestinian leadership make its peace with the United States, with Clinton. What a shame, what a waste, that they were not making their peace with us.

I do believe that Arafat is ambivalent about terrorism. The interviews I've had, the information I've gathered, suggest that he made a token effort to crush the Hamas militants—their leadership toughened thanks to Israel's misguided 1992 mass deportation—soon after he came "home" to Gaza from Tunis in 1994: his troops killed sixteen Hamas supporters outside a Gaza City mosque that November. But he was deterred by the furious reaction among ordinary Palestinians, perhaps 20 percent of whom are involved with Hamas's extensive network of mosques, schools, and social organizations, and by the personal humiliation and trauma of having his keffiyeh knocked off his head and being threatened when he tried to attend the funeral of another Islamic extremist, Hani Abed, killed by Israel at around the same time. Since then, he has taken action only when it was clear that without a crackdown there would be no more peace progress, no more land relinquished by Israel.

Not long ago, I had the opportunity to talk briefly to a very senior former Israeli military figure who had worked very closely with Arafat between 1993 and 1996. Yes, he told me, Arafat had made "a big mistake" in 1994 and 1995 in failing to stop the Hamas bombings. When Arafat, in those years, received "hard information" of an imminent suicide bombing, he sent his security operatives to thwart it, but he did not attempt to dismantle the Hamas infrastructure. He had not been prepared to tackle Hamas head-on, said this former senior official, had not recognized until it was too late how deeply traumatized Israel was becoming because of the bombings, had refused to concede that the extremists might come to constitute a threat to him, too.

This same informant said that because Arafat had personally benefited so much from violence, had seen how it had helped his cause over the years, he was reluctant to abandon it altogether. "There was also the fact that his own security chiefs, people like Muhammad Dahlan in Gaza, have relatives and longtime friends who are active in Hamas. Tackling them was more complicated than people are prepared to recognize."

Why didn't you push him harder? I asked.

"I pushed, believe me I pushed," came the response. "The Palestinians are still talking to this day about some of the meetings I had with him in 1995." But to no avail. For the trailblazer who genuinely wanted a relationship of equals, for Yitzhak Rabin, Arafat was not prepared to take on Hamas. "Yes it was a big mistake," he sighed, with the weariness of hindsight.

How different might our recent history have been had Arafat shown more determination to root out the bombers: The suicide attacks might have been halted; Israeli support for peacemaking with Arafat might have stayed at the 60 percent level it reached around the time of the first 1993 handshake on the White House lawn, or risen even further; the settlers and other hard-liners would have been pressed firmly to the margins; perhaps Rabin would not have been assassinated. Wistful hypothesizing? Sure. But this was a possibility, an opportunity, that got blasted away by a sequence of indoctrinated, frustrated, misguided young Palestinian men, for whom the promise of martyrdom and a heavenly future surrounded by adoring young girls was unsurprisingly more tantalizing than the reality of unemployment and poverty and sleeping six to a refugee-camp shelter with a stream of foul-smelling sewage running down the center of the alley outside.

The bombers killed 279 Israelis in the first five years after the 1993 Rabin-Arafat handshake, 279 men, women, and children in ninety-two attacks—more murders than in the fifteen years before the handshake. Hundreds more people were injured, scarred for life. Hundreds of families torn apart.

The Cohens, who live a few doors down from us, lost their son, a soldier, in a suicide bombing in 1995. Mrs. Cohen told her next-door neighbor, a good friend of ours, that the loss was unthinkable to her, something she had utterly refused to conceive could happen. Had anyone had the nerve to suggest to her, years before, that her family was not immune, she said, she would have physically attacked that person. The Cohens keep themselves indoors a lot of the time now, with a giant German shepherd barking in the yard outside, and the neighbors, mindful of the tragedy, never wishing to object.

Rinat, one of our baby-sitters, in her late teens, was wounded in the face in another bombing, in 1996. We only realized the source of the scars after she told us that her army service involved teaching physical education to young recruits at the Givat Ram university campus across town. Wow, marveled Lisa, how did you get an assignment so close to home? Because the army wanted to make her life a little easier, she began, explaining how it was shattered when a Hamas activist happened to choose the Ashkelon bus stop where she was waiting as the venue for his attack.

So it is hard not to be wistful, to wish for what might have been, for what might so easily have been.

And yet, all my reservations about Arafat notwithstanding, in full cognizance of his flaws and of the volatility of those Palestinians who were capable of putting out the flags to welcome Clinton one day and burn them three days later to denounce the U.S. bombardment of Iraq, it still seems clear where Israel's interest lies.

There are, I suppose, three principal elements in the arguments against the alliance: the one that claims that granting the Palestinians control of most of the West Bank grievously harms our security; the one that revolves around the belief that Arafat is playing salami tactics—first slice the Gaza Strip, next slice the West Bank, then munch into East Jerusalem, the Galilee, West Jerusalem, and Jaffa until he has swallowed all of Israel; and the one that says the land-for-peace barter is un-Jewish, a breach of God's promise.

I do not think the first argument holds up. After all, which better serves our security: Making a deal with the Palestinians to divide the territory we both want to live on, putting up a big fence, and staying the hell out of each other's lives for a few years while hostilities recede, or maintaining our rule over them, no border, no fences, and tens of thousands of them building our homes, washing dishes in our hotels, picking our fruit, and one or two nasty characters among them blowing us up and knifing us when the mood takes them? Most Israelis, in their heart of hearts, would be perfectly content never to see another Palestinian. I am sure that a friend of mine who works in a restaurant in central Jerusalem would be more comfortable if there were Israelis, rather than Palestinians, in his kitchen, close to all those big carving knives. I know that Lisa, like every Israeli mother, kept a particularly anxious eye on the kids playing outside when Palestinians were building the house across the street.

Because of the fear of suicide bombers, the very process of allowing Palestinians to cross into Israel to work is unbelievably unpleasant and can only breed hostility. The Erez checkpoint between Gaza and Israel is like something out of a bad 1950s Cold War spy movie, with long, winding, narrow corridors of iron fencing and huge concrete barriers so forbidding that no screenwriter could have dared invent them. Every individual is scrutinized, every entry pass closely examined, every bag and parcel rummaged through. A group of border policemen, based at Kibbutz Yad Mordechai just north of Erez and charged with checking the cars of Palestinian VIPs before waving them through, once told me that *they* felt embarrassed and uneasy having to demand that people like Nabil Sha'ath, the Palestinian planning minister, present personal ID papers and open the trunks of their cars to prove that they are not secreting Hamas bombers alongside their spare tires.

Which is more likely to produce a Palestinian society ready to live peacefully alongside Israel: today's situation, in which, for want of alternative employment, many Palestinians come here to work in appalling conditions or, worse still, endure the abject humiliation of building homes for settlers on land they covet in the West Bank, or a future in which Israel could encourage the international community to invest in Gaza, to rehouse refugees, to set up industry in the West Bank and benefit from Palestinian intellect and low labor costs—to boost an independent Palestinian economy in which there would be no incentive to martyr yourself or to exhort Saddam to send his Scuds into Tel Aviv, and every incentive to learn computer skills or engineering? Let the Palestinians cook and build in the West Bank and Gaza, fuel their own economic growth—and wean Israeli contractors and restaurateurs off their cheap labor force, have them pay a decent wage to Israelis, and thereby reduce our jobless rates.

Recently, a group of us from the *Jerusalem Report* spent a day in Gaza, courtesy of a U.N. organization. We saw the squalor of the Rafah refugee camp, visiting a family of six with a handicapped father and a helpless mother sharing two rooms of unfinished concrete, and sewage rolling past outside—an entirely typical refugee family whose own leadership

187

should have long since rehoused them but instead criminally allows the camp to fester, the better to blame Israel as the cause of the squalor. Then we drove to a Palestinian school a few miles away. Yossi, typically, went off to investigate their maps and found, to no one's great surprise, that "Palestine" was still shown to cover not merely the West Bank and Gaza but all of Israel as well. For Yossi, this is more proof that the Palestinians are not ready for peace and that we would be foolish to continue facilitating their progress toward independent statehood. For me, the map is a holdover from another era—a holdover it is in our interests to render irrelevant. You just cannot expect the maps to change before the reality does, before peace is stable, lines of separation drawn, refugees rehoused. If you insist on having the maps altered first, you will never alter the reality.

By early 1999, for all our misgivings over Arafat, a majority of Israelis were telling the pollsters they supported the establishment of an independent Palestine; a realistic two-thirds were saying such a state was inevitable. And hundreds of thousands of Israelis have actually already demonstrated a willingness to subjugate themselves to Palestinian authority—myself among them. How so? By visiting the only legal casino in our area, the Oasis, built by an Austrian-Palestinian conglomerate and located in Jericho, deep inside Arafat territory.

Every night of every week, thousands of Israelis make the perilous trek on the unlighted road from Jerusalem for the dubious pleasure of throwing away their money in a smoke-filled room with fake stars glimmering from the ceiling. We went for a friend's birthday, a surprise outing organized by her husband. And after Lisa and I had lost our pitiful thirty dollars' worth of chips—mainly in the slot machines, quarter by quarter, but also through a single mad, extravagant ten-dollar roulette bet on the number thirteen, the sum of the kids' ages at the time—we stood and marveled at the four-figure sums being frittered away by impassive, hardened Israeli gamblers, apparently immune both to emotion and to common sense. Here they were, giving the Palestinians their money. More than that, here they were, submitting themselves to Palestinian control. To get into the casino, we had been required to give our names and proof of identity to the unfailingly polite Palestinian clerks in the entrance lobby, and then we were asked to stand still for a moment in a certain spot in front of a desk. Why? I inquired. The clerk who was registering me motioned to the smoked glass panel behind him. "So that we can take your photograph," he explained. ID checks and photographs—a measure of sweet revenge, I'd say, for the checks, arrests, and confrontations throughout the years of occupation.

Those who still insist that our security depends on maintaining control of the West Bank are nowadays reduced to using racist, delusionary arguments to justify themselves— depicting the Palestinians as radically different from Jews, as a people uniquely immune to the attractions of a reasonable paycheck and the possibilities of foreign travel and the joy of improved education, bent only, irrevocably, interminably, on the elimination of the Jewish state; a people with elephantine memories of perceived historical injustice to whom peace treaties are meaningless and compromise means capitulation; a people, that is, who bear no resemblance to the real men and women out there—not to the *Jerusalem Report*'s various correspondents in the West Bank and Gaza, not to the parents we would chat with as our kids bounced around at "kindergym" at the Jerusalem YMCA, not to my curly-haired Arabic teacher from Beit Safafa, not to Hassan, the gentle father of twins who used to work with Lisa at the Village Green restaurant on Ben-Yehuda, or to Sami, who was still working there when the Hamas bombers came to blow it up. It is so much easier to dehumanize—and to turn off the radio, as my taxi driver did after the winter 1998 suicide bombing of the Mahaneh Ye-huda vegetable market, when a relative of one of the two dead Palestinian bombers was expressing his sorrow at the act of barbarism while explaining how the dead man had been in and out of Israeli jails since being wounded in a clash with Israeli soldiers early in the Intifada. Who wants to hear about his life history, as though that had anything to do with the bombing?

Because we need to separate, I feel that the pistol-packing settlers, especially those who have made their homes deep inside the West Bank, in remote areas where their presence does nothing to boost our security, far from constituting an asset to Israel, amount to a liability. They are my generation's misguided pioneers, placing themselves, their children, and those Israelis obligated by the army to protect them, in unnecessary danger. How facile to quibble, as some settlers do, about whether there are two million or three million Palestinians in Gaza and the West Bank, as though, if there are "only" two million, their aspirations to independence can be countered more efficiently. And how foolish for the Netanyahu government, even as it was forced into territorial concessions, and as settlers near the areas being evacuated were clamoring for financial compensation to enable them to up and leave, to still have been providing economic incentives for more Israelis to make their homes in the West Bank. What a waste of money to send hundreds more families, like most of their settler predecessors motivated not by ideology but by the prospect of a better quality of life—larger homes, bigger gardens, and cheaper mortgages—into the West Bank when, a few years down the line, they will all have to be rehoused at great government expense inside sovereign Israel.

Argument two against the partnership: Arafat is a lying, cheating cad, and so is the rest of the Palestinian leadership. Clinton was duped. Netanyahu was cowed. The Gaza gathering of December 1998 was not, as required by PLO protocol, a "special session" of the Palestine National Council convened for the express purpose of amending the Covenant. No formal vote was taken, and so no clear two-thirds majority of PNC members could be calculated. The Covenant was never really revoked. The professed desire for peace that won over Rabin and Peres and Clinton and the world is part of the 1974 "phased plan," under which the Palestinian leadership resolved to establish its rule "on every part of Palestinian land to be liberated," and from there to continue the struggle until all of Palestine was freed.

So what? Why should our reservations about Arafat's eventual goals force us to compromise our own best interests? We can negotiate a final deal, and as he walks away from the table after affixing his signature, he can dream all he wants about breaching the accord and continuing a quest for ultimate rule over the country we like to call our own. We can see to it that he doesn't have the wherewithal to turn that dream into a reality. We can ensure that his independent state is largely demilitarized, deprive him of the tanks, missiles, and other weaponry he would need really to hurt us. We have the means to monitor his elegantly domed, Moroccan-style airport, and his seaports, and his border fences, to stop the Iraqi army sneaking into Jericho, and Scuds slipping over the Allenby Bridge. If we do get into a conflict, it might well be painful and costly, but, united in the belief that we had done all we could for peace and that violence was being forced upon us, we would prevail. We don't need to kill off our chances of peace because we are paranoid about Arafat's ultimate aspirations.

Argument three is the argument that killed Yitzhak Rabin. The way I remember it from Jewish day school, virtually every other Orthodox Jewish principle, no matter how cherished, went out the window when lives were at stake. But that is not the way some of our most learned spiritual guides see it or teach it. To them, the land comes first—Hebron, burial place of the patriarchs and matriarchs; Shiloh, pre-Temple home of the Holy Ark; Nablus, purported last resting place of Joseph. These were ours, are ours, and must remain ours, all these links to our glorious history. Never mind how many living, breathing, soaring souls must die in the cause of their retention. (They don't say that last part, Heaven forbid; instead, they argue that if we give up holy Hebron more lives will be lost, because we will have shown the Arabs that we are willing to forgo our heritage, positively inviting them to try and rid the area of us all.) So overpowering has this passion for the land become in some quarters that I have actually heard a Jewish mother who lives in a West Bank settlement, whose son had just been shot and was dying in the hospital, ignore a reporter's question about her boy's medical condition to hammer the government for contemplating further territorial compromise.

For too long in Israel, perhaps because somewhere in our psyche we half-believed these rabbis' and their followers' argument that they were living on the authentic holy land and should not be removed, they have been allowed to set the agenda here—to delegitimize Rabin and Peres and (in his occasional peace mode) Netanyahu, to invoke centuries-old and misinterpreted dictates that imply a divine sanction for violent resistance to withdrawal, to escape prosecution for encouraging a climate in which one assassin has already fired his weapon and others may now be preparing theirs.

Natan argues passionately that maximizing the Jewish presence in the West Bank is not a question of putting land above life, but of holding land to save life. "I find this leftist nonsense that we [settlers] care more for land than for human life insulting," he says. "Did it ever occur to you that we feel that, by giving up the land, we will be putting more people in danger? From the security point of view, giving back the heartland, and leaving yourself with territory fourteen miles wide, is not so smart. No country in the world would be willing to do that. None. Also, one doesn't give up on one's water sources, when water is so scarce in the Middle East."

While many Israelis hold to Natan's positions, many more, Barak's resounding election victory proves, are edging toward a consensus on peace. It's an entirely workable consensus, in my opinion. Yes, we are two peoples who want to live on much the same land. But as things stand now, for the most part, despite the best efforts of the settlers, we don't actually live in the same place, and that means separation is not just desirable, not just attainable, but a fact of life. About six million of us live down the left-hand side of our disputed area (the state of Israel); about three million of them live down the right-hand side (the West Bank) and in the bottom left-hand corner (Gaza). Even in Jerusalem, the Palestinians reside in the eastern half of the city, which three decades of concerted Jewish neighborhood-building have not managed to dislocate from the West Bank, and the Jews populate the western half, an integral part of sovereign Israel. Most Palestinians want their capital in East Jerusalem, full control of the West Bank and Gaza, and the means to travel from one to the other.

Like most Israelis, my family has hardly set foot in East Jerusalem in the past few years—it's an adventure, with a frisson of danger, to go shopping on Salahhadin Street, or pop into a pharmacy in the Old City, or ride the gloomy-faced camels outside the Seven Arches Hotel on the Mount of Olives. My great-uncle and several cousins are buried in a cemetery on the Mount of Olives; the last time I attempted to visit their graves, I came back to the car to find that a rock had been hurled through the driver's window. As for Gaza, since the Intifada, Israelis have gone there only for army duty, and the few thousand hardy Jewish ideologues who insist on settling there are completely isolated from the rest of the strip. In the West Bank, meanwhile, Arafat is already in formal control of much of the territory, and informally runs still more, while those settlements close to heavily populated Palestinian areas are looking more and more like heavily protected army bases.

So we have separation in Jerusalem, separation in Gaza, separation in the West Bank. Since the vast majority of the 150,000 West Bank settlers live fairly close to the Israeli border, a minor adjustment of the pre-1967 lines would bring 70 percent of them into Israel. The 30 percent of settlers living deeper in the West Bank could take their chances under Palestinian rule—much like one million Arabs have done in Israel for fifty years—or be offered alternative housing inside Israel. Add in an assortment of joint-security arrangements along the Jordan border, agree on jointly patrolled west–east roads across the West Bank, sort out a deal on West Bank water allocations, designate Jerusalem's Old City as nonsovereign territory administered by representatives of all relevant world religions, and present the whole package to the people of Israel and Palestine—and a vast majority on both sides, whatever their private reservations, would give it a cautious thumbs-up.

If it all sounds terribly simplistic, so be it. That is hardly a serious complaint when the present hostile complexities have given us daytime nightmares featuring flying dislocated body parts. And don't tell me that coexistence is unworkable, impossible, because I have visited "the Saddams of Jericho." And I have seen how the impossible, given the right conditions, can become the commonplace. . . .

"The Saddams" arrived in Jericho in the spring of 1994. They didn't call themselves the Saddams, of course. They called themselves the fighters of the Al-Aqsa Brigade of the Palestine Liberation Organization. But they had spent the previous five years training in Iraq and, for all I know, fighting for it. They had grown to respect, admire, perhaps even love the local dictator. The evidence of this affinity was plain to see, etched into their features—each of the several dozen Al-Aqsa Brigade members I met on a visit to their prefabricated military head-quarters, just outside the sleepy, ancient West Bank oasis town of Jericho, affected the Saddam slightly wavy, not quite army-cut hairstyle, and the Saddam broad, matte-black mustache.

Their presence in Jericho was, quite obviously, ridiculous, an aberration. They had been sent in from Iraq—the nation that, a mere three years earlier, had been vowing to turn all of Israel into toast—as the guinea pigs in the Israeli-Palestinian effort at joint security. They were to conduct jeep patrols in convoy with Israeli troops in and around Jericho, the first West Bank city being handed over to Arafat's control. As incongruous matches go, it made Arthur Miller and Marilyn Monroe look perfect.

They arrived in an assortment of uniforms, without beds or basic communications equipment, and with only the hazi-est notion of what Arafat had let them in for. They knew noth-ing of the finer points of the Oslo peace accords they were supposed to be implementing. As longtime exiles, they knew nothing of the terrain. Needless to say, they were not instinc-tively well disposed toward Israelis.

And yet, this thoroughly implausible cooperative venture proved perfectly successful. The Israelis supplied the beds, walkie-talkies, and lectures on the minutiae of the peace deal. Hesitancy and unfamiliarity gave way to confidence and expertise. Within weeks, the Al-Aqsa boys and the Israelis were hopping into their respective jeeps as if they had been at it for years, the Israelis leading the way until the convoy entered Arafat territory, the Palestinians then overtaking, a constant burble of Arabic conversation on the walkie-talkies. Whatever their private views of the peace accords, the musta-chioed men of the Al-Aqsa Brigade were used to following or-ders. There were hiccups—disputes between the Palestinian patrolmen and Israeli settlers crossing to fields in the area; a water tanker boxed in; rude gestures and rocks thrown at the Israelis by Jericho locals—but improving communication between the respective senior officers gradually reduced even these minor incidents. A permanently staffed, three-room liaison office was established—two Israeli teens in their room at one end, listening to Hebrew pop and reading the tabloids; two fortyish Palestinians at the other end, heads buried in the *Al-Quds* daily; and a vacant area in the middle for emergency get-togethers whenever a crisis broke out.

So successful was the Jericho experiment, in fact, that when, in the fall of 1995, Israel was poised to hand over a series of other West Bank cities to Palestinian control, the Israeli and Palestinian security forces sent the prospective joint patrolmen for these cities to Jericho for lessons. And these recruits, in turn, drove off together around Jenin and Tulkarm, Kalkilya and Nablus, and Ramallah and Bethlehem, and grew accustomed to one another's habits, and picked up one another's names, and drank coffee together, and maybe even got to telling their families when on home leave that those Israelis or those Palestinians weren't quite the vicious, devious devils they'd always thought they were.

The bubble burst in September 1996, because of the Jerusalem tunnel. Whether genuinely concerned for the safety of their mosques atop the mount or provoked into protest by their leaders, Palestinians across the West Bank, Gaza and East Jerusalem relapsed into the stone- and Molotov-cocktail-throwing demonstrations of the Intifada years, the Israelis fired at them, and this time—unlike the Intifada period—the Palestinians had their own guns and fired back. The Saddams of Jericho, along with Palestinian policemen elsewhere in the West Bank and Gaza, fired at and were shot at by their erstwhile traveling companions. Many Israelis, and many more Palestinians, were killed. It was a mortal blow to the improbable camaraderie that had developed among the uniformed men. The joint patrols were suspended for months; when they resumed, both groups were plainly far more worried by their partners than by any security threat they were supposed to be jointly deterring. It will take years for trust to be restored to those fragile relationships. The innocent good faith of 1994–1995 can never be recaptured. Of course, the Saddams should never have opened fire. Of course, Netanyahu's misjudgment over the tunnel shouldn't have triggered the bloodbath. But don't tell me that the very idea of a partnership for peace with the Palestinians is impossible, because fragile though it may have been, it was developing. I saw it.

Chapter Seven

On the Other Hand . . .

So far as the Arabs are concerned . . . I hope they will remember that it is we who have established an independent Arab sovereignty of the Hedjaz. I hope they will remember it is we who desire in Mesopotamia to prepare the way for the future of a self-governing, autonomous Arab State, and I hope that, remembering all that, they will not grudge that small notch—for it is no more than that geographically, whatever it may be historically—that small notch in what are now Arab territories being given to the people who for all these hundreds of years have been separated from it.

—Arthur James Balfour, July 1920, three years after his Balfour Declaration pledged British support for a Jewish national home in Palestine

I came to Israel first. My older sister, Miriam, came a short while afterward. I met Lisa, the American daughter of a Holocaust survivor, who had been fed affection for Israel—the one safe haven for the Jews—with her mother's milk. Miriam met Natan, the child of a second-generation American mother and a German-born father, Reform Jews, who were desolated by his decision to move here in defiance of their contention that Israel was for refugees, not nice Jewish boys from New York. "My parents had visited here in 1969," says Natan, "and, back then, it was, 'Israel is a dream, Israel is wonderful.' They even bought the record of 'Jerusalem of Gold.' Then, when I moved here, of course, it was, 'Israel stole my son.'"

198

Part of Natan's inspiration to move came from his late grandmother. He had told her about Israel after a long visit he had made here in 1981, and she had told him how, growing up in a village outside Frankfurt at the turn of the century, she had looked at Israel as a dream, a place no one seriously believed they would ever be able to go to. Natan thought about the generations of righteous Jews praying for the right to go to Israel, and about the fact that this generation, finally, had that right. How could he not seize it?

Natan wanted to be a farmer. He wanted to make orchards bloom on the land of his forefathers. On one of several pre-immigration visits, he had done some archaeological work at Pisgat Ze'ev, on the outskirts of Jerusalem, an area the Palestinians regard as occupied West Bank territory but that Israel has incorporated into its capital. The dig was part of an archaeological survey being carried out prior to the construction of a new Jewish neighborhood there. Along with Crusader and Roman remains, he had uncovered Jewish tombs from the Second Temple period and a Jewish industrial site from the First Temple period. With his own eyes, with his own hands, he had rediscovered the historical Jewish connection to the Holy Land—to land that the Palestinians were claiming as theirs.

When he came here to stay at the age of thirty-two, in the late spring of 1984, with no relatives or friends in Israel, he was offered work in a fruit orchard at Ofra, half an hour's drive north from Jerusalem, near Ramallah, deep in the West Bank. As his interest in Israel had intensified over the years, he had become fairly expert in its politics and had come to feel strongly that the West Bank, the biblical Judea and Samaria, was Israel's by historical right and by right of liberation in the 1967 war. It would, he felt, be a privilege to plant fruit trees there. A few months later, when he and my sister had met and decided to get married and it seemed likely that he would be able to purchase land of his own at the settlement, Ofra was the choice for their permanent home.

"I didn't set out to live on a settlement," he says, "but I also didn't set out not to. And living there, now, is very important to me. It's my land. Our land. This is where our history is. This is our raison d'être. There's a story told that a member of one of the British commissions investigating how to deal with Palestine asked David Ben-Gurion what right the Jews had to be here. And Ben-Gurion took a *Tanach* [the Holy Scriptures], put it on the desk, and said, '*This* is my right to be here.' Now I don't know if that story is true, but the point it makes is. If you look at the parts of the Torah [the Five Books of Moses] that deal with the land of Israel, most of it takes place in Judea and Samaria—in Hebron, Jerusalem, Nablus. . . .

"Look at 'Lech Lechah' [the third portion of the first book of the Torah, Genesis], where God tells Abraham to journey to a land that will be given to the Jewish people. God leads Abraham to a mountain between Beit El and Ay. On the highest peak in the area, where you can see from the Mediterranean across to the Jordan Valley, God tells him to look across the land, that this is the land that will belong to him. Well, that spot is right by where we live, the mountain of Ba'al Hatzor, which overlooks Ofra. There's an army base there now."

I speak to Miriam every week on the phone, but Lisa, the kids, and I don't see her, or Natan, or their four children, too often. This is a terrible shame, because the fact that they are Orthodox and we are not, that they live where they live and we live where we live, doesn't intrude in the slightest on a personal level. We are one family, and we feel it and look it: Their quartet of children and our trio are virtually interchangeable, all blond hair and freckles. All the kids are young enough, still, to talk only about the unifying things young kids talk about—Barney and Beetleborgs and bikes, and collecting stickers, and who beat up whom in school—not the divisive, argumentative stuff we grown-ups go in for. We all love each other, we respect each other, and we are only forty minutes away from each other. But it's forty minutes into another world, into the wild West Bank. And I am reluctant to drive out to Ofra, even though the "bypass" roads—constructed in the West Bank in recent years to enable settlers to travel to and from sovereign Israel without going through Palestinian-controlled territory—have made the journey safer.

Some of our relatives who live abroad would not visit them on principle, would not want to confer presumed legitimacy on their presence there. One family member actually wrote a letter to my sister a few years ago, urging her and Natan in all seriousness to give up their home to Palestinian refugees. I am not quite that hysterical. I just do not want to place my family at additional risk.

Natan, too, worries about the safety of his kids. "Up until now," he notes, "it has been safer at Ofra than, say, living near the Lebanese border. But we are in a situation where there's a possibility of danger. I can't say we're no different from Tel Aviv. We have to live with the danger, and that's the way it is. We have our faith in God, and we hope that everything will be all right. Our kids are probably at more risk than those in Tel Aviv, and less risk than those in Hebron. Each set of parents makes its own decisions about what's important. If we run from here, then we might as well give up on the whole country."

I adore Natan—a warm bear of a man, light-haired and stocky and bearded, with laugh-lines crinkling from behind the sides of his spectacles. He is open, generous, and decent. He loves my sister. And from what I've seen, he's a wonderful dad. He is also extremely firm in his views and more than happy to discuss them.

Once, I asked him how his children relate to the Arabs.

"Arabs come in here, to Ofra, to build houses," he said. "We explain to the kids that, as in any group, there are good Arabs and bad, just like there are good Jews and bad. And that you never know who's good and who's bad. One day, they may say hello; the next, they may stick a knife into you. And so, unfortunately, you have to limit your contact with them.

"We're careful at home to stress that we don't hate Arabs. We explain to our children that the Arabs view us as their enemy—because we are living on land which they claim as theirs. But the suicide bombings, the bus bombings, do produce a negative impression of Arabs—for our children, as for any child in Israel. Except that here, I'd say, there's less of that. Because our kids see how the Arabs live, which is very healthy. We try to tell the kids that we're in a war situation, so they have to be careful. That's not to say that there aren't kids at Ofra who don't get a very negative impression of the Arabs from their parents. But we're very careful about that."

I asked what kind of values he felt he was passing on to the kids. "We give them the education we think is right for them," he replied. "We try to set an example. But when they're older, they'll make their own decisions. Hopefully, we'll be proud of them. As long as they're good people, we'll be proud. I'd prefer that they be Orthodox and contribute to the advancement of the people of Israel and to the Land of Israel. But they'll have to make their own decisions. A few children from Ofra have turned out non-Orthodox. But, interestingly, all have stayed to the right politically."

What if they turned out to be ardent leftists, "Peace Now" supporters? I asked. He laughed, then got serious: "If that's what the kid truly believed in, I'd be disappointed," he said. "But what's most important is that they be decent, honorable people. Everything else is secondary."

. . .

When we cityfolk do get to Ofra, it is a joy. The air is fresher. There is a sense of space—absent in so much of Israel. My sister's home is on the fringes of the settlement, so it doesn't feel hemmed in. An entry road runs near their house, but there is hardly any traffic on it. So our kids, and theirs, actually play more freely at Ofra than we would let them in Jerusalem. My sister doesn't panic too much when one of the kids goes missing, not the way we would if our gate was open and Josh was nowhere around; hers are bound to turn up somewhere on the settlement. Where else are they going to go? They know better than to head off to Ein Yabrud, the Arab village five hundred yards away.

The homes themselves are spacious by Israeli standards, detached, red-roofed houses with gardens larger than postage stamps. There are playgrounds for the kids, a grocery store, pizza to go, a mini–industrial zone, a gas station, caring neighbors, no shortage of babysitters, schools just a minute or two away. It is a veritable world unto itself. Suburbia.

Only, remember, it is half an hour into the West Bank, into territory gradually being relinquished to the Palestinians, and I wish they lived somewhere else.

Natan, who should know, says Jewish-Arab coexistence used to work just fine out there and can be made to again, without evacuating the settlers. He says he would not oppose Palestinian statehood in Gaza, but that Israel should extend its sovereignty through the West Bank and then restrict the Palestinians to limited autonomy—a stance, it seems to me, that has long been overtaken by events.

"I have no problem granting autonomy to Ramallah, Nablus," he said. "Certainly, occupation is a problem. They should be able to run their own lives. But the Israeli army should have complete control of security. And if there has to be a Palestinian police force, it shouldn't be the quasi-army it is now. There should be very few of them, carrying a sidearm only. The Arabs should have 'city-level' control, taking care of local taxes, development, health, and education. But Israel should be the sovereign power.

"Now people say that, in a democratic country, you can't have a situation like that. You have to treat the Palestinian Arabs as equal citizens. And my response to that is, 'Tough.' A democratic country can't be so democratic that it kills itself. Since we are living in a Zionist country, in a Jewish country, the majority has to be Jewish. I don't believe we should be a binational state. That's not to say we should deny basic human rights to the people who live in this country."

This all sounds well and good, except that the Palestinians won't accept it. Natan's response is that you can't please everyone. But we have seen what happens as a consequence of occupation. We have seen wars, the Intifada.

"The Intifada would have been finished in three days," Natan asserted, "if we'd handled it correctly—with force. Let me backtrack a minute. The popular leftist media impression of the settlers is that we're all crazy racists, religious fanatics, that we hate Arabs. That's totally false. Yes, there are a few crazies among us, just as there are crazies in any large population. But the great majority of us don't fit this stereotype. Those on the left talk about coexistence, but what relationship do the lefties in Tel Aviv have with the Arabs, except that the Arabs build and clean their apartments, do the gardening, and clean the plates in restaurants? In day-to-day life in this area, before the Intifada, one man from Ofra used to go to Ramallah to get his hair cut, another member used to take Arab buses to Jerusalem. On the way to work, I myself sometimes stopped in Ramallah to buy the *Jerusalem Post*. Many others did their food shopping in Ramallah. Coexistence was a fact. It was only because of the Israeli left and the fanatics on the Arab side that this was ruined. Quite a few people in Ofra speak Arabic. I'm not saying that we'd have the villagers from Ein

Yabrud over for tea every night, but there were some casual relationships and some business relationships. After the Intifada started, this one person from Ofra, who was very friendly with someone in Ein Yabrud, was driving through the village, and he saw his friend standing with some other Arabs off to the side of the road. He stopped his car and he honked at him. And the guy just ignored him. So he honked again. Finally, his Arab friend walked over to him and said to him, 'Don't speak to me anymore. It's dangerous for you. It's dangerous for me.' And that was the end of that. It's very, very sad.

"Before the Intifada, if there were problems that occurred between our two villages, the mayor of Ofra would work things out with the *mukhtar* of Ein Yabrud. But then, after the Intifada started, the *mukhtar* said he had no control over the *shebab* [the rebellious Palestinian youths] anymore, and there was nothing he could do about stones being thrown at cars from Ofra or any other problems.

"As far as the occupation is concerned, I had a lot of problems with it myself, and so did other people at Ofra. We'd travel to Jerusalem, and there'd be a roadblock, for security reasons. And we'd go through, and the Arabs would be stuck waiting on line to be checked. And I always felt very uncomfortable with that. It creates resentment."

So the occupation was mishandled? I asked.

"When I did reserve duty," he replied, "my experience was that the people who mistreated the Arabs were not from the settlements, but were kibbutzniks and people from central Israel. Those people that, for the most part, have no exposure to Arabs except for what I said before. They unnecessarily humiliated the Arabs. Once, when I was doing reserve duty, we were spot-checking cars [in the West Bank]. I have no problem with that. You just say, 'Sir, may I see your ID card?' Or, 'I am sorry, but I have to open up your trunk.' You should try to be polite. One person in the unit was very abusive, and if the Arab didn't answer him the right way, he'd slap him. I would get very upset. So I saw firsthand how the occupation was humiliating. I think the whole idea of 'preventive detention' is disgusting, completely undemocratic. [During the Intifada, Israel kept thousands of Palestinians in jail without trial for months on end; more recently, the number has fallen to a few dozen.] I am sure that innocent Arabs suffered because of that. If someone is suspected of doing something wrong, he should be given a lawyer and brought before a court. Due process.

"So mistakes were made. I certainly understand Arab resentment. That's not to say that everything was terrible. The Jordanians didn't allow any universities [in the West Bank, between 1948 and 1967]; it was Israel that allowed Birzeit and all the other universities to open. Infant mortality dropped considerably. Health care improved, regardless of what the Arab propagandists say. Not everything was negative. Their standard of living very much improved."

My view is that from 1967 to 1987, the occupation festered, and the resentment grew, and finally the Intifada exploded. And the fact is that, even though the Palestinians had their universities and their health care, they just didn't and don't want to be occupied. What, I asked Natan, was he going to do when, ten years down his limited-autonomy road, it happened again. "When a violent demonstration occurs," he answered simply, "you put it down immediately with as much force as is needed."

But wasn't that precisely what the army did during the Intifada?

"They certainly did not do that," Natan retorted. "If live fire was necessary, live fire should have been used. Do you think for a minute the Americans or the French would tolerate riots like these in their own countries?"

But live fire *was* used when lives were in danger.

"But what did they define as lives in danger?" Natan asked. "I would say that if someone is standing with a rock, about to throw it at you, I would say that your life is in danger. Therefore you shoot. I've seen the damage firsthand that a well-aimed rock can do.

"There's an expression in the Talmud, 'If you're merciful to the cruel, you'll be cruel to the merciful.' I suggest that if the correct amount of force had been used, and violent demonstrations put down when they had occurred, hundreds if not more lives would have been saved in the long run—Arab and Jewish.

"So, yes, from time to time, this festering of national aspiration will erupt. And we have to put it down by force. And those who are not willing to live peacefully, you throw them out of the country."

I think I have driven out to Ofra, myself or with Lisa and the kids, no more than four or five times in the past decade—and I have been worried the entire journey that someone is going to pop out from atop a hill or around a corner and hurl a rock through my windshield. I half want to leave the window open and scream out, "I'm a leftie, I'm just visiting" at passing Arab motorists, to forestall potential drive-by shootings. This is ridiculous. Most of the breadwinners of Ofra and other settlements cheerfully travel these freshly tarred West Bank roads every day. Hardly anybody gets stoned or shot at (although that doesn't stop foreign journalists, in their own adaptation of my "don't hit me" inner cry, from placing a keffiyeh prominently atop the dashboard and large signs in the rear window proclaiming "PRESS" in English and Arabic). Still, even when Natan drives us out for a rare visit, collecting us in Jerusalem in his settler car with its reinforced windows, I get nervous at every mini–traffic jam, check out the drivers of every overtaking car, and feel relieved when we finally spot those red roofs up ahead.

Even at times of high national drama—of assassination, or suicide bombing, or West Bank withdrawal, or elections—my sister and I barely talk politics in our phone calls; come to think of it, *especially* at times of high national drama. We are not going to convince each other of anything, and we will only upset each other. With Natan, the sensitivities are less acute. That is why it was with Natan—who is now doing data-processing work full-time in Jerusalem but has also been growing first nectarines and now cherries at Ofra in most of his spare time—that I set out to understand the values and the motivations that see him and my sister bringing up their family where they do. The views he expresses here, I should stress, are not necessarily those of my sister.

I hope I'm not so arrogant as to be certain that all of my thinking is right and all of Natan's wrong. He certainly lives in more of an Arab environment than I do. But boy, do we see the region differently. While I believe that the Arab mindset is fundamentally no different than ours, Natan's mistrust of the Arabs is profound. While I believe that Israel and Palestine can ultimately coexist peacefully, and that we can complete our circle of peace with Syria and Lebanon if we will pay the territorial price, my soft-spoken brother-in-law is convinced that neither the Palestinians nor the wider Arab world is interested in long-term reconciliation with us. And somewhere between my readiness for compromise, for believing that the "other side" ultimately clings to the same humane values, and Natan's stance—his conviction that the Arabs will always be determined to rid the Middle East of our Jewish state, his firm attachment to biblical land—swirls, I would say, much of the spectrum of Israeli opinion.

Had we behaved toward the Palestinians in the way you have suggested, I said to Natan, we would never have achieved peace with Jordan and the peace deal with Egypt would have fallen apart. We would always be at war with the entire Arab world, not just with the Palestinians.

"Don't misunderstand me," Natan responded. "I don't want to be at war with these people. But I want them to accept me on my terms, that I live here, and that I have the right to live here."

But the Jordanians only made peace with us because we were trying to make peace with the Palestinians.

"The Oslo accords," he said, "allowed the Jordanians the cover they needed to publicly formalize a relationship that existed de facto. And the Egyptians made peace with us because they knew they couldn't destroy us and because we gave in to every one of their demands. What does the peace treaty with Egypt have to do with the Palestinian Arabs? And in return for that, they gave us a piece of paper that is pretty much worthless. Incitement against us is common in the Egyptian media. Look at Azzam Azzam [an Israeli Druse jailed in Egypt for fifteen years, convicted of spurious-sounding espionage activities including transferring top-secret material using invisible ink written on ladies' undergarments]. Look at Ras Burka [the shooting of Israeli tourists on an Egyptian beach by an Egyptian soldier in 1985]. Egypt is not a place where Israelis can feel welcome. I went to Egypt in 1982, and I remember how nice it was. I was on a bridge over the Nile, and an Israeli flag was flying. And the people I was with took a photo of me under the flag, and I was wearing an Israeli army-style coat. And the Egyptians who were passing were saying, 'Shalom, Shalom.' And there was a definite positive feeling. But that doesn't exist today, because of incitement and hatred mainly from the government. Still, there have been no hostilities between us and the Egyptians since the Camp David peace treaty, and that is certainly a better situation than one of war."

Did Natan think that the Arab regimes would forever seek to eliminate us?

"When they feel that they are capable of doing it, they will try."

So any concessions we make are stupid, counterproductive? I prompted.

"No, it depends on the concession. It doesn't mean don't try."

Well, were we wrong to give up the Sinai to Egypt?

"No," he said, "I'm not going to say that. Take the treaty with Jordan. Our situation security-wise before the treaty and after the treaty did not change. We haven't put ourselves in any danger. If it works, great. If it doesn't, we haven't lost anything. As for Egypt, the buffer zone still exists because there are warning stations. So it's not the end of the world. I think we made a tactical mistake in relinquishing every inch. That's a dangerous precedent. But I'm not one of those who say the treaty was a mistake. Still, I don't believe it will last. I'm very pessimistic. If you look at how many jet fighters Egypt is producing, you ask yourself, who are they planning to use them against? Libya? I doubt it very much. Their rearmament does not bode well."

Syria, though, was a lost cause. "We certainly can't afford to take a risk on the Golan Heights," said Natan. "And by the way, for those who say the Golan is not Jewish, take a visit to the old synagogue at Katzrin, or to the ancient city of Gamla, which dates back to before the Roman occupation."

I set out an alternative outlook: Israel had fought wars every decade of its existence. In the late 1970s, we eliminated Egypt from the array of enemies. In 1994, we reached a deal with Jordan. Under Rabin, we were trying to reach an accommodation with the Palestinians, in which they would gain most of the West Bank, and some kind of subsovereign status in East Jerusalem. We were negotiating with Syria, toward a deal to exchange the entire Golan for a peace treaty. We would have been reduced in size, but we would have had treaties with all our neighbors. There would still have been ideologues on the Arab side who clung to a phased plan for Israel's destruction. But a new reality would have begun to take shape. Eventually, Israel would have become another normal country, an accepted part of the Middle East.

But then, along came an assassin. Along came a different government. And under Netanyahu, the goodwill ebbed away. We relinquished more land, but grudgingly, under American pressure—an enemy reluctantly returning some of the spoils. Peace was not coming any closer. No relationship of equals was being built.

Natan, it need hardly be said, saw a different picture, and he mocked me gently: "I think you may have read too many books that ended with, '. . . and they all lived happily ever after.' You are also applying your Western cultural outlook and projecting it onto the Arab mentality. Different cultures have different ways of looking at life. Your way is not their way, and vice versa. The point is, their education and tradition tells them that we are on their land and that we must be removed. Even after all these years, if you ask an Arab, in any of the refugee camps, where he is from, even if he was born in a refugee camp to parents who were born in the same refugee camp, he will answer you, 'Lod,' or 'Haifa,' or 'Jaffa.' He has not forgotten, nor will he forget.

"The majority of Israelis are tired of wars," he acknowledged. "They're tired of reserve duty. They're tired of sending their sons to fight. They're tired of terrorism. They travel the world a lot, and they want to live like a normal country. But just because you want something doesn't mean it exists.

Reality isn't all roses. Before Netanyahu got elected, during the wonderful Rabin and Peres years, when everything was just beautiful with the Palestinians, they, in their media, on their TV, incited against us. Nothing changed. When Baruch Goldstein did his terrible deed, 99.9 percent of Israelis stood up and condemned what he did in no uncertain terms. When [Hamas bombmaker] Yihya Ayash did what he did, and was killed by us for it, he was considered a martyr to the Palestinian people. And Yasser Arafat, our peace-loving partner, went to the demonstrations in his honor and proclaimed him a martyr."

True, I said to Natan, the Palestinians' attitude toward Israel didn't change overnight. But give it time.

Fine, Natan countered, but don't give up any land until they've changed their attitude.

But you cannot say, "I'm not going to give you anything until you love us." The Palestinians are not going to "love us" until they see us moving toward them.

Then, said Natan, you are naive, foolish—because you are giving something concrete for something theoretical that, until now, has not materialized.

But we are never going to change things, I insisted, unless we take the first steps. And remember, if it becomes clear that attitudes are not changing on the Arab side, if compromise proves unworkable, we are still incredibly strong. We have a strong army.

Natan wasn't as sanguine. "You've provided them with an army," he charged. "And from what I've read, they've been smuggling all types of weapons into this autonomous area that you've given them. And the war that will take place will be a catastrophe. Too much is made of the strength of the Israeli army. The Israeli army is very strong and very capable. But there's a difference between fighting a war across a border and fighting a war within your own country, which is basically what you're going to do. The Palestinians could, if they planned it well, wage a very successful war against us.

"Even from your point of view, I would say, you don't give up something concrete unless you get something concrete back in return. You people on the left, you talk out of both sides of your mouths. First of all you say that Arafat is strong, that he can fight against terrorism. On the other hand you say, he's not strong, it'll take him time, the people have to be won over. . . . The point is I've seen nothing on the Palestinian side to indicate that things are heading in the direction you want them to head. In fact, I see the opposite. The Palestinian mindset is that it's a matter of time until they get rid of us. And they'll take whatever they can get, any way they can get it, until then."

And are they going to get rid of us?

"I don't think so. But there's a possibility that they can do a tremendous amount of damage. There may even be a situation where there's peace for a few years. We'll give back half of Jerusalem, everything they want. But eventually they'll attack us, with plenty of Arab support."

Peace treaties notwithstanding?

"That's irrelevant," Natan scoffed. "Since when has a peace treaty with the Arabs meant anything? Did Chamberlain's 'peace in our time' treaty with Hitler hold up?"

They want to be rid of us simply because we're Jews?

"Not because we're Jews, but because they say we're occupying what they consider Arab land."

And there's nothing we can do about that, ever? Nothing we can do to change that fundamental Arab mindset?

"No," said Natan.

The bottom line for the Arabs remains and will always remain that we have to get the Jews out?

"Tell me something," Natan said. "How many peace deals have there been between Arab nations themselves? And how

213

long have they lasted? Look at the other conflicts that have occurred in the Middle East in the not-too-distant past. Egypt against Sudan. Egypt against Libya. Iraq against Iran. Iraq against Kuwait. Syria against Jordan. North Yemen against South Yemen. And you expect them to love us more than they love each other?"

In our conversation, which unfolded one fall afternoon at a Jerusalem café, after a day at work for both of us, Natan shattered quite a few of my preconceptions—for better and for worse. I'd have supposed that, at Ofra, regarded as a "hard-core," ideological settlement, there would be people determined to resist any eventual evacuation—by force, if necessary. Natan was adamant that this was not the case. If the government of the day came along and ordered him and the other four-hundred-plus families to evacuate because the area was being handed over to the Palestinians, the settlers would demonstrate long and hard, he said. They might have to be dragged away physically. But go they would. No one would resort to violence against the troops come to evict them. "There is no such thing as fighting against the army. Everyone would eventually go."

This was no theoretical musing, either. In the provisions for West Bank land hand-overs as set out in the Wye peace accords, Ofra is one of about twenty settlements left iso-lated—Israeli-guarded islands in a Palestinian sea. As soon as the first phase of the Wye deal was implemented, in November 1998, residents of the two settlements most directly affected, Ganim and Kadim, complained with some justifica-tion that they had been abandoned and that their lives were now in real danger. This assertion was strengthened just a few days later when a settler there was shot and badly wounded on the road home. Since the ninety families at Ganim and Kadim had moved there largely because housing was cheap, gardens were spacious, and the area was particularly tranquil, without much apparent thought for the political consequences, waking up one Friday morning to find Palestine on the doorstep was something of a shock, and the majority of residents immediately signed a petition—ignored by the government—asking for financial compensation and a rapid relocation inside Israel. Ofra residents are hardier folk, and, as is evident from everything Natan says, deeply committed to living precisely where they live now. But if even a right-wing government was prepared to countenance isolating their settlement in 1998, it may well be that subsequent governments would contemplate evacuating it somewhere down the line.

"In the Rabin years," Natan remembered, "Ofra was under a dark cloud. We didn't know what the future would bring. The trees that we'd planted, the houses that we'd built, we really didn't know what was going to happen. . . . And there was a program on Ofra's internal TV station, and the panel, which consisted of the leaders and big shots in the settlement, were saying, 'If we have to leave Ofra, we'll leave Ofra. We will continue to believe in the Land of Israel, even if for the present, our ideals and values have had a setback.' The option of establishing a settlement in the Galilee or Negev was even mentioned. And I want to tell you something else. At that time, I didn't hear one person say, 'If we are forced to leave Ofra, we're leaving the country.' That just isn't a possibility with us. This is our country. Whatever happens, happens. A few of us were joking about where we would go. One friend said Vermont. I said Tahiti—no news and no Jews! But we were joking."

But if it was encouraging for me to learn of that fatalism at Ofra, that readiness to accept whatever decision a democratically elected Israeli government sought to impose on them, I was shocked, to put it mildly, when we got to talking about democracy, and Natan endorsed the argument that the

Rabin government had not had a legitimate right to negotiate territorial compromise with the Palestinians.

"You can't have a situation," Natan maintained, "where a minority imposes its will on the majority, which is what happened under Rabin. You can't have a situation where the vote on Oslo B [the 1995 agreement giving Arafat control of the major West Bank cities] was decided on two Mitsubishis [a reference to the defection before the vote, from the opposition to the government benches, of two Knesset members who were rewarded with government jobs and cars]. That causes a problem with the legitimacy of that government."

I pointed out that Rabin was the democratically elected prime minister of Israel.

Natan: "Let me ask you a question: When Rabin ran for office, what did he say about giving back the Golan?"

He said he wouldn't give it back, I acknowledged. And some people feel he misled them. But that's not the point, I said. We had an election, and people voted for him. So they could vote him out next time.

"But there's a problem with that," said Natan. "Theoretically speaking, you're right, that when a government gets elected, it has the right to do what it wants. Theoretically speaking. The problem is that if you have a situation where the government that's elected, which said it was going to do A, goes and does B, it loses its mandate. What does that mean? Not that the people should overthrow the government. But that the government itself should go back to the people for a new mandate. From a strictly theoretical point of view, it was perfectly legitimate. But from a nontheoretical point of view, it was not legitimate."

After two hours with Natan, I had to conclude that we live in two distinct Israels—not just geographically, but in our minds. I don't think his Israel can last. And he doesn't think mine can last. I don't think we can afford to be intransigent where Palestinian independence is concerned, whatever the historical rights and wrongs. And he doesn't think we can afford not to be. I think his worldview sentences us to endless conflict, and quite possibly ultimate defeat, and he thinks mine positively invites conflict. I don't think there is any moral value, any raison d'être, in a Jewish state that has to quash another nation to survive. And he thinks we dare not allow that other nation to flourish, because we will pay the price, and we have no other Jewish state to run to.

Barak's defeat of Netanyahu suggests that Israelis are shifting from Natan's stance toward mine. But I know that if both our families stay in this country in the years ahead, the gulf in our attitudes will remain just as wide, and the sensitivities as acute, because I don't doubt for a second that Natan believes he is right with every fiber of his being. You don't live where he lives if your heart and soul aren't there with you. And if there is another huge round of killing, another war, a lot more bombing, he will argue that it's because of stupid people like me, who wanted to give the Palestinians guns and independence. And I will argue that it's because of stupid people like him, who insisted on planting themselves deep in the West Bank and prevented a process of disengagement and slow-building friendship. And much of Israel, at the same time it is fighting, will be arrayed across those divided lines.

I'm not sure all Israelis are as resilient as Natan. As he says, Israelis travel, see the world, know what the West is like, aren't ready to go off to war every ten minutes as they once were. And the Palestinians, by Natan's own admission, are more committed, have more fixed ideals, are not as hedonistic, as materialistic, as the rest of us. It sounds to me that, from where Natan is standing, one should deeply fear for Israel. I do not think the people are ready to fight the wars he envisages as inevitable.

"Israelis from all political sides are very attached to this country," he noted. "I am, though, very worried for Israel. When the youth today knows nothing about its history. Nothing about its religion."

Perhaps, I ventured, they just don't want to get killed.

"Do you think I want to get killed?" he said. "Do you think I want my children to get killed?"

But if the Arabs will always retain this desire to kill us all, as Natan claims, and that means that my children and my kids' kids are all going to have to go off to war, and have losses, it's just not worth it. Life is too precious. Life is more precious than the fact that Abraham spoke to God on Natan's West Bank mountain. My kid should be killed for that? And yet I want to live here, in a Jewish state at peace with its neighbors, at the price of giving up the West Bank and Gaza and the Golan and East Jerusalem. And before I abandon that option, I'd like to see if we can have reconciliation with the neighbors, compromise instead of constant domination.

"If only we could live in peace," Natan sighed. "But I don't believe that's possible, for the reasons I've mentioned. And even if the majority of Jews in the country don't take the position that I take, so what? I believe that, in the end, they're going to learn a very hard lesson. There's going to be a lot more death this way. Please God that I'm not right. Please God that you're right. But I don't believe that. Besides which, this is my home. After two thousand years, we have our home."

I am sorry, I said. I'm not the representative of the entire legions of Jews down the centuries, who has to stay put on a patch of West Bank land at all costs. I am one man, with my kids, who would like to be part of a new Jewish state if it is feasible, if it can have a peaceful future. But I don't want my kids to have nothing to look forward to but fighting wars here. If that's the case, I'll live elsewhere.

"I *do* think that I am a link in the chain in the history of my people," said Natan, "and that my kids are the next link. And yes, I do believe this little piece of land is worth fighting for; and no, I am not willing to go somewhere else. I look at it that if my children have to go to war, heaven forbid, and even if they have to die. . . . I'm not crazy, I give my kids cuddles and kisses every night, but if that's the price that has to be paid, well, that has to be left in God's hands. I don't want it to appear that I'm some crazy extremist, willing to let my kids die. But if all of us felt the way you do, we wouldn't be here now in the Land of Israel having this discussion."

Don't get me wrong, I urged Natan. I am willing to fight, if it's necessary. I am willing to send my boys to the army. But not if we didn't give peace a real chance; not if we were so pig-headed and unwilling to compromise that we got ourselves into unnecessary wars; not if people with Natan's mindset are setting the agenda—certainly not, if they're the majority. I won't send my kids to fight for the expansion of West Bank settlements.

Natan had the last word: "I could turn your argument around and say, either, Why should I stay here if Israel is willing to give up its heritage? or, Why should I stay here if those lunatic lefties are putting me and my kids in terrible danger with their suicidal policies? But I don't say either of those things because this is my country and I will stay and, if need be, fight for it, even if its government decides, God forbid, to do something stupid. I am Jewish and my lot is with this people, here in the land that belongs to the Jewish people. I'm not saying we shouldn't try to make peace. We pray for peace three times a day. We should even compromise if that will secure a true peace. But we have to be realistic."

Chapter Eight

Honeymooning with the Neighbors

Well, look what happened to him.

—Apocryphal response of President Assad, when asked in the
1980s and '90s why he had not followed in the footsteps of
Egyptian president Sadat and flown to Israel to make peace

The road to Eldoret, winding north and across the equator
from Nairobi, is one of the best in modern Kenya—a pothole-
free, two-lane highway that cuts through maize fields, potato
farms, and green hills evocative of Scotland. In marked contrast to gridlocked Jerusalem and Tel Aviv, the midafternoon
heat keeps most of the native drivers indoors, leaving the
highway free for strolling sheep, slight women lugging impossibly large loads of firewood, and bony young men, two to a
bicycle, freewheeling down and pedaling painfully up hill after
hill. Just outside the town, rows of brightly dressed women
stand patiently by the roadside, offering milk by the can and
potatoes by the bucket. A big yellow sign proclaims the glad
tiding that we have arrived at ELDORET—HOME OF ELDORE
MUSHROOMS. Another placard, planted appropriately outside
the Uasin Gishu Memorial Hospital, implores: DRIVE CARE-
FULLY—BLOODLESS ROAD LOOKS GOOD!

Eldoret proves to be a compact, bustling town, population
100,000, with a technical college, a few hotels, snack bars,
grocery stores, several churches, and even a dry cleaner. What

it does not have, however—and the matronly woman at the front desk of the local library is quite adamant on this point—is a synagogue. Indeed, she and the two colleagues to whom she immediately relays the inquiry evidently find the notion delightfully absurd, collapsing into gales of laughter that shatter the reverential quiet of the reading rooms.

After a good deal of this hilarity, followed by much patting of the eyes with a pocket handkerchief, she pulls herself together and even looks up a trifle guiltily, as though in apology, toward the sober black-and-white portrait of Kenyan president Daniel Arap Moi, hanging in pride of place above the entrance. And when absolutely certain that the threat of a further relapse into hysterics has been averted, she manages to frame a polite response: "Why would we have a synagogue in Eldoret?" Once the words are out, though, she disintegrates again. And one cannot but sympathize. After all, it is a pretty bizarre idea—a synagogue, out here.

Except that, actually, it isn't. Joseph Chamberlain, the British colonial secretary in the early years of this century, didn't think so. In the spring of 1903, he returned from touring Britain's extensive possessions in Africa and, at a meeting with the Zionist leader Theodor Herzl in London, suggested that six thousand square miles of the Uasin Gishu Plateau in which Eldoret is centered—in those days part of the British Ugandan Protectorate—might be just the place for the persecuted Jews of Russia to find refuge. Herzl was not ecstatic. "East Africa," he acknowledged in an address to delegates at that year's Sixth Zionist Congress in Basel, "is indeed not Zion and never can become it." But he did beg his colleagues not to reject the plan out of hand. Perhaps, he mused, Africa might serve as a temporary homeland, "an antechamber to the Holy Land," as he put it. "A place of apprenticeship."

While the Jews were deliberating, the British expatriates in the area were going apoplectic. A certain Lord Delaware

cabled the *London Times* tersely: "Feeling here very strong
against introduction of alien Jews." In purpler prose, another
wrote to the local *East African Standard:* "To read of this beautiful land being reserved for foreign Jewish paupers is enough
to make one wish for a big nose and a name like Ikey Moses."
A rally was organized in Nairobi, at which one speaker is said
to have observed that Jews have always "rendered themselves
obnoxious to the people of every country they went to."

Defying that kind of invective, a handful of intrepid Jewish
pioneers nevertheless moved in. Two of them, Messrs. Hotz
and London, established farms to the south of Eldoret. A
third, Abraham Block, became a hotelier in Nairobi and a bas-
tion of the tiny Jewish community that has flickered there ever
since. But the "Uganda Scheme" was abandoned within two
years, after a three-man commission funded by Christian
friends of the Zionist movement returned from an exploratory
visit with the assessment that the land would not be able to
sustain more than about five hundred families and that it was
singularly ill-suited "to consolidate the bonds uniting Jews."

Tubby Block, Abraham's son, says his father thought that
the commissioners were wrong, and not just because, as another of the Eldoret roadside signs proclaims, the region
enjoys THE BEST CLIMATE IN THE WORLD. If the Jews had
given a prompt yes in 1905, he muses, deftly filleting his sole
in the restaurant of the family's Norfolk Hotel in Nairobi,
there is no telling how many of the European Jews who perished might have found refuge in Uasin Gishu Plateau three
and a half decades later. "My father always thought it was a
terrible wasted opportunity," says Tubby, a dapper gent in his
late seventies. "He believed the Jews could make something of
that land. He thought it had great potential. He'd always say,
'We could have grown anything there,'" Tubby recalls. "And
he'd grumble that, 'Instead, they gave us a bit of bloody
desert.'"

There was and is, however, one more drawback involved in settlement around the Eldoret area. It has always been, and remains, the focus of frequently violent disputes among various native tribes with conflicting claims of ownership. Indeed, in clashes that continued into the 1990s, two such tribes—the Kikuyu and the Kalenjin—were hammering away at each other with good old-fashioned bows and arrows, yielding annual death tolls in the hundreds. Perhaps not the best neighborhood after all. . . .

. . . But then again, not that bad when compared to the neighborhood we ended up with instead. If it is not claustrophobic enough living in a country you can travel the length of in a workday, and across in a coffee break, take a look at the immediate vicinity: the Palestinians on the doorstep, the Syrians over the hill, and the likes of Algeria, Libya, Iran, and Iraq just beyond the horizon. No wonder every Israeli who can afford to heads to the airport once or twice a year, that a year's travel break to somewhere exotic is de rigueur for twenty-one-year-old soldiers immediately on their being discharged, that whenever there is a crisis vote in the Knesset two dozen parliamentarians have to be rounded up and flown home from fact-finding tours of Finland or the Ivory Coast. And no wonder that, for a brief honeymoon period, when the ties did bind, Israelis in their hundreds of thousands delightedly hopped across to Egypt (in the early 1980s) and Jordan (in 1994 and 1995) to sample the sights, to breathe some different air. How sad that the honeymoons had to end.

With Lisa, I popped over to Egypt in the mid-1980s for the briefest of visits—just a few days in Cairo and its immediate surroundings. We went on an Israeli tour bus with four of our more enterprising friends, heading for the border directly through the Gaza Strip—unthinkable nowadays, quite routine back then, before the Intifada and the hand-over to Arafat. I have memories of a border crossing that, bureaucratically, was no more than routinely nightmarish. I vaguely recall one of our party being body-searched. And I have photos, after our brief voyage across the Suez Canal, that show we had entered another world—for one of our number, who shall remain nameless, of excruciating stomach complaints and the odd bout of dehydration; for the rest of us, of awe-inspiring antiquities and incredible Cairo traffic jams, of six- and seven-year-old kids working full days weaving rugs, of eating an exorbitant, slow-moving meal on the Nile, buying radically overpriced papyrus wall-hangings, marveling at the high quality of the local cream cheese, feeling very small in the shadow of the Sphinx and the pyramids.

The hot Israeli band Tea Packs has a song about how, wherever you go in the world, it is best not to tell them you are from Israel, just in case. Well, in Cairo back then, most of the Egyptians we spoke with assumed we had a Palestinian connection because Sid, one of our gang, spoke Palestinian-accented Arabic. And we were happy to correct the misapprehension, to acknowledge our Israeli affiliation. And we connected as Israelis: We organized a soccer kick-about with a bunch of street kids in the parking lot of the Nile Hilton (we lost); we somehow found ourselves testing out various scents in the inner sanctum of a Cairo perfumery; I have a picture of three of us smoking I honestly don't remember what through a water-pipe on the floor of a carpet showroom, and another of us all posing on one of the Nile bridges with four middle-aged, black-clad, smiling women. We had got talking because they spotted the rubber-ring "bracelet" Lisa was wearing and excitedly pointed out that they wore them too. (The bracelets, actually part of a tank-firing mechanism, happened to have become fashion statements simultaneously in Cairo and Jerusalem.) Emboldened by a few too many beers, one afternoon Sid (aping Bill Murray and Harold Ramis in *Stripes*) even persuaded the bemused but game denizens of an overcrowded textile market to learn and sing along with the chorus of Manfred Mann's "Doo-Wah-Diddy Diddy" ("Here she comes, just a-walking down the street, singing doo-wah-diddy-diddy-dum-diddy-dum. . . .").

But then, in 1985, came the shooting. On a Saturday afternoon that October, an Egyptian soldier—subsequently, inevitably, to be characterized by the Egyptian authorities as "deranged"—opened fire on Israeli tourists on the Sinai beach of Ras Burka, about twenty-five miles across from the Israeli border, killing seven of them. Compounding the tragedy was the fact that some of these lives could have been saved, were it not that other Egyptian soldiers refused to allow fellow Israelis to drive the injured back to the border at Eilat for immediate treatment. Adding insult to fatality, President Hosni Mubarak, a few days later, dismissed the incident as a "small matter."

Not a great deal has happened since to encourage Israelis to return confidently to the Sinai, or anywhere in Egypt. There have been Israeli tour buses shot up, spies arrested on the flimsiest of evidence, and a spate of Islamic extremist attacks on tourists of all nationalities.

A former colleague at the *Jerusalem Post* happened to be at Ras Burka that day in 1985. He, his wife, and their young son were only about one hundred yards away from the "deranged" soldier's position, playing in the sand, when the shooting started. Not long afterward, my colleague emigrated with his family to Australia.

With Jordan, though, things were going to be different. It took Amman and Jerusalem only one hundred days, from King Hussein's first public handshake with Yitzhak Rabin at the White House in the summer of 1994, to negotiate a peace treaty—so both sides must really have wanted it. In contrast to

the Egyptians, who held out for every last inch of Sinai territory, most definitely including the luxury hotel on the Taba
border, Jordan made concessions—dropping a demand for
direct access to the waters of the Sea of Galilee, agreeing to
"land swap" arrangements along the border, even giving the
farmers of Kibbutz Ashdot Ya'acov Ihud continued access to
the fields they had been farming before the treaty, although
these were formally restored to Hashemite sovereignty. And
while Rabin's funeral was the only time President Mubarak
has set foot in Israel since succeeding Anwar Sadat (murdered
for making his peace with Israel), the king was a frequent visi-
tor—in all kinds of disguises on secret missions before 1994,
and as his smiling, public self on a series of trips after the full
treaty was signed one blustery day in the desert.

In the first heady months of warm, new friendship, Hussein invited a group of amateur radio hams to visit him in
Amman and gave them all gold watches. He encouraged two-
way tourism and turned a blind eye to the uncouth vandalism
of Israeli visitors, who developed an unhealthy reputation for
stealing hotel bathroom fittings and crashing Amman society
weddings. We waved to him once from our office balcony as
he piloted his plane over Jerusalem. He telephoned Rabin
from the cockpit. And you could tell that Rabin loved him. At
that first public White House encounter, only the trademark
Rabin shyness, I'm sure, prevented the hug both men must
secretly have wanted. "Why didn't you kiss him?" an Israeli
reporter asked Rabin when he got home. "I don't go in for
that kind of thing," he said. A shame.

But then, in a hail of bullets that echoed as loudly as those
fired at Ras Burka, and had precisely the same impact, a Jordanian killed seven Jews and the Jordan honeymoon was over,
too. Hussein, unlike Mubarak, did everything he could to
repair the damage. There were inconceivable scenes: an Arab
king on his knees before the bereaved parents of seven slain

Israeli schoolgirls, thanking them for receiving him, urging that they treat him like a brother, pledging that "if there is anything left in this life," he would use it to try to further peace.

But respect and affection for a remarkable king can't blot out the newspaper images of those who were mown down by a Jordanian border guard, the Hashemite kingdom's contribution to the list of "deranged" gunmen: Adi Malka, a thirteen-year-old who served as the bridge to the world of her deaf-mute parents, Shimon and Alia, and took care of her eleven-year-old twin brothers; Nurit Cohen, who lost an uncle in the Hamas 1996 Jerusalem bus bombing and whose dying act, a bullet in her chest, was to fall on a classmate, saving her life; Natali Alkali, who had phoned her parents just before the shooting to bubble about what a wonderful time she was having. . . .

On the morning of March 13, 1997, the parents of these three and four other teenage girls from Beit Shemesh had sent them off on the annual class field trip, along the newly peaceful border. The highlight was to be a brief sojourn inside Jordanian territory itself, at Naharayim, site of an old hydroelectric plant on the Jordan and Yarmuk rivers, a small enclave that had become known as "the island of peace." That same night, those same parents said Kaddish, the mourner's prayer, over their daughters' fresh graves.

I am looking at photos of Josh and Adam at Naharayim now, sitting on the hood of a Jordanian army vehicle just like the one from which the gunman fired his opening volleys. I am looking at their sunny, trusting features, gazing unconcernedly out from beneath their newly snipped hair. I am remembering what a lovely day out we had there, a few months before it all went sour, how we clambered onto the roof of the abandoned railway station, how we looked out across the Jordanian hills, how we tried to make conversation, in our inept

Arabic, with the Jordanian soldiers on duty. And I am reflecting on my ex-colleague's move to Australia.

Just days before the killings, our then–prime minister's eighty-four-year-old mother had been quoted in the *Washington Post* scoffing at the notion of lasting peace between us and the Arabs. "Ridiculous," Mrs. Cela Netanyahu had snorted. "There'll be peace . . . when we're not here." Amid the wailing in Beit Shemesh on the night of the killings at Naharayim, there were many who agreed with her. There were many, too, who blamed the king for the whole affair. The king who had just sent and publicized an extraordinarily harsh letter to Netanyahu, accusing him of leading the region to the "abyss of bloodshed and disaster," deliberately humiliating the Palestinians to prompt them into "inevitable violent resistance" so that "your powerful armed forces" could then "commit wanton murder and mayhem" in Palestinian towns. Distraught and defensive, the king now insisted he was not responsible. "When I warned a couple of days ago against what I perceived as danger, of despair, and the possibility of violence," he explained, standing small and alone, clutching one hand in the other as he faced a phalanx of television cameras, "I never thought it would break out the way it did today. But I was fully within my responsibilities to try and warn one and all." There were a few, on our side, who tried to think a little deeper, to consider our role in the breakdown of faith that presaged the shooting. Netanyahu had written a considered, statesmanlike reply to Hussein's letter, defending his policies, and taking exception to the personal tone of the king's assault. But his officials had also reportedly muttered something about a history of mental illness in the royal family—infuriating the royal palace and, presumably, Hussein's loyal subjects and soldiers.

It may be that peace with Jordan will prove viable. Though young and untested, it survived not merely the strains of Netanyahu's years in power but also Hussein's death and the surprising transfer of power to his son, the unknown Abdullah, rather than to his brother, the familiar Hassan. On a personal level, Hussein was genuinely beloved here, the more so after the Beit Shemesh condolence call. His dramatic presence at the White House signing of the Wye deal, when he made light of his loss of hair and eyebrows to chemotherapy, was incredibly moving. There is affection too for the former Lisa Halaby, Noor al Hussein (Light of Hussein), the ex–Princeton architecture student who quit the cheerleading squad in protest of the skimpy outfits, lived in a hippie commune, demonstrated against the Vietnam War, and gave up a career in her father's airline business for life with a man married three times before, eighteen years her senior, in an obscure desert kingdom where a woman is expected to know her place—in the shadows, several paces behind her husband. If Abdullah proves as personally warm to Israel as was his father, that reservoir of affection awaits him too.

But restoring the people-to-people peace, the trust that enables me to take my kids to Naharayim, or Amman, or Petra, that is going to take time.

Several months before the Naharayim tragedy, I got a phone call from Melitz, a pluralistic Israeli educational institution that, among other things, provides guides and lecturers to visiting tour groups. Melitz had thirteen busloads of twenty- to forty-year-old Diaspora Jews coming in for a tour of Israel, and they wondered if I would like to spend two weeks on one of the buses as a "scholar in residence"—a kind of backup to the main guide, on hand to offer historical context, geographical insights, and general analyses of what was being seen.

It was, to put it mildly, a challenge. I can barely find my way from central Tel Aviv to the Jerusalem highway, let alone pontificate on the precise travels of the children of Israel through the Holy Land. But you know that old cliché about the people who live in a country never getting to see it as well as the tourists do? I felt a bit that way about Israel. I had been to the Metulla and Eilat northern and southern extremities many a time. But there was an embarrassing amount in between that I had never quite got around to seeing.

My busload turned out to comprise three dozen singles and a few married couples from Montreal, prone to excruciating renditions of the Macarena dance hit on the bus microphone but otherwise quite charming. Initially taken aback, on their first morning in our lovely country, to encounter a driver, the sour-faced Ezra, who considered it beyond his duty to assist in the loading of their suitcases into the underbus storage compartments, they devoted the first hour of their sojourn to the forbidding task of extracting a smile from his granite features. And they succeeded, inveigling him into taking the mike for his own Moroccan childhood favorite and responding with enough extravagant applause to melt a waxwork.

In twelve frenetic days, we completed the full "Israel Experience" in all its frequently surreal glory. Not only did we tour the big cities, cry in the Holocaust museums, inspect kibbutz dairies, and learn about Negev desert-irrigation systems, but we took coffee with a Bedouin family in the gravel-paved parking lot of an ethnic museum, barbecued on the Lebanese border while the army and Hizbollah guerrillas exchanged gunfire a few miles to the north, and grabbed a planeload of newly arrived, utterly uncomprehending immigrants from the Ukraine for an impromptu *horah* dance on the tarmac at Ben-Gurion Airport.

And then it was time to cross into Jordan—our two-day bonus at the end of the trip. We had spent the previous night at an outrageously expensive hotel in Eilat so that our convoy could be the first at the Eilat-Aqaba border crossing. We headed off a little after six, and two hours later we had bidden farewell to Ezra, surrendered our passports, passed our worldly goods through the X-ray security machines, and gotten the all-clear to clamber aboard our blue-and-white Jordanian bus, complete with Haitham, our Jordanian driver, and our very own police escort vehicle, for our thirty-six-hour Hashemite adventure. Two hours might sound like an inordinately lengthy time to while away at a border crossing. But by the prevailing standards, it apparently represented express treatment. The tour organizers had prepared us with ominous accounts of past mishaps, the daylong delays occasioned by the presence of one too many or one too few on a bus, or of an exotic, obscure border stamp in a passport.

My relief at our having safely negotiated the crossing was short-lived, however. No sooner had the elderly bus cranked up to speed for the three-hour journey to our first stop, at the ancient red-rock city of Petra, than a young Canadian whom I'll call Janine, crying plaintively, threw herself down next to me in the front row and begged for us to turn back. "I can't be here," she wailed. "I don't feel safe. We're in an Arab country. Anything could happen to us. I want to go back to Israel."

Janine was one of the few married members of our party, and her husband, Jacob, was with us on the bus. But sadly, in this, her hour of need, he was, literally, taking a backseat. So I tried my best to reassure her. Everything was going to be just fine, I promised. Stay here next to me, take deep breaths, get some rest, and if you're still feeling unhappy when we get to Petra, I said, we'll see what we can do about getting you home early. This last pledge was unrealizable. Given the limitations of Jordanian bureaucracy, there was scant prospect of Janine, having entered the country as part of a tour group, being allowed back into Israel on her own. But it did pacify my troubled tourist; she even calmed down sufficiently to manage a nap before we pulled up at the splendors of Petra.

If you have been there yourself, you know just how

magnificent it is. If you have not, I have no desire to spoil it for you by describing that marvelous sensation of riding on horseback along the narrow pathway to the ancient Nabataean city, that sense of time standing still as you pass along the narrow rift between the towering rocky walls on either side, that unforgettable moment when the vast, exquisitely carved, redrock treasury building first comes into view. I won't mention any of that. Suffice it to say, in the rush of emotion, the fascination, the awe that Petra engenders, I quite forgot about Janine.

We spent much of the day exploring in the heat, then trailed wearily back to the bus in midafternoon for the long haul to Amman. As we followed our police escorts toward the capital, the scenery mirrored the Israeli desert route just to our west: endless golden rocky desert bisected by a single road, the King's Highway. Showing unexpected *jeunesse*, our aged bus was eating up the miles until, about halfway through the journey, with night falling, at a particularly desolate juncture, there was a dull thump and we began to lose speed. Evidently, we had sustained a flat on our nearside rear. Haitham nursed the bus along for a few more minutes until, either guided by a sixth sense or impressively familiar with the roadside amenities in the area, he pulled up outside a nondescript, unfinished, gray concrete building that proved to be a garage. From this and the other, similar one-story buildings dotted nearby, about one hundred Jordanian males of all ages emerged in a great curious wave: ninety-nine of them to gawk at us, and one poor sap whose job it was to change the tire.

First he attempted to use an ordinary tire iron. But our wheel nuts, doubtless embedded in years of desert grit, were disinclined to budge. So he tried adding a small wooden stick, for leverage. Still no luck. Now he disappeared into the garage for a few minutes and emerged triumphant, dragging a solid steel bar more than a yard long. He heaved one end onto the tire iron, left the other on the sand, and began jumping on the bar. The wheel nuts were unimpressed. Haitham, our driver, got out to assist. Unfortunately, though, he strayed too close to the high-tech wheel-removing operation, and the iron bar slipped off the tire-iron and smashed down across his instep. Massive bleeding ensued, a red fountain erupting through his left sock. Our police escort pulled up with a screech of brakes, Haitham was manhandled into the backseat, and the vehicle sped away.

So here we were, a group of Jewish tourists on our first day in a strange Arab country, with night falling, in the middle of the desert, surrounded by one hundred male natives, with no driver, no means of transportation, and no police escort. Anybody with a modicum of common sense might have been alarmed. Anybody uncomfortable in the first place about being in Jordan would be downright panic-stricken. At which point, a sudden, terrible thought occurred to me: Janine!

I looked around for her, half expecting to find her cowering in terror in the baggage compartment, or fainted clean away under her seat. Instead, in the doorway of the bus, perched jauntily on the third of the four steps leading up to the driver's seat, Janine was holding court. It need hardly be said that she spoke no Arabic. And yet she was entertaining perhaps a dozen giggling Jordanian boys, playing some kind of improvised version of charades. Janine was miming theater curtains parting, cameras whirring, books opening. It is doubtful that Janine and her audience had been to many of the same shows, seen many of the same films, or read many of the same books. But somehow they were bridging the language and culture barriers. And they were having fun.

I will never forget that tableau, especially in the wake of incidents like that at Naharayim. Here was a young woman disposed, by a lifetime's absorption of dubious conventional Jewish wisdom, to expect the very worst from the Jordanians.

So worried was she about being in the country that she would have turned back if she'd had the chance. And yet, just a few hours later, in a situation where she might have had every right to feel concerned, she had conquered those instincts. She had relaxed, subtly calmed by the unobtrusive politeness of our hosts, the no-fuss welcome. And while it might be extravagant to construe that if that is what the Jordanians could do for Janine in less than a day, then the rest of the region's problems cannot be insurmountable, and horrific acts of violence such as the shootings at Naharayim should be dismissed as atypical moments of mayhem, it is certainly tempting to believe that a tad more ordinary personal contact and a shade less rhetorical grandstanding could go a long way toward easing tensions.

As for our bus, the combination of leverage and brute force did ultimately dislodge the wheel nuts, and the tire was eventually replaced. The police came back with Haitham after mere minutes, his wound cleaned and bandaged. He hobbled back to his seat, cheered on by passengers and locals, and managed to drive another twenty minutes or so to a gas station, where a relief driver, magically conjured up, was waiting. Late and exhausted, but bubbling from our little adventure, we arrived at an Amman restaurant to dine like kings and queens on couscous and grilled fish. It turned out that the fish was off. And most of us awoke with stomach agonies the next morning. But nobody, and least of all Janine, could get too upset with the Jordanians.

Our two other immediate neighbors, Syria and Lebanon, have never voluntarily opened their borders to us—not yet, at least. That hasn't prevented Israelis from visiting, but not as tourists: The Golan Heights, openly accessible residential northern Israel for the past three decades, were captured from Syria in the 1967 war; the south Lebanon security zone, home to a rotating deployment of Israeli troops and their intermittent journalistic visitors, is the last unhappy vestige of the 1982 invasion, a buffer zone designed to prevent pro-Iranian guerrilla groups from targeting towns and villages across the international border.

Israel, under any government, would have readily relinquished the security zone and pulled the troops back to the border if it could have been assured that Hizbollah and the other gunmen wouldn't try to follow. But only when Barak came to power did a government seriously entertain the notion of pulling back unilaterally—mindful of how skilled Hizbollah had become over the years, and how high the army death toll had soared. Barak, essentially, played a complex game of chicken with Syria: If Damascus wanted to talk peace, fine, Israel would even put the entire Golan Heights on the negotiating table. But if President Assad waited too long, Israel would withdraw from Lebanon—and then Assad would have a real dilemma. Should he, the dominant power broker in Lebanon, allow Hizbollah to raid and shell civilian targets in northern Israel, he would risk furious Israeli military retaliation, directly against Syria. On the other hand, were he to rein in the guerrillas, Israelis in the north would finally sleep easy, and there would be no particular pressure on the government in Jerusalem to sign a peace treaty with him. Either way, Assad's leverage in Lebanon—using Hizbollah to fight a proxy war, to keep killing Israeli soldiers and reminding their parents that there could be no tranquillity there until the Golan was restored to its rightful Damascus owners—would be gone. No wonder that, in December 1999, he consented to resume peace talks.

Under Rabin, Israeli and Syrian negotiators have since claimed, a Golan deal was all but signed and sealed. Rabin himself hinted broadly that something was taking shape. Having pledged in his election campaign not to relinquish the

Golan, he began talking about holding a referendum on the issue, indicating that he was getting ready to give up the Heights as part of a peace treaty that would normalize Israeli-Syrian ties and allow for a solution in Lebanon. The icy Assad gave signs of starting to thaw—sending his foreign minister to be interviewed on Israel Television, hanging up signs all over Damascus hailing a new struggle for peace, beginning a reeducation program in his army and his schools to the effect that the Zionists weren't quite so intolerable after all.

But Assad was cautious, afraid to commit himself. An American diplomat who knows him quite well told me at the time that Assad was prone to mentioning the fate of Sadat, and his desire not to have his life ended in the same way. He may have felt that, as the last holdout against the Israeli-American peacemaking bulldozer, he was feared and respected, whereas once he put his name to a treaty, he would be just another balding old bully, running a minor Third World country with outdated infrastructure and no raw materials. He may also have calculated that peacemaking could put tremendous pressure on his minority regime, reducing the chances of his installing his reportedly somewhat unsuitable ophthalmologist son Bashar as heir, with his citizens wondering why it was they had suffered economically over the decades to feed a war machine that was now being deactivated because the enemy was actually a friend. And he may have feared that peace would bring Westernization, demands for a free press (the kind that might have complicated his 1982 assault on the townsfolk of Hama, where his army killed an estimated twenty thousand of their brethren to quash a feared nascent Islamic revolution), satellite television, and exposure for his people to the notion of democracy (Assad does hold periodic elections, but there's only one candidate). Perhaps most of all, after nearly thirty years of happy totalitarian power, the status quo had a certain reliable appeal.

I think that, had he gone for a deal, and Rabin held his referendum, Israel would have voted for it—provided, by then, that Assad had himself done what Sadat did: come to Jerusalem, spoken in the Knesset, invited Israeli leaders and journalists to visit his capital. Now that the talks have begun again, I still think the electorate will vote yes in the promised referendum—so long as we feel the necessary security arrangements are in place to guard against surprise attack, so long as we feel our water sources are protected, and so long as Assad displays a personal commitment to neighborly relations. The opinion polls don't back me up unequivocally. But the opinion polls in the early 1970s showed a vast majority steadfastly opposed to trading the Sinai for peace, and the whole picture changed when Sadat flew in.

Even though Assad held back during the Rabin era, there were some beneficiaries of that mild flirtation with Damascus: Syria's Jews, who finally got to leave for Israel and other places west, and Mohammad Badwan.

Badwan is an Israeli Arab who grew up poor in the village of Ein Nakuba, fifteen minutes outside Jerusalem on the way to Tel Aviv. His father was a cleaner at the Jerusalem municipality, and Mohammad was working hard himself before he had even reached his teens—mixing cement at a Jerusalem cemetery. By fourteen he was a trainee baker in Jerusalem's Mahaneh Yehuda market, and by sixteen he had left the village and gone to work at a bakery in Tiberias, on the western shore of the Sea of Galilee. One Saturday in May 1962, Badwan went boating with two Jewish friends. A strongish wind sprang up, and the boat was pulled inexorably toward the eastern shore of the sea—in those days, Syrian territory. The two Jewish boys, who could swim, dived in and headed back to safety. Badwan, who could not, drifted helplessly into Syrian captivity. He was picked up, bound and questioned by Syrian police, and placed in solitary confinement. His family had no idea what had become of him. When it became clear to the Syrians that he was not an Israeli spy, he was put to work in a hotel, and later at a restaurant and a bakery. Not long after he went missing, an uncle in Jordan managed to track him down, but there was no way to extricate him. After ten years in Syria, he married a local girl, Miriam, and they moved to a refugee camp just outside Damascus.

As the years passed, the couple had eight children, and Mohammad forgot his Hebrew, but he never abandoned the dream of being allowed to return to Israel. The Syrian authorities, though, blocked his applications to travel abroad, never supplying him with Syrian papers to replace the Israeli identity documents they had confiscated on capturing him. Finally, in 1994, he and his family were granted exit visas—ostensibly to visit relatives in Jordan. And on November 11, 1995, the fifty-year-old Mohammad, his Syrian wife, and their children crossed the Allenby Bridge and headed back to Ein Nakuba, to a welcoming party at the village he had last seen thirty-three years before. Both his parents had died while he was away. He had been forced to leave his eldest son behind in a Syrian jail, imprisoned for refusing to serve in the army. But he was, he declared, overwhelmed to be back in the country he had always considered home, and his only hope, he said, was that Israel and Syria would soon make peace, so that he could be reunited with his boy.

The Syrian people in general could do with the profits of reconciliation, the rise in living standards that would result from a little less spending on defense and a little more on education, health, and social services. And our people could do with peace. We could even live without our renowned Golan Heights winery.

We could certainly do without losing a soldier a month in the miniwar inside south Lebanon. All wars are stupid, but this one has been stupider than most, a low-level conflict involving two countries that have no particular desire to confront each other, wasting life after life after life: Hizbollah gunmen who have grown up on horror stories of the Israeli invaders, teenage Israeli soldiers desperate to get home safely, and their generally older south Lebanese "allies," pressed into uniform in return for more money than they could earn elsewhere and jobs inside Israel for their wives. All of them locked into a cycle of violence that cannot ever be ended by anything they do but that could always have been halted overnight if politicians in Damascus, Beirut, and Jerusalem had willed it.

Barak is proving that he wills it, having been elected partly because of his pledge to bring Israel out of south Lebanon, to dismantle a military infrastructure that looks so depressingly permanent. On a press trip a while back around the security zone, we were taken to Marjayoun, the joint headquarters of the Israeli army and the allied South Lebanon Army (SLA) militia, and though we were deep inside Lebanese territory, there was nothing temporary about the Israeli presence. A Lebanese flag fluttered above the metal gateway that led to the concrete French-built compound, but the "standing orders" on the notice board inside were written in Hebrew, as were all the inevitable army placards calling for ACTION, NOT PROMISES! and urging soldiers to PREVENT FIRES! In the lush recreation area, kept emerald green by a fountain that sprayed water out of twelve machine-gun barrels, there was even a plaque acknowledging the generosity of the Jewish National Fund.

We were driven to Mansura, twenty minutes to the west, for a display of firepower. SLA soldiers prepared missile-like shells for a row of five howitzers. But when one of my colleagues, visibly uncomfortable, inquired nervously as to whether they planned to "fire one of those things" into the gray yonder, our Israeli liaison officer host responded curtly, "Not likely. They cost two thousand dollars each." Asked how long he anticipated Israeli troops being kept out here, the officer shrugged and said there would be no pullout until "the central government in Beirut can maintain rule here. Then, you won't find so much as a single Israeli adviser."

But the central government in Beirut couldn't act until its parent government in Damascus gave its assent. And Damascus is only now starting to budge, because Israel, finally offered the promise of normalized relations with Syria, is getting ready to give back the Golan—to return the land we captured in a war, for a peace we simply could not have achieved without that bloodshed. It is a heavy price, most of all for those 17,000 Israelis who have built their lives on the Heights. But the alternative is there for all of us to contemplate in black on white. Pick up an old newspaper at random, and just read. October 10, 1998: Nineteen-year-old Yarom Amit, hit in the head two days earlier by an artillery shell while on duty at the security zone outpost at Carcum, is still unconscious in the hospital fighting for his life. Go back two weeks: two paratroopers killed by a roadside bomb. Go back another two weeks: two more paratroopers laid to rest, their armored personnel vehicle having toppled over a ridge.

On November 26, 1998, I was watching the nightly television news with our neighbor's son, Amitai Sawicki, just turned thirteen, an unusually considerate and intelligent boy. The lead story concerned the two soldiers killed that day in Lebanon, Nitzan Balderan, twenty, and Uriel Peretz, twenty-two. Peretz had been at home the previous weekend, on leave, and got it into his head to make a video, but his mother, somehow fearing that this would bring bad luck, refused to appear in it. They screened the video on the news—the close-cropped, bespectacled Peretz, in uniform, smiling and carefree, imploring his mom to get into the frame. "Okay, you don't want to be filmed? So don't be filmed," he told her, giving up. "Mum doesn't want to be filmed, because she's scared," he then said. "Don't worry, nothing's going to happen to me." Yes, I'll vote to relinquish the Golan—to open the Middle East to Israel, to give us peace on all our borders, to save Amitai Sawicki and tens of thousands like him from that Lebanon nightmare.

Chapter Nine

What Kind of Jewish State?

Twenty-two soldiers were killed in Lebanon this year. Not a single ultra-Orthodox draft-dodger got killed studying the Torah. . . .

—From a December 1998 ad campaign mounted by "A Free People," a movement professing itself dedicated to "pluralism in religion, conscience, education, and culture"

The ultra-Orthodox community doesn't realize the extent of the Nazism developing against it in this country. . . . The Nazi hostility is taking root among an entire generation of youth in high school and in the army, who are incited by the media and anti-Orthodox educators.

—From a December 1998 newspaper article by Rabbi Yisrael Eichler, a leading ultra-Orthodox spokesman, in one of his community's newspapers (Eichler subsequently retracted the Nazi comparison)

My father was born in Germany, into an Orthodox family, a rabbinical family, but one that was also very much a part of its adopted homeland: His dad, a lawyer, was an officer in the German army, was badly wounded in World War I, and was awarded the Iron Cross for bravery on the French front.

In the mid-1930s, my grandfather paid a monthlong visit to the Holy Land, to pre-state Palestine. He came here not to check out a potential escape route, but to see with his own eyes what he called "this blessed and longed-for land." He described the experience in an address he gave to Jewish friends in his hometown of Frankfurt in 1935. Translated into English (from German) by my Aunt Selma, it makes for extraordinary reading all these decades later.

Amusingly, even way back then, my grandfather picked up on the casual approach to personal discipline that still characterizes the Israeli mentality. He observes, I think with a twinkle, that despite a notice on all buses forbidding smoking and spitting, "the driver often welcomes one with a cigarette dangling from his mouth and a perfect curve of saliva to the floor." Bus schedules are not strictly adhered to, he points out (his German efficiency-consciousness coming through loud and clear). More seriously now, he notes that people talk loudly to each other even at memorial services, there are many complaints about "sharp practices" in the business community and a "lack of professional solidarity" among doctors and lawyers, and a mistaken respect for permissiveness means that children are allowed to disobey their parents. "The constant 'I don't want to' is heard from *every* child."

But while he is somewhat concerned by such peccadilloes, the central theme of my grandfather's address, along with his awed delight at simply walking on land that has for centuries been the focus of Jewish "hopes and yearnings," is his dismay that the pioneers of Jewish statehood "have introduced a lifestyle that is far removed from tradition." They are not living as Orthodox Jews—not following the halachic code of Jewish living as set down in the Torah and understood through the chain of Jewish tradition, with its provisions for resting from work on the Sabbath, its kashrut or dietary laws, its prayer schedule, its framework for family purity. Almost everywhere he goes, while he marvels at the pioneers, he encounters "opposition to all religious observances, even the maintenance of Sabbath and kashrut." Boys do not celebrate their bar mitzvahs. On Sabbath eve, rather than congregating in the synagogue, people of all ages travel to the Dead Sea, to moonlight parties with "seabathing and subsequent dancing to jazz music."

His sad realization is that "these glorious young people, who are dedicating the prime of their youth to the soil of the country and who number among themselves the most excellent models of humanity, goal-orientedness, and dynamic idealism, have strayed so far from the Jewish way that they believe observance of the law to be a burden, or anyway not essential, even on this holy ground." What is needed, what the Holy Land is crying out for, he says, is lively young rabbis and teachers who can combine the pioneering spirit with a traditional, Orthodox outlook. "They will find a great and difficult job ahead of them, but also a gratifying one." (Although he bought land here, subsequently nationalized, in the Carmel forest, my grandfather apparently gave little serious thought to moving here himself. He brought his family to England in 1937, having stayed in Germany as long as he could to help other Jews escape.)

Sixty years later, my grandfather would be surprised at how things have changed. The unhappy irony is that some of the shifts in attitudes to Orthodoxy that might have gratified him, a Diaspora Jew, are somewhat less gratifying to the grandson who came to live here.

This has hardly turned out to be a godless Jewish state. And its official relationship with God is organized by the Orthodox establishment that my grandfather found so lacking here sixty years ago. Despite feisty opposition from the less rigid Reform and Conservative streams of Judaism, the Orthodox rabbinate has managed to exert a monopoly on birth, marriage, and death in the Holy Land—only Orthodox rabbis, using their unbending criteria, can determine whether one's newborn is to be considered Jewish by the state's various institutions; only Orthodox rabbis can perform state-recognized marriages; only Orthodox rabbis can decide whether a recent Russian immigrant who falls defending his new country in the uniform of its army may be buried in a Jewish cemetery or, because of doubts about his parents' Jewish heritage, must be laid to rest in a separate section for outcasts.

My grandfather would have found this hard to believe, but the fiercely secular state that he witnessed in the making has seen one government (Rabin's in 1977) fall because it ignored Orthodox sensibilities and accepted a delivery of American warplanes on a Sabbath eve, and another (Netanyahu's in 1996) given a critical boost toward election by the massed support of an Orthodox community that deemed its fundamental mindset more traditional, closer to the Torah, than that of the opposition. And while almost a million overwhelmingly secular immigrants from the former Soviet Union have arrived here in the past decade, even that vast influx cannot obscure a trend in parts of Jewish Israel toward a return to Orthodoxy, an abandonment of secular values in favor of halachic, Jewish spiritual ones.

In the quest for some meaning to this life, or just for a crutch to help them through it, many Israelis have looked to the East; yearlong pilgrimages to India, Indonesia, and Thailand are highly popular among soldiers discharged after their compulsory service. Some have tried to extract the spiritualism from Judaism without the commitment to ritual practice—enrolling, for instance, in courses in Kabbalah, the mystical higher form of Jewish study that the sages reserved only for the most exceptional and mature scholars. A relatively small number have embraced the Jews for Jesus cults, a brand of the faith that has always left me particularly cold—I mean, Judaism and Christianity are each complex enough, and thoroughly mutually exclusive, so why complicate matters further by trying to meld the two? (Strictly for reporting purposes, I attended a quite pleasant Jews-for-Jesus service in London a few years back, where the words to psalms were spelled out on a projector screen, with a jaunty, bouncing white dot to help the congregation follow along, and where the rabbi struck me as a particularly jovial fellow. I ran into him again quite recently. He has renounced Jesus and rededicated himself to the Jews and was working as a building contractor at one of the larger West Bank settlements.)

In by far the greatest numbers, however, previously secular Israelis are exploring Orthodox and ultra-Orthodox Judaism, swapping Saturday soccer for synagogue, forsaking nightclubs for yeshiva classes, shedding their jeans and T-shirts and letting their beards grow. My uncle has made returning Jews to the roots of their faith his life's mission; he runs a yeshiva for *hozrim be'tshuvah*—for those "returning in repentance"—in Har Nof, a fast-growing ultra-Orthodox Jewish neighborhood. One of my childhood friends, now also a rabbi, teaches at a similar establishment. He describes what he does as "reacquainting people with what it's all about, why we're here." I respect both of them immensely. I know them to be decent, considerate people. But I adamantly refused when, in my late teens, it was suggested by some of my Orthodox relatives that I might want to go and study at my uncle's yeshiva. I did not and do not want to immerse myself in that world. I cherish my freedoms and I fear its certainties.

My grandfather died nine years before I was born. Since I never knew him, I cannot know what he would have made of me and of my Judaism—my confused attachment to the faith that sustained my people over thousands of years, my reluctance to honor all its rituals, my fear of its extremes and indignation at those I see as seeking to coerce Israel into more Orthodox practices, my fear that my own children might become attracted to an ultra-Orthodox lifestyle that would see them renounce their parents' upbringing. His late wife, my grandmother, whom I was fortunate enough to know for many years, was completely certain in her faith and serene in her certainty. She, I am sure, felt sorrow that I was missing out on the lifestyle she found so valid, but I think she loved me just the same.

My Aunt Gustel assures me that my grandfather was tolerant in his Orthodoxy and that he favored a melding of observant Judaism with Westernization. If so, I think he would have been dismayed to see that the intolerance he noticed here in the 1930s has, if anything, deepened. If the fiercely secular state-builders were ill disposed to Orthodox Judaism, then many of their descendants remain equally ill disposed and now find themselves matched by the bitter descendants of those who were mocked fifty and more years ago—the leaders of the increasingly numerous and powerful ultra-Orthodox community. If the energetic pioneers were adamant in their rejection of all things traditionally Jewish, then we are paying a heavy price all these decades later, because the closed-mindedness is mutual: Secular Israelis, in great part, aren't interested in hearing the ultra-Orthodox argue about why their young men should be exempted from army service; ultra-Orthodox Israelis, on the whole, are indifferent to the affront they cause by ignoring the solemn soldiers' Remembrance Day siren.

The dialogue of the deaf was never manifested so clearly as in the 1999 elections, when ultra-Orthodox politicians urged their voters to come out and support them so that they could muster enough influence to prevent the country's being overrun by "non-Jewish, Russian immigrant crooks, prostitutes and pork-butchers." Countering them was a journalist and Holocaust survivor named Tommy Lapid who campaigned on the delegitimizing platform of demanding ultra-Orthodox exclusion from government, and whose Shinui party won six seats in the Knesset. In one especially telling and depressing televised exchange, after Lapid had leveled a string of allegations of ultra-Orthodox greed at the then interior minister, the ultra-Orthodox politician Eli Suissa, Suissa retorted by remarking that Lapid evidently hadn't "learned his lesson" in the Nazi death camps. In no "democratic" country save our riven Jewish state would someone like Lapid be allowed to campaign on his exclusivist platform; in no other country would a leading politician dare make a comment like Suissa's to a Jew.

There is not an absolute desert between the two poles. In the last few years at the *Jerusalem Report* we have carried a series of articles highlighting two new trends: the emergence of Orthodox-secular movements that try to bridge the decades of mutual antipathy and develop what has been termed a "common Jewish language"; and the coalescing of non-Orthodox study groups seeking to "retrieve" Jewish sources from the Orthodox—to study the Bible and other religious literature and create "new variations of a Jewishly rooted secular identity." First tens, then hundreds, and now thousands of non-Orthodox Israelis have joined educational groups that study the holy texts, reversing the pioneers' rejection of our literary heritage. Five years ago here, you would not have found many such students insisting on their right, their obligation, to involve themselves in Judaism, rather than entrusting it solely to the Orthodox. Five years ago, too, I would not have heard, as I did recently at a panel discussion in which I was participating, the left-wing secular Knesset member Anat Ma'Or talking of the need for religious tolerance, for non-Orthodox and Orthodox freedoms, for debate and open-mindedness among the various streams of Judaism. Rabin, it must be noted, never bothered to reach out to the ultra-Orthodox community in the way that Barak did immediately as prime minister—by formally allying himself with a moderate Orthodox political movement, Meimad; by making the symbolic effort of praying at the Western Wall the day after his election success; and by invoking Talmudic sources in his victory speeches.

Among many on the left, immediately after the Rabin assassination, anyone wearing a skullcap was almost automatically regarded as some kind of coconspirator, and there were several cases of Orthodox Jews being attacked on that basis. Part of the change may be a belated political correction: an attempt to woo traditional Jews, who were scared away by the virulently anti-Orthodox rhetoric of some left-wing politicians. But part of it, too, may reflect a gradually dawning awareness among non-Orthodox Israelis that blame doesn't all flow one way; that maybe non-Orthodox Israel, which rightfully demanded soul-searching and reform among Orthodox educators and leaders after the Rabin assassination, had cause for introspection of its own.

Early in 1998, I visited the site on the Tel Aviv University campus where a new synagogue was being completed. At its donor's insistence, it was to be made available for use by all streams of the faith. Resembling nothing so much as a pair of oversized grain silos, it is actually a prayer house of two halves—a unified structure in theory and in potential, with its Orthodox section, in practice, at Orthodox insistence, kept severed from the Reform and Conservative heretics next door by a partition. You could look at the "Cymbalista Synagogue and Jewish Heritage Center," with its central partition, as evidence that the Jews of Israel are never going to make peace with themselves. Or you can argue that at least the Orthodox and the others are sharing. And perhaps, in our polarized Jewish state, that is the best we can hope for.

On a recent Friday night, Sabbath eve, Lisa and I took a glimpse from both sides of the religious divide in our holy home city. As the light began to fade, we put a white summer dress on Kayla. We persuaded Josh to put away his basketball. We scraped most of the chocolate ice cream off Adam's hands, cheeks, and eyebrows. And we set off, first, for our synagogue.

By Israeli standards, Kol HaNeshamah (the name comes from the final verse of Psalm 120: "Let everything that breathes praise the Lord") is an extremely unusual Jewish prayer house. For one thing, a few of the congregants, ourselves included, drive to the Sabbath services. For another, men and women sit side by side. Sometimes, women lead the service. Some of the men do not have their heads covered with the traditional Jewish skullcap. Some of the women do. All of this violates the halachic code.

In North America, indeed in much of the Jewish Diaspora, none of this would be remotely out of the ordinary. The overwhelming majority of practicing Jews there follow the Reform and Conservative approaches to the faith—more lenient than the Orthodox, less zealous, more pluralistic, less chauvinistic. In Israel, Jews are either ultra-Orthodox (perhaps 10 percent of the population, living according to Jewish law, and seeking to separate themselves from the modern world), modern-Orthodox (another 20 percent or so, living according to Jewish law, but as part of the modern world), on the road to Orthodoxy, still clinging to faint strains of Orthodoxy, or lapsed and possibly virulently anti-Orthodoxy. Reform and Conservative Judaism have made next-to-no impact on the general Israel psyche. I think that plenty of secular Israelis, disaffected by establishment Orthodox Judaism, might well be attracted to these two options—if those Israelis could shed their ingrained assessment of Orthodoxy as the only "real" Judaism, and if they knew these options were out there. But the Orthodox establishment is doing its best to keep Reform and Conservative Judaism firmly marginalized.

For much of the Orthodox establishment, the Reform or Conservative Jew has rebelled against the "true faith" and is thus reviled. To some in the Orthodox world, hard though this may be to believe, Reform rabbis are actually despised even more than the spiritual leaders of radical Islamic movements such as Hamas, who encourage their supporters to murder Israelis. Rabbi Eliahu Bakshi-Doron, one of Israel's chief rabbis, for instance, has been known to send emissaries to talk conciliation with Hamas's founder, Sheikh Yassin, advocate of violent resistance to the presence of the Jewish state on the land of Palestine, patron of the suicide bombers. The same Rabbi Bakshi-Doron has been adamantly opposed, however, to opening a dialogue with Reform rabbinical leaders—they are farther beyond the pale than the bombers, for they seek to murder the Orthodox Jewish spirit. They constitute "a bridge to assimilation," to the "loss of millions of our people."

That my synagogue even exists is a triumph over extreme adversity. While the location of the Orthodox synagogue tends to get penciled in early on new neighborhood blueprints, and government funding swiftly allocated, it took years of lobbying (with the support of then mayor Teddy Kollek) to pry a small plot of land for Kol HaNeshamah from the clutches of Jerusalem City Hall, and many more years to separate wealthy North American philanthropists from enough of their cash to finance its construction. So accustomed did its congregants become to praying in its spartan, cash-starved concrete shell, that when a belated injection of funds facilitated the installation of mildly ornate marbled flooring, a minor rebellion ensued, with some aggrieved members passionately arguing that the synagogue was losing its basic, rootsy feel and becoming just another ostentatious American-style temple. Such internal objections, though, were as nothing by comparison to the fevered opposition to our presence exemplified by local residents who, while many of them were not particularly Orthodox themselves, professed themselves deeply offended by our Sabbath parking, regarded the Reform practice of letting women handle the Torah scrolls as veritable blasphemy, and occasionally felt the need to demonstrate their commitment to "authentic" Judaism by punching congregants outside the synagogue gates.

When I moved to Israel at the age of twenty, I was wearing a skullcap, but I had laid aside almost all the trappings of my Orthodox upbringing. Pretty soon, I took off the skullcap and inserted an earring. Certainly, I trusted and trust that there must be higher powers than those known to mankind, and I am happy to think of those powers as godly. The basic tenets of Judaism are beautifully formulated, and I would almost certainly be a finer human being were I to follow more of the rules. But while ready to try and love my neighbor, and happy to commit myself to neither killing him nor coveting his wife, I was not prepared to conform to the regimented lifestyle of observance prescribed by Orthodox Judaism.

Indifference to Orthodoxy gave way, in my early years here at least, to outright antipathy, largely in response to the rabbinical involvement in politics here—a corrupting involvement that stains Orthodoxy. Eschewing the option of remaining separate from the democratic institutions of the state, and thus retaining a pure, nonpartisan voice on key religious issues, Israel's Orthodox rabbis have plunged their noses as deeply into the murky political trough as any other minority interest group—extracting, as their price for propping up various coalition governments through the decades, laws on everything from banning the import of nonkosher meat to halting archaeological digs at the first hint that ancient Jewish graves may be disturbed. The rabbi-legislators have become political manipulators par excellence—which may be all well and good for the growing community they represent, but it doesn't do a whole lot for their image among the rest of us. This is especially true when, inevitably, some of these purportedly holier-than-we leaders of the faith are found to be salting away their tendentiously won government allocations to finance the additions of new stories to their luxury villas or, in one particularly extravagant case of misuse of funds, the survival of a bankrupt national carpet monopoly.

The ultra-Orthodox Shas party, in particular, has made an art of both acquiring political influence and returning "traditional" Jews of Middle Eastern and North African origin, the Sephardim, to their faith, Sephardim who feel they were patronized and discriminated against by the 1950s Labor Zionist establishment. Shas is giving them back their pride, burgeoning into a huge political force, with its own rabbinical hierarchy and a large education network that offers cash-strapped parents genuinely free schooling lasting late into the afternoon for their kids—as opposed to the costly, short-day state system—and subtly throws in ultra-Orthodoxy along with the reading, writing, and arithmetic. It is a simple cycle: More recruits means more votes, more political influence, more government money, more recruits.

Shas is a thoroughly modern ultra-Orthodox party—the weekly sermons delivered by its spiritual leader Rabbi Ovadia Yosef are broadcast via satellite to synagogue halls nationwide. Its embrace of technology also has a dark-age twist: Come elections, not only does it woo voters with "holy" amulets, purportedly blessed by its spiritual leaders, which are supposed to bring their bearers good fortune, but it offers "telephone blessings," personalized recorded messages by Rabbi Yosef and his colleagues, to reward its loyalists. More troubling, Shas (in common with its more internalized Ashkenazi ultra-Orthodox equivalents) appears to have little commitment to democracy and pluralism. Its fealty is to its rabbis' rulings, not to the laws of the state. Its sages and spokespeople deride women's equality, condemn homosexuals, furiously resist religious pluralism. It is incessantly seeking to use its political power to pass ultra-Orthodox legislation to legitimize practices the Supreme Court would otherwise invalidate. Its spiritual leaders regularly scorn the Supreme Court's legitimacy and urge their adherents to look elsewhere—that is, to the rabbinical courts—for justice.

In the spring of 1997, it even sent its supporters to march on the Supreme Court building, to protest what it claimed was the discriminatory targeting by the courts of its leader, Aryeh Deri, over corruption allegations. Deri, a former minister of the interior, had whipped up a crowd of thousands, gathered in the Hebrew University soccer stadium, by telling them that Zionism was "a movement of heresy . . . determined to annihilate the Torah, our religion, and the culture of the Sephardi Jews." To what should be their abiding shame, in recent years, both our main political parties, Labor and Likud, preoccupied with their rivalry with each other, have kowtowed to Shas and backed some of its legislation, in order to bolster their respective governing coalitions. Only after Deri was convicted of bribe-taking and ordered jailed for four years, and after he had used the claim of false conviction at the center of a 1999 election campaign that saw Shas become the largest rising political force in Israel, did some mainstream politicians finally recognize the danger and make Deri's removal from the party helm a condition for further contacts.

I also became aware, as I took in my surroundings here in the 1980s, of a nauseating arrogance in the pronouncements of too many Orthodox leaders when disasters befell us. When a school bus stuck at a railway crossing is hit by a train and children die, a rabbi will pop up to tell us that the mezuzot—the small cases of holy texts affixed to doors—at the school must have been faulty. When military helicopters collide and soldiers die, another sage will emerge to blame the deaths on the recent proliferation of pork butchers in the country or our national failure to observe the Orthodox Sabbath.

It was the sense that I was rooted to this place and this people, through my religion, that had brought me here in the first place. But in my early years in Israel I came to behave as though living in the Jewish nation-state was all that was required. My Jewishness consisted in being an Israeli. And then the kids came. And a horrifying thought dawned. Were I to shelter my children from all exposure to the intricacies of Orthodox Judaism, might they not, one day, walk into an Orthodox synagogue, or Talmud class, or my uncle's yeshiva, and feel that this was their authentic home? Might they not fall prey to the Orthodox "pickup artists," those smooth-talking hucksters who peddle their faith like contraband jewelry to the hapless secular Jewish innocents they chance upon at the Western Wall, gazing at the foundation stones of their forgotten religion? I had seen the pickup artists in action myself trawling the cobbled streets of the Old City in search of the day's catch: a rootless youth they could invite to a warm Orthodox home or to their yeshiva for a wholesome Shabbat meal and a gentle introduction into the centuries-old traditions their parents had kept hidden from them. Friends had even succumbed. The rugby-playing hulk I used to know as Sam, the guy who hit on every female student at Mount Scopus in our university days and is immortalized in my photo album with a maniacal grin and a tampon hanging out of either nostril, wears black now, studies in yeshiva, and prefers that you call him Shmuel. It's more biblical.

God forbid, if you'll pardon the expression, that such a fate should befall one of my offspring, that they should know so little of their faith as to be seduced down one of its narrower alleys by an Orthodox dogmatist. In too many families that I saw in my first years here, a return to the faith, the observance of new commandments by one family member, had been accompanied by an abandonment of at least one of the top ten: Out the window went respect for the parents; the newly Orthodox son wouldn't eat with Mum and Dad anymore, for the food wasn't kosher enough, which meant that family Shabbat and Passover get-togethers were no longer feasible. The best way to avoid this eventuality was clearly to ensure familiarity with observant Judaism but prevent total submission.

That was the rationale that led me to Kol HaNeshamah, the belief that I would be exposing my children to a mild strain of the faith and thus guaranteeing their avoidance of the full, terrifying outbreak. And, of course, that rationale—the rationale of a lapsed Orthodox Jew who had always assumed that Orthodox Judaism was the only real Judaism and had chosen to eschew it—was false. For at Kol HaNeshamah, I found a rabbi, Levi Weiman-Kelman, like the long-retired Orthodox rabbi in the local London synagogue I had loved as a boy, who managed to communicate gravitas and warmth simultaneously; I found a community spirit in tune with my own sensibilities, a place to mourn in quiet unity the assassination of the prime minister (unique in increasingly right-wing Jerusalem, where few stores downtown even bothered to post death notices mourning Rabin); and I found an atmosphere relaxed enough to accommodate mine and everyone else's kids dashing in and out at the start and end of services, yet sufficiently fervent at the height of the prayers to create a genuine sense of *Kavanah*, of heartfelt, communal devotion finding a distant echo. I have found myself eagerly anticipating Friday-night services, even though the touchy-feely, deep, cleansing breaths and eyes-closed communal singing are entirely alien to my usually repressed nature. And I also quite like sitting next to my wife, rather than having to peer at her around a separating curtain or crane my neck to some distant upstairs balcony—the synagogue purgatory to which women are sentenced in Orthodox establishments.

Now, my daughter is about to join the kindergarten at Kol HaNeshamah. Adam is at preschool at Beit Shmuel, and Josh is in first grade at Tali Bayit V'Gan, the next steps up the Reform-educational ladder. They pray briefly in the mornings. They bake challah, the ceremonial Shabbat bread. They make improvised menorahs for Chanukah, the festival of lights. They build and decorate little *sukkot*, flimsy huts, to mark the festival of Tabernacles. They are learning Jewish history, about the Temples built and destroyed three and two millennia ago in the Old City down the road from them, about the heroes and villains of our ancient past whose stamping grounds and some of whose purported tombs they can visit on the weekends. They are learning, slowly, to read Hebrew. Where many of the secular state schools teach Judaism by rote, a reviled curricular necessity, and ultra-Orthodox schools overload the curriculum with classes exclusively devoted to religion, Tali seems to offer a middle ground. My children are being exposed to a Judaism that values women as highly as men and is open to every individual's relationship with God and the faith. Josh has taken to wondering aloud about God—whether He exists, whether He's a he, who made Him, how He made us. So somebody at Tali must be opening his mind, but nobody is forcing a specific interpretation into it.

I'm not sure if the Kol HaNeshamah–Tali approach to Judaism would have worked for me in England or North America, where much of the Reform service may be conducted in English and the sense of distance from the Hebrew roots of the faith would have been unbridgeable; but here in Jerusalem, it is Hebrew that we employ inside the synagogue as well as outside it, and using the language of daily life as the language of prayer heightens the sense of authenticity.

My numerous Orthodox and ultra-Orthodox cousins would doubtless argue that this is not authentic Judaism, that it is watered-down Judaism tailored to the demands of the cosseted modern citizen too lazy and lacking in self-discipline to accept the entire code.

And my Reform friends would cite statistics "proving" that Judaism would have all but disappeared in the nineteenth and twentieth centuries had it been left in the hands of the inflexible Orthodox, that only Reform and Conservative adaptation—evolution—gave it the relevance to maintain its appeal.

Better a core of the genuinely devout, imbibing the true, immortal brew, the Orthodox might reply, than millions drinking a diluted version with none of the essential nutrients.

Yes, but it is doubtful the Orthodox practitioners would have brought us independent statehood. Judging by my grandfather's survey, not many rabbis were draining the swamps in the pre-state pioneering years.

Anyway, until the lightning strikes, I am sticking with Kol HaNeshamah, where, on that recent Friday, the service was invigorating even in our rabbi's absence (he was temporarily ministering to the Jews of Hong Kong). For once, only one of the kids insisted on staying outside for most of the service (Josh, playing on the climbing frames with some friends and their determinedly nondevout dads). And for once, there was no visiting busload of American Reform tourists, come to lend temporary moral support to our close-knit band of local worshippers, so we could actually find seats on the comfortable chairs, rather than the plastic ones. Reenergized, imbued with spiritual fervor, we drove home in cozy near-silence, unloaded the children into the baby-sitter's safekeeping, and set off for the other side.

It is a twenty-minute drive from our house to Bar-Ilan Street across town; ten minutes on Friday nights, when a great many Jerusalemites won't use their cars. As we approached, I slowed down. I had not driven here during the hours of Shabbat before, and I didn't know exactly how close I dared come before I'd be risking a stone through my windshield. If the graffiti-laced streets of Hebron and Ramallah are the front lines of the Israeli-Palestinian conflict, innocuous-looking Bar-Ilan Street is the battlefield on which one of the landmark skirmishes of the intra-Jewish war has been fought—using much of the same ammunition: hatred, intolerance, and rocks.

In the early 1980s, when I arrived in Israel, Bar-Ilan was just another unremarkable section of the main road that took you from the central bus station at the entrance to Jerusalem to the university campus on Mount Scopus in the north of the city. I remember seeing placards on some of the balconies, as I wheezed past on my asthmatic motorbike, urging me to REMEMBER THE SABBATH DAY, TO KEEP IT HOLY. But that was about as persuasive as attempts at religious coercion got, back then. The following decade and a half, though, evidently radicalized the locals. While ultra-Orthodox Jews were long a majority in this area, nowadays there are no non-ultra-Orthodox Jews here at all. Every apartment—on either side of the main road, and deep into the neighborhoods that wind off it—is occupied by families whose menfolk dress in the garb of the Poland of four hundred years ago, whose bookshelves sag under the weight of well-thumbed Jewish texts. These are people who have seen the would-be First World, the secularly governed, hedonistic, materialistic Israel we have built for ourselves these past fifty years, and averted their gaze in horror. These people cling to a purer lifestyle, a lifestyle dedicated to walking in the shadow of the Lord, amassing good deeds in His honor, dedicating themselves to His service. Well, that's the theory. In practice, sadly, there seems to be no shortage of ultra-Orthodox swindlers, wife-beaters, sex offenders, gamblers, and smokers too—which has always struck me as particularly reprehensible, given the lovely Jewish concept of the human body as a temple to the Lord, and thus worthy of better upkeep than the nicotine wallpapering of the smoker's lungs. But it's easy to mock, and the truth, of course, is that there are many fine, honest souls in the ultra-Orthodox community, as anywhere else. It is just that, when it came to Bar-Ilan, those good souls seemed to be in short supply.

Having established a universal presence on both sides of Bar-Ilan, the ultra-Orthodox locals began demanding, not unreasonably from their point of view, that the road be fenced off during the Sabbath, closed to traffic to prevent the desecration of the Seventh Day calm in their pocket of Jerusalem. Non-Orthodox Jews, equally reasonably from their point of view, expressed horror at the notion. This was no minor side-street, no ultrasuburban dead end, but one of Jerusalem's main highways, a vital link between the entrance to the city and the north. All deference to deeply Orthodox locals notwithstanding, the road had to stay open. How else could a non-Orthodox resident of Mount Scopus, or adjacent French Hill, get out of the city on a Saturday for an afternoon's sunbathing break on Herzliyya beach?

And so the battle lines were drawn. When ultra-Orthodox spokesfolk highlighted the two not particularly inconvenient alternate routes connecting northern Jerusalem to the rest of the country, secular advocates retorted with talk of principles and precedents: If it was Bar-Ilan that got closed in 1997, it would be other major roadways in '98 and '99. And when would-be mediators suggested an apparently divine compromise—a subtle, soundproofed, subterranean tunnel under the junction for Sabbath drivers, affording crosstown access with no cost to neighborhood tranquillity—ultra-Orthodox leaders paled at the prospect of long-buried Jewish bones being desecrated by the mechanical diggers, and the city council blanched at the cost.

An impasse had been reached. And while the politicians agonized, the rival camps, with their conflicting concepts of Sabbath-day rest, went to war. Jerusalem's dwindling ranks of secular activists organized themselves into convoys and set off on provocative Sabbath-day vehicular parades, driving through Bar-Ilan each weekend to emphasize that the road had to stay open, that it symbolized a Jerusalem open to all. The local residents hit back by shouting "*Shabbes, Shabbes*" at the unholy drivers, turning the Yiddish word for the day of rest into a term of abuse. And when words failed to break the drivers' bones, some ultra-Orthodox extremists upgraded their weaponry to sticks and stones, and feces. "Loaded diapers" were thrown at the Sabbath-day motorists, and then at the unfortunate policemen called out on what should have been their day off to keep the warring sides apart. Saturday after Saturday, for years, tranquillity was the last thing you would find on Bar-Ilan Street. While the confrontations raged, the protagonists petitioned the courts, the Knesset weighed legislation, and learned committees wrestled with the parameters of possible compromise. And finally, in the spring of 1997, a solution was imposed.

By ministerial decree, Bar-Ilan Street is now officially open on the Sabbath . . . except around prayer times on Friday night, Saturday morning, and Saturday afternoon. The idea was that Orthodox worshippers walking to and from their synagogues would be spared the carbon-monoxide-belching secular intruders, but that, in between prayer times, the traffic could flow as normal. In practice, this means that the street is closed about as much as it is open—a situation that pleases neither side particularly, and that therefore can't be too awful.

It reminds me of my own particular battle with creeping ultra-Orthodoxy in Jerusalem. And like that battle, I think it ultimately signifies an ultra-Orthodox victory, and another defeat for Jerusalem as the city of all Israelis. Before we moved to our present home, we lived in a neighborhood known as Old Katamon, a happily mixed district of ultra-Orthodox, more traditional, and thoroughly secular Jews. One bright summer's morning, a yeshiva moved into the building next door—a study center filled with boisterous acned youth from the United States, here for yearlong all-day courses in religious study and, by the sound of it, all-night same-sex partying, beer-drinking, and arm-wrestling contests. The then Labor-run city council took the yeshiva to court, arguing that its presence was a breach of zoning regulations, that the building was intended for ordinary residential use.

The judge was elderly, irritable, hard of hearing, and Orthodox. Deeming the case too insignificant to necessitate the slow shuffle to the adjacent courtroom, he elected to contemplate it, briefly, in his chambers. It need hardly be said that he did not smile on the fresh-faced young attorney representing the city, and that he had no desire whatsoever, thank you very much, to hear testimony from nearby residents who wished to stress that they had no ax to grind against the yeshiva per se, but whose quiet evenings in the tree-lined neighborhood were now so regularly disrupted by whooping, vomiting noises, screams of pain, and scraping furniture. Instead, our learned judge glanced briefly at the city's zoning map, snorted, and waved his hand to indicate that the room should be cleared while he prepared his verdict.

All of ten minutes later, the parties were summoned back in, and our beloved judge delivered a masterpiece of balanced legal wisdom. There was, he concluded reluctantly, no getting around the black block letters on the city map. The building was indeed designated solely for residential purposes. And, therefore, he announced triumphantly, he was instructing the proprietors of the insurgent yeshiva that its students could—here he paused for additional dramatic effect—sleep there, but woe betide them were they to study there! Any studying would be a clear breach of the law. And with a broad satisfied smile, the judge raised his arm again, dismissed us all, and shuffled the files on his desk in search of the next case so fortunate as to merit his Solomonic attentions.

Obviously, the yeshiva made no effort to abide by his ruling; the judge knew full well that no such effort would be made. The city's lawyers briefly considered an appeal, realized they would be wasting their time, and threw up their hands. Within the year, the Labor-led city council had been voted out of office; the current right-wing/religious council now champions the pro-Orthodox zoning changes its predecessor tried to halt. And so, with our yeshiva as with Bar-Ilan Street, an apparent compromise would appear to presage ultimate ultra-Orthodox control. For now, Bar-Ilan is only closed for part of the Sabbath, and Sabbath drivers on the Friday night that we were there waited in a patient line for prayer-time to end and for the police to back up the van they had parked across the disputed carriageway and give them the okay to drive through. But pretty soon, the Sabbath drivers won't bother; they will use the alternative routes. Then the locals will argue reasonably that, since no one is using it, there is no longer a real need to keep Bar-Ilan open at all on the Sabbath. The road will close altogether. And a few more, or a few thousand more, non-Orthodox Jews will get the message that they are not really wanted in Jerusalem anymore.

Not overnight, but over a decade or two, the capital city of Israel is becoming a no-go area for Jews who do not take literally the biblical injunction to rest on the Sabbath day. From some points of view, non-Orthodox life is flourishing more widely than it was twenty years ago, when Jerusalemites fled for Tel Aviv on a Friday night to catch a movie and there was next to nowhere to eat out on a Saturday. Now, most of the movie houses are open on the Sabbath, as are a whole lot of restaurants. We may have to buy the entrance tickets, bizarrely, almost secretively, from a van rather than the main box offices, which are shut by Orthodox order, but we can take the kids to the Israel Museum, the Science Museum, and the zoo on the Sabbath. And if, on a Friday night, you walk around the bars in the Russian Compound downtown, or in the Cinemathèque area, or in the Talpiot disco district, there is no room on the sidewalk for all the teens being squeezed out of the clubs. When we come home, around midnight, from a Friday movie, our baby-sitter checks her lipstick and heads out to the clubs.

But the longer-term picture is less rosy. Entire neighborhoods that, when I came here, were non-Orthodox or mixed secular-Orthodox, are now Orthodox or ultra-Orthodox, areas where you dare not play music or drive on Shabbat. Only in my current neighborhood, Talpiot-Arnona, and a handful of others, can you still spend your Saturdays as loudly as you wish without provoking the wrath of the ultra-Orthodox. We are not being stoned to death for gathering firewood on the Sabbath. But a few of the less fortunate among us have been stoned for driving in the wrong areas on the holy day by the extremists who stain ultra-Orthodox Judaism.

Women can get paint, ink, and eggs thrown at them by self-styled ultra-Orthodox "modesty squads"—thugs in anyone else's language—if they are spotted walking in a shortish skirt or a short-sleeved blouse anywhere near an ultra-Orthodox area. In the winter of 1998, a trio of Swiss women, tourists suspected of engaging in the heinous crime of missionizing, had their apartment in an ultra-Orthodox neighborhood of Jerusalem trashed by a mob of ultra-Orthodox men. (I saw an

American tourist in Jerusalem not long afterward wearing a T-shirt blaring ASK ME ABOUT JESUS. I wanted to warn her that she was displaying inflammatory propaganda and might get beaten up for it.) Just a few days later, Benzion Karni, a seventeen-year-old Jerusalemite who had committed the yet more heinous crime of renouncing his ultra-Orthodox up-bringing and opting for a secular lifestyle, had his home trashed and set on fire, its outside walls daubed with graffiti, again by an ultra-Orthodox terror squad. And soon after that, a seventy-nine-year-old man was beaten up in his neigh-borhood by four ultra-Orthodox men for the crime of pos-sessing a TV set, a set he insisted he never turned on during the Sabbath.

As with the Bar-Ilan rioters, or the rabbis discussing a halachic death sentence for Rabin, the police seem uncon-scionably complacent about all of this, unconscionably re-luctant to prosecute the offenders, to take action. Maybe, somewhere deep in the secular Israeli psyche lurks a sense of shame, a feeling that we are the sinners, and that we do not have the authority to impose our democratic laws on the authentic, ultra-Orthodox Jews. Or maybe the police are cowed by ultra-Orthodox political influence at the local and national levels.

Anyway, the result of the growing ultra-Orthodox domina-tion is that thousands of disenchanted Jerusalemites are head-ing off to more liberal climes, and especially to Tel Aviv, where the city that likes to claim it never sleeps is prepared to con-ceive that the God of fifty-year-old modern Israel might find seventh-day rest and relaxation watching television, playing computer games with the kids, or going go-cart riding—pur-suits that just were not available in those far-off days when the Bible got written.

Noting that opinion polls show that most Israelis fear and dislike ultra-Orthodox Jews more than they do the Arabs,

Ze'ev Chafets, a colleague at the *Jerusalem Report*, wrote a series of columns late in 1996 proposing that this country be divided into two: the state of Judea, its capital in Jerusalem, ruled by the laws of the Torah as interpreted by a body of "great Orthodox rabbis"; and a state of Israel, its capital Tel Aviv, "ruled by the principles of Western democracy." Mixed together, he argued, our two Jewish worlds in our one Israel "are incompatible and dangerously combustible," bound to bring us civil war and eventual self-destruction. "Side-by-side, though, they are complementary." Most of us at work, initially assuming that he was kidding, were horrified to realize that he was not. Obviously, the notion of formally cutting up our tiny Jewish state is unrealistic, crazy, we said. What a terrible failure it would reflect. Almost everyone I work with or am friendly with here would belong in neither of Ze'ev's polarized states. I am not the only Jerusalemite, and Kol HaNeshamah is not the only communal hub, for Israelis making a Jewish life somewhere between Orthodoxy and secularism. Where would someone like me fit within his two-state solution? You would vote with your feet, responded Ze'ev: Judea, Israel, or the Diaspora.

Two trends are now gathering force in Israel, and there is no telling yet which will prevail. On the one hand, you have the non-Orthodox effort to resist ultra-Orthodox coercion and stake a claim in Judaism—to study it, to achieve rights for the Reform and Conservative movements, to get non-Orthodox representatives onto local area religious councils, to defend personal freedoms from ultra-Orthodox straitjacketing—in Jerusalem and nationwide. At the same time, you have Ze'ev's vision—geographical separation—slowly coming to pass, albeit informally. The Tel Aviv area *is* a world away from Jerusalem. In the capital, in the early summer of 1999, we considered it a great victory that a new grocery store had opened up on Shabbat downtown, a beacon of secular commercial life on the otherwise silent Ben-Yehuda Street, flourishing despite ultra-Orthodox efforts to close it down. North of Tel Aviv, one Shabbat that summer, meanwhile, we bought plates and cups for Josh's birthday party at a jam-packed Toys "R" Us and dropped in for lunch at a restaurant on a nearby farming village that happened to be hosting an annual show-jumping contest, with jockeys immaculate in their black uniforms, a large crowd of onlookers, and a blaring loudspeaker rendition of the "Hatikvah" national anthem to round off proceedings that would have been unthinkable in Sabbath-observant Jerusalem. Driving out of the holy city that day, and every Shabbat for months, we passed an elderly, bearded Hasid, fur-hatted and gold-robed, who sat from late morning to mid-afternoon under the last traffic light on the city's edge, wagging an admonishing finger at every godless vehicle that flashed past him. During the week, his metal chair remained in place, chained to the traffic light, awaiting Shabbat duty.

As non-Orthodox Israelis leave Jerusalem, and neighborhood after neighborhood turns black-hatted, the shops they used to patronize are closing down; Intel recently abandoned plans to build a vast factory here; the city center looks more slumlike with every passing year. And our mayor, Ehud Olmert—who came to power in 1993 with the support of ultra-Orthodox leaders, to whom he gave control of such key city portfolios as planning—knows it. Seeing the number of his residents who work and pay taxes dwindling, he has been seeking to annex outlying secular cities, like the thriving Mevasseret Tsiyyon, ten minutes away on the road to Tel Aviv, to bring its taxpaying residents into his cash-strapped orbit. Locally, as nationally, the ultra-Orthodox influence would be balanced if Olmert's right-wing secular Likud got together with the moderate-secular Labor party. But no, the historical enmities run too deep, and the two dinosaurs are so busy clawing at each other that they do not notice the ultra-Orthodox politicians quietly rising to render them both extinct.

Many in the ultra-Orthodox community feel that it is the rest of us who are intolerant, who are trying to tell them how to live their lives, in Jerusalem and elsewhere. For every charge we lob at them, they have a counteraccusation. My first cousin Shai, whose father heads the Har Nof yeshiva for "returning" Jews and who works for an ultra-Orthodox "information center," has reams of material detailing incidents of secular violence against the ultra-Orthodox community. When I visited his office, near the Mahaneh Yehuda market, photos of elderly sages on its walls, he whipped out clippings concerning this Jerusalem yeshiva ransacked on a Friday night, that yeshiva student in Bnei Brak, Tel Aviv's ultra-Orthodox suburb, pelted with rocks and then stabbed. He dug out a report on an early 1990s survey among secular schoolkids, who sneered at ultra-Orthodox Jews for being smelly and having dirty beards. He gave me a 157-page booklet highlighting the nasty distortions in the secular media—including the photograph that ran in *Ma'ariv* in February 1995, to take just one example, of an ultra-Orthodox man walking past a billboard of posters inviting the public to a first-anniversary memorial ceremony for the Hebron killer Baruch Goldstein, the false implication being that the ultra-Orthodox world identified with the murderer.

If non-Orthodox Jerusalemites complain that the ultras are grabbing too much of the education budget, the ultra-Orthodox produce figures to show that they get a disproportionately small slice and note that most schoolkids in this city are now ultra-Orthodox, which only annoys their critics even more. We tend to brand the entire ultra-Orthodox community as corrupt because of the illegal, immoral antics of a handful of high-profile leaders—the kind who will hijack a housing project intended for the most needy Jerusalem families. They argue that we would never descend to such generalized castigation of other sectors of the population. We despise them for not serving in the army. They argue that full-time yeshiva study is no picnic, and that it is the best way they know to keep the Jewish nation alive. Our media finds an ultra-Orthodox kid burning the state flag on Independence Day or cooking a barbecue lunch on the stone base of a military memorial, and it's front-page news. But how much space do the same newspapers give to the voluntary ultra-Orthodox-staffed groups that run soup kitchens or offer medical assistance to needy Israelis, observant and secular?

The tide isn't all flowing one way. The Orthodox intransigence on religious pluralism is being challenged by an increasingly vocal coalition that includes some unusually open-minded Orthodox politicians. And while we feel the ultra-Orthodox influence especially keenly in Jerusalem, elsewhere in Israel, the right to non-Orthodoxy is being vigorously, and more successfully, defended. For instance, there are the entrepreneurial spirits of Kibbutz Shfayim, on the coastal road north of Herzliyya, who struck deals with Ace Hardware and Office Depot (in addition to Toys "R" Us), leased them land for warehouse stores, and attract vast crowds of Saturday shoppers from across the country. The former mayor of Tel Aviv, Ronnie Millo, zealously protected his city's nonkosher restaurants and Sabbath entertainment industry, and his successor, Ron Huldai, has done much the same. The entire town of Eilat is so conspicuously godless that tour operators safely advertise it without reference to Israel, confident that American and European package-tour groups can spend ten days there without ever discovering that they have been tanning in the Jewish state.

In a rough-tarred courtyard just off a narrow street in

obscure if picturesque Zichron Ya'acov, there is a small "antique" store that is waging the battle too. Although it is called Antiquon, what it really sells, the small print on the sign tells you, is "original fashions" created by its owner, Alice Meroz. And these original fashions are not exactly to my taste— "antique-style" porcelain dolls reclining in "antique-style" mini–rocking chairs, uninspired still lifes, china tulips. The appeal or otherwise of the merchandise, however, is not the point here. The point is that Meroz formally owns her store only six days a week. On the seventh day, just as the Lord commanded, she rests, so to speak. In practice, on the seventh day, Meroz acts as a "volunteer helper" to Rasmi Kaysee, a Druse friend from the nearby town of Faradis, who becomes the official proprietor of Antiquon as soon as dusk settles on Friday evening, and who relinquishes his responsibilities the moment the third star is sighted on Saturday night. It is a deliciously sneaky scam, one that could only be conceived and necessitated in Israel—a devilish adaptation of the Orthodox Jewish practice of selling forbidden bread to a non-Jew on the eve of Passover.

When the State of Israel was founded, the Orthodox guardians of the faith wrestled with the question of how to relate to the secular intruders who had taken control of soil many of them thought ought to remain bereft of Jewish sovereignty until the arrival of the Messiah, whenever that might be. Those unable to reconcile themselves to the premessianic resurrection of Jewish rule in the holy land pronounced themselves non-Zionists or even anti-Zionists. Some of them, reasonably, simply boycotted the upstart, remaining in their Diaspora communities. Others organized themselves inside the new nation but cut themselves off from its administration—creating Jewish ghettos in the Jewish state. And still others, despicably, happily lived their comfortable ultra-Orthodox lives in Israel, protected by the Jewish soldiers of

the new state, while actively working to undermine its existence. The best known of these anti-Zionists are the members
of the small but vocal Neturei Karta sect, who could always
be relied upon to encourage Yasser Arafat's Palestine liberation struggle—in the years *before* he replaced the pursuit of
the "armed struggle" with the more palatable ideology of coexistence.

Most of Orthodox Jewry, however, fully embraced the secular pioneers of the young state, opting for a partnership to
the benefit of both. Together with David Ben-Gurion, our
first prime minister, and the other early state leaders, who felt,
one suspects, the odd twinge of unease about their lack of Sabbath observance and readily acknowledged that it was the
pious, traditional Jews who had kept the faith alive through
centuries of Diaspora dispersion and persecution, they formulated a recipe for domestic coexistence, a framework within
which Orthodox and non-Orthodox Jewish lifestyles could
flourish. That foggy framework came, with the decades, to be
enshrined as the "status quo," a tissue of national and munici-
pal laws, open to myriad interpretations, that managed to gov-
ern the relationship between Orthodox and secular life with
something approaching relative harmony. The Orthodox
guardians of the law were given their monopoly over such
matters as birth, marriage, divorce, and death. The brightest
ultra-Orthodox talmudic scholars were exempted from army
service provided they studied all day. And regulations were
formulated over Sabbath observance in the state: buses to run
in Haifa, but not in Jerusalem; some cafés open, but no grocery stores; some cinemas open, but not theaters. Don't ask.
Antique stores were definitely a no-no. Jewish antique stores,
that is—hence Mrs. Meroz's Druse ruse. Nowhere in the
multitudinous regulations governing Sabbath observance is
there any suggestion that an Israeli Druse can't open his or
her antique store on Saturdays. The notion would be absurd.

The Labor Ministry itself uses Druse inspectors to carry out checks on the state of Sabbath observance nationwide, issuing warnings and fines to shops and businesses that defy the regulations.

Alice Meroz's ploy has been drawing hundreds of fiercely secular Israelis to her somewhat remote store on even the wettest of weekends, boosting sales of her china tulips by hundreds of percent. It's foolproof. The Druse inspectors can hardly fine the store's temporary Druse "owner." But it's not threat-proof. One weekend, somebody parked a hearse across the courtyard entrance in front of the store. Meroz and her husband, Amos, have received death threats. They have proved reluctant to cave in, but the publicity surrounding the hearse incident means few other Israelis are likely to try and emulate them. Zichron Ya'acov isn't about to spark a Sabbath revolution.

In November 1998, the Orthodox and ultra-Orthodox population of Jerusalem tightened its grip on the city still further. In local elections, while the overall turnout was barely 40 percent, adults among the city's 200,000-strong ultra-Orthodox community (about a third of the overall population) voted en masse and helped elect fifteen ultra-Orthodox and Orthodox members to the thirty-one-seat city council. The vote prefigured the following year's national elections, in which Shas would rise so dramatically from ten Knesset seats to seventeen, and a second ultra-Orthodox party, United Torah Judaism, would also be strengthened. As in the national elections, antireligious snipers in the Hebrew press suggested that the ultra-Orthodox had cheated in Jerusalem, that thousands of ultra-Orthodox voters miraculously rose from the dead, dusted off their identity cards, and showed up at the polling stations to cast their ballots before disappearing underground again. As in the national elections, the allegations proved impossible to substantiate and were likely exaggerated or unfounded.

The fact is that, in Jerusalem's ultra-Orthodox community, leading rabbis issued an order to vote, and more than 80 percent of their loyal followers did as they were told. Many in the rest of Jerusalem, apparently resigned to the growing ultra-Orthodoxification of their city, did not bother. And unlike in previous years, when part of the Palestinian population of the city had turned out to vote for secular parties, this time Arafat's increasingly powerful Palestinian Authority ordered an election boycott, to avoid conferring legitimacy on the Israeli claim to sovereignty throughout the city. The Arabs stayed home.

Coincidentally, on Jerusalem's local election day, I had arranged to meet with my cousin Shai, who, though ultra-Orthodox, has a less-than-orthodox past. He and his eight brothers and sisters grew up in an ultra-Orthodox Jerusalem neighborhood, with the boys expected to spend much of their time studying, and to keep that emphasis on holy study at the center of their adult life too. But in his midteens, Shai re-belled. He left his yeshiva, left his home, changed out of the customary dark suit, stopped praying three times a day, and exchanged his lifestyle for a secular one. And he didn't stop there. For a number of years, he was actively doing the reverse of "returning" Jews to their faith—he was helping disillusioned ultra-Orthodox Jews break out of the confines of their society into the secular world. In the secular-dominated mainstream Israeli media, depressed by evidence of the one-way trend toward greater religious observance, Shai, a rare mover in the opposite direction, became a minor celebrity—the subject of television documentaries and newspaper interviews.

After about five years taking university philosophy courses in jeans and a T-shirt, though, Shai went back home. He made his peace with his parents, married, had children, and now combines working for his ultra-Orthodox "information center" with several hours a day of yeshiva study. He says he feels terrible about having eased a passage out of ultra-Orthodoxy for other troubled youths but comforts himself with the knowledge that many of them, like himself, have since returned whence they came. Having been through his personal journey, he has been able, since his return, to advise other parents about how to deal with their troubled kids—to compromise, to give them some space and warmth and love and, above all, "not to push them away." There is a concept in Judaism, he notes, that the left hand, the weaker hand, pushes away, and the right, stronger hand brings people close.

The ultra-Orthodox community is a world apart, a world I admit to mistrusting because of the certainties it appears to offer, because of the speed with which it is growing, because it appears to threaten my own. If anyone could help me understand it, and help me understand what this increasingly numerous and powerful community wants to make of Jerusalem in particular and Israel in general, it would be Shai—someone I have known throughout his life well enough for us to talk openly to each other, someone who has stood on either side of the invisible wall between our two worlds.

Except that Shai outlined an ultra-Orthodox worldview so benign and constructive and warm that I find it hard to accept that he speaks for his whole community. If he does, then I and many other Israelis are indeed guilty of what he calls "ultra-Orthodox-phobia," and have become overly cynical, victims of a distorted perception of ultra-Orthodox life. If he doesn't, it is still impressive to realize that the other community, on the other side of the wall, includes people who think like he does.

When I asked him, my fresh-faced cousin, with his childhood Manchester accent and his shy toothy grin, what his lifestyle gave him that mine lacked, he told me that he lived in a theological world, a complete world, a "Torah-rich" world, and that spending day after day learning holy texts sharpened the mind and made you look at life differently. You grew, he said, absorbing into the essence of your being the Torah's values about dealing morally with your fellow humans, about respecting them and interacting honestly with them. Immersion in those values gave you a better chance to be a better person. It helped him in his marriage, in the way he treated his wife and sought to spare her unhappiness, in the way he treated his children. Plus, of course, he added, it was "the truth."

And what, I asked him, did that mean, "the truth"?

He tried to answer, but it wasn't easy. We went from English to Hebrew and back again, but language wasn't the obstruction. Mindset and environment and experience and context were. We didn't seem to have concepts in common that would enable him to convey to me what he was trying to convey. So he tried to explain by personal example. As you know, he told me, "I was forced out of the framework because of problems at home and at my yeshiva. Several factors combined. I was a fifteen-, sixteen-year-old rebel. And it wasn't that I suddenly developed for myself a whole new humanistic, secular worldview, a new 'truth,' that I'd left a world where everything was bad and entered one where everything was good. No, the pressure forced me out—pressure from home, from the yeshiva. But then, naturally, I sought justifications for my new path. I couldn't lie to myself about the way I was living. I got very involved in humanistic movements . . ."

I interrupted: You tried to find values as powerful and complete and convincing as those you'd grown up with in the ultra-Orthodox world?

More than that, he said. "To find answers to the key questions—about the creation of the world, whether the Torah was genuinely God-given. I met all kinds of people, enrolled in university courses, studied some philosophy, read a lot of books—and built myself a world that had a lot of contradictions with Judaism, that saw the Torah as something manmade, not divine. And that's the worldview I lived with.

"And then, at some stage, I met someone who had become Orthodox, and who said to me, 'Listen, let's check if you're right.' And he and various others really forced me into a corner. They presented me with truths that I had no answer for. That I knew were truths. That the Torah is true. That there is a God. I'll give you an example. They constructed a proof that the Torah was given by God to Moses at Mount Sinai. They used proofs that are inside the Torah itself. And proofs about the chain by which it has been passed along the generations. Let me try to explain like this:

"Today, already, there are people who deny that the Holocaust took place. In a hundred years, there'll be even more of them. So what can you do to ensure that the world will know forever that the Holocaust happened? Let's say, theoretically, that a group of people, at the Yad Vashem Holocaust memorial, at the Wiesenthal Center, wherever, decide that they're going to immortalize the Holocaust. They set up a network of Holocaust survivors. And they decide to meet at some huge place. And to invite all those with Holocaust numbers on their arms. And they gather together and write a huge book describing their experiences. And the leader of the movement tells them that, 'We, here, swear that every word of this is true. And we take on ourselves the responsibility to construct a system to ensure that this truth is passed from generation to generation.' And a copy of the book is given to every survivor. And an excerpt is pinned on every door. And every kid carries an excerpt. And every week, say, a portion of the book is discussed and debated. And once a year, each family gathers, and the grandparents and the parents and the kids discuss what happened. All over the world. And every day, the book gets put to the heart and to the head, to ensure it's not forgotten.

And two hundred years from now, there'll be a court case. And the Holocaust deniers will come and say, 'It never happened.' And then all the descendants of the survivors from all around the world will come forward with all the genuine eyewitness testimony, all the identical accounts passed down through the generations. And that great mass of evidence will be incontrovertible. The courts will know whom to believe. Well, the same goes for the giving of the Torah on Mount Sinai, an identical text passed down through the generations, cherished and discussed and revered. I think the metaphor is clear.

"So all these proofs placed me in a position where I was in internal conflict. And I became convinced that you can't just take part of Judaism. There's a whole lifestyle, a whole way of life here. I learned more. I realized its depth, this entire theological, philosophical system. I came along as someone looking for holes, as someone who didn't want to live an ultra-Orthodox life, a grown man, coming from the outside. And I came back in."

As Shai spoke, I began to feel increasingly admiring of the passion with which he had examined his life and its purpose—the reasons why he had been put on the planet, the responsibilities that the divine provision of his life placed on him. This is someone who changed his entire lifestyle because he was having difficulty in determining the nature of the relationship between man and God; left his comfortable, enclosing background; struck out on his own; sought and evaluated alternative approaches; wrestled with alien ideas and with his own conscience; and returned to a path he had now rediscovered. I, on the other hand, have mused vaguely that there has to be a God, a force more powerful than we are, existing before we did, because, even if you buy the big bang theory, something must have caused the bang. I have concluded that the sum of human knowledge cannot account for the universe, and that since my personality does not appear to be located behind my knee or under my arm, perhaps there really is some kind of "spirit" or "soul" inside me that might conceivably be able to exist separately from my physical being. I have mused vaguely and gotten on with life, without seriously considering whether that force more powerful than I might require me to conduct that life with a certain code, toward a certain purpose.

So what was that purpose? I asked Shai. Why were we put on earth?

To enjoy it, he told me simply, savoring my surprise, before killing it by adding that, "Coming close to God is the greatest joy." When God created man, said Shai, with the utter certainty of one who feels that he has almost witnessed the scene, He made him out of two components—taking the soil and filling it with divine spirit. And man's whole life is the struggle between those two components—the struggle to be a better person, to learn more, to respect one's fellow man; to conquer the base inclinations and glorify the spiritual; to impose the intellect on the urges. Learning Torah and following that whole life-code gives you the tools—and also means you are fulfilling life's covenant with God, following His "operating instructions."

I asked him, though, why his world had to be so closed off from mine, why he didn't read the newspapers, why he had no television in his home. Was his community afraid that it would be unable to resist secular temptations if it was more directly exposed to them?

Television, he answered, was not important and was corrupting. If he had a TV in his home, he acknowledged, he would be tempted to watch it—to the detriment of spending time with his wife and his children. He would be bringing all the corruption of the outside world, television's idealization of negativity, of violence, into his home, into a family he was trying to raise with higher ideals. He said he would not go to extremes to stop his kids watching TV at someone else's house. He had learned from his own experience that coercion didn't work. But, at the same time, you did have to place limits. Kids needed to have bedtimes, to be told how to treat their parents. And he'd probably ask them not to watch TV; he just wouldn't go check up. "Sealing them off hermetically," he said, "I don't think it helps. . . ."

Sealing them off, I offered, meant running the risk that, one day, they might break out and discover this entire new world, my world, and be bowled over by it. The reason I was sending my children to schools and kindergartens where they would learn a little about Judaism, I told him, was partly so that, one day, they wouldn't have their eyes opened to a new and totally unfamiliar world of Orthodoxy and get swept away by it. Maybe the reverse had happened to him, I wondered, maybe he'd been attracted to the secular world because he'd grown up so sheltered from it, and he was now repeating the same mistake with his children?

No, Shai was adamant. He had not been seduced by secular attractions. He had been "pushed out" of his world, not "sucked in" by mine. Ultra-Orthodox Jews didn't need to leave their insular world to see what secular life had to offer. "They know what it has to offer, and that it's not for them. What do secular people do? They go to the beach? So do the ultra-Orthodox. Go to higher education? So do the ultra-Orthodox, albeit through their own, yeshiva, framework. Watch TV? So, here and there, ultra-Orthodox people might see a little TV. They'll read a bit [of non-Orthodox literature]. That's the great big world, for which they'll give up the entire value system they grew up with? An ultra-Orthodox Jew doesn't need to leave his world to know that this is sugar, and this is artificial sweetener."

I told him I thought I was leading the fuller life, the richer life, a life in which I faced up to the challenges he'd spoken about, rather than avoiding them. I watched plenty of television, things that were funny and fascinating, and was still, I hoped, good to my wife and my kids. I was doing my best to bring up my kids to be kind and honest and considerate people, and my wife and I were doing that while also pulling our weight within the state, working and paying our taxes and, in my case, serving in the army—unlike most ultra-Orthodox Jews.

He nodded a trifle wearily. Yes, he said, there were always people claiming that the ultra-Orthodox have it easy: They know what prayers to say in the morning, to wash their hands before eating. . . . But his way of life, he said, was central to his being a more moral person. And the same could be said of his society as a whole, as compared to mine. Without that element of respecting God's will, of a relationship between man and God, he said, people could and did justify anything, even the most horrific behavior. "A society that is based on man-made ethics," he stated flatly, "is corrupt. It has no limits. The red lines are always moving. Take the extreme example of German culture in the Weimar republic, a highly developed culture. Music, art, philosophy. And see where that culture led. To corruption.

"Now, you don't have to be Orthodox to be moral," he stressed. "You don't have to be Orthodox to treat your wife and your children properly." Even when he lived a secular life, he said, he always thought of himself as a moral person—"I didn't steal, I didn't lie. I respected other people. So I thought I didn't have to keep the 613 commandments, the Sabbath, to pray three times a day, to keep all the commandments between man and God, to wash my hands on waking, to put on tefillin in the morning, to keep the laws on family purity, to keep kashrut. I didn't need all that to make me a decent person, because I saw myself as a decent person."

But the fact was, he now acknowledged, that every man has his weaknesses. And Orthodox Judaism gave him the formulas, the golden path, the model for life—to build himself better; to build his personality. "And," Shai added again, "it is the true path. And that's what gives it its strength."

Still, I persisted, it was parasitic, wasn't it? I mean, if everyone in Israel lived an ultra-Orthodox lifestyle, the economy would collapse, there'd be no army, there'd be no money to collect the garbage. . . .

Shai pleaded guilty on the army—he said he had been turned down for medical reasons—but he noted that three of his brothers had, quite unusually for ultra-Orthodox Israelis, served shorter or longer terms in uniform. As for taxes, he earned a reasonable salary, paid his taxes and his mortgage, didn't get a penny from the state.

There were, he said, a lot of misconceptions about the ultra-Orthodox world. In 51 percent of ultra-Orthodox families in Jerusalem, he told me, for example, at least one parent was at work. He showed me a survey in which 81 percent of ultra-Orthodox Jews professed no objection to living alongside non-Orthodox Jews, while only 48 percent of non-Orthodox Jews said they'd be prepared to live next to the ultra-Orthodox. And he tried to put the record straight on the issue of the army. Most ultra-Orthodox men were studying in yeshiva full-time, he insisted, only because the rest of the Jews were not.

Come again?

If all the Jews were ultra-Orthodox, only a small proportion would be studying, only the best and the brightest. The rest would be out there building and housepainting and computing and fighting. That's what is was like at the time of the Second Temple, he noted (albeit without the computing). The entire Jewish people strictly observed the commandments, the descendants of the tribe of Levi got on with the holy studying, and the rest of the Israelites staffed the army and got the hard labor done.

Shai and his community are apparently today's Levites, studying to defend the rest of us. "We think of ourselves as a unit of the army," he said. "We *know* that our studying is what protects the Jews. I have a map up at work showing tiny Israel surrounded by Arab states. Tiny Israel. If they wanted to, I'm sorry to say, they could wipe us out like that. [He snapped his fingers, and we were gone.] So why haven't they? Because the value of the Torah protects and saves us. Artillery and airplanes aren't enough by themselves."

Since we were talking misconceptions, I asked him about coercion. Soon, I wanted to say, given the way Jerusalem was turning ultra-Orthodox-black, Shai's communal leaders would doubtless have all the roads, cafes, and cinemas closed on Saturdays—Shabbat observance by decree. Not long after that, I wanted to ask, could sinners like me expect to be stoned to death, in the best biblical tradition, for such crimes as turning on the lights on the Sabbath? How, I might have inquired, when the Jewish ayatollahs held sway, could our adulterous prime minister Netanyahu expect to be punished for breaking Commandment No. Seven? But this was my cousin I was talking to, my candid, earnest cousin, so I kept clear of my own hysteria and just told him about my sense that the ultra-Orthodox were bent on imposing their lifestyle on the rest of us—banning nonkosher meat, closing roads, shutting down businesses on Shabbat.

He insisted that "there is no religious coercion in Israel," that all the laws now being imposed were enshrined in the original Ben-Gurion–negotiated "status quo." He also said that there was "no such concept" in Orthodox Judaism as coercion. From a "pure" Orthodox perspective, Bar-Ilan Street, he said, should have remained open—since its closure was requiring Shabbat drivers to exacerbate their "sin" by driving still farther, via alternate routes, to reach their destination. It was just, in this case, that the safety of ultra-Orthodox children walking to and from synagogue across the junction, and the need to spare them the sight of people breaching the laws of Sabbath, took precedence.

If these struck me as somewhat unconvincing justifications, I was much more taken with what Shai said was the widespread ultra-Orthodox stance on territorial compromise with the Palestinians. The most respected ultra-Orthodox sages, men like the venerable Rabbi Eliezer Schach, he said, had ruled that "saving life outweighs everything"—"that you give up territory, you give it all up" if that will spare a life. He said he didn't know how some modern-Orthodox rabbis had the nerve to discuss, even theoretically, whether Yitzhak Rabin, Shimon Peres, and, more recently, Benjamin Netanyahu might have merited the death penalty for their alleged crime of abandoning the settlers. "That inflated Yigal Amir," he said bitterly, "who thought himself such a big shot. You think he went to a rabbi and got an okay? Then that rabbi should sit in jail. There's nothing Orthodox about that. These rabbis are putting the Land of Israel ahead of the Torah. Now the Land of Israel is important in the Torah, but it's not a supreme value. The state has value, but it is not something to sanctify, to revere. The sanctity of God is more important. And to see people from the modern-Orthodox community going to live in the West Bank, raising the flag, and simultaneously pressing to draft yeshiva students, cutting them off from the Torah, that's a world with misplaced priorities. Rabbi Schach has said that, if they decide to conscript yeshiva students, we'll raise our right hand, we'll say, 'If we forget thee O Jerusalem, cut off our right hand,' and we'll emigrate."

But then tell me, Shai, why, why, why did the great mass of

ultra-Orthodox Jews vote for Netanyahu over Peres (as they were to do again, for Netanyahu over Barak), the right-wing land-loving ideology over the left?

Here, too, Shai, or rather his rabbis, had a Solomonic explanation: "Well that's because, while Rabbi Schach said you should carry out all the peace agreements in the world to save a single life, Torah is the supreme value. And the left, the secular left, is further from the Torah than the more traditional right."

Where does democracy fit into your world, I asked him, into a world of unquestioned fealty to the rabbis, rabbis answerable only to God?

"Democracy is a critical value," he said. "A halachic state is a democracy. This idea of an Orthodox Khomeinist regime does not exist as a halachic concept."

Excuse me, a halachic state would stone a Jew to death for gathering sticks on the Shabbat?

"No, the Sanhedrin [the political and judicial body of sages that presided in Orthodox Jewish states of the Temple times] can only operate when the entire people keep the commandments. A Sanhedrin that imposed a death penalty more than once in seventy years would be closed down. By definition, it would have proved that it didn't have the authority to exist. There can be no halachic state unless the people want it. The spiritual leadership, the judges, have to be responsive to the people."

But isn't that the goal? To make us all Orthodox and take us back to the days of the Sanhedrin? Isn't that the mission?

"No," Shai protested. "In halacha, there is no suggestion of forcing people to keep the commandments. God placed man here to struggle, and then put a gun to his head to keep the commandments? Where's the free choice in that?"

Shai made it all sound so reasonable that, for a few minutes, I quite forgot about those loaded diapers at Bar-Ilan

Street, about ultra-Orthodox fanatics throwing rocks and excrement, too, at Reform and Conservative groups who try to pray at the Western Wall, about the stones thrown through Reform synagogue windows, the swastikas daubed on their walls, the torching of a Reform-run kindergarten outside Jerusalem the weekend before the school year started. I almost forgot how, when I see the armed security guard outside Adam's kindergarten, I wonder to myself whether he is there to protect my son from Palestinian attackers or from the ultra-Orthodox shock troops. I'm sure Shai would have condemned the fanatics, assured me that they were a minority who were harming the image of the rest of a sensitive, God-fearing community. And I'm sure that is the case. And I'm sure that, although his is a society ruled by rabbinical hierarchy, where every major decision is taken with deference to the rabbinical will, he would have explained that some hotheads are beyond even the rabbis' control, that the rabbis aren't a law-enforcement agency, but that they do condemn violence, through speeches and articles and posters.

My cousin was still talking. "I'll happily help someone who comes to me and wants to know more about Orthodoxy," he was saying. "That's my obligation. We are all responsible for each other. Maybe your kids, one day, will hear a brilliant ultra-Orthodox lecturer, who'll blow them away, and they'll think, 'Wow,' and want to know more. Who knows? Maybe even you yourself . . . !"

He laughed good-naturedly. I tried to smile.

Chapter Ten

A Certain Tension

The fate of Israel depends on two factors: her strength and her rectitude.

—David Ben-Gurion, Israel's first prime minister

In mid-November 1998, for the first time in its sixty-seven-year history, the General Assembly—the annual get-together of the leaders of organized North American Jewry—convened in Jerusalem. This not altogether logical venue—the GA is in the business of determining the future for North American Jews, not Israelis—was chosen, in part, to mark Israel's fiftieth anniversary. But more especially, it was selected in an attempt to tackle the widening rifts between these two centers of the Jewish world—by bringing together three thousand North Americans and more than two thousand Israelis.

Israel and the Diaspora have always had divergent priorities. While Israelis have been preoccupied with their physical survival, Diaspora Jews are preoccupied with their spiritual survival—the battles being fought, respectively, against two very different enemies, Arabs and assimilation. But that is not the reason for a worsening divide. That has been the case for decades. Rather, the worlds are growing apart because, over recent years, Israel has been developing into a country that fewer and fewer Diaspora Jews feel strongly about, feel they wish to identify with.

To some extent, this is a function of the Holocaust receding into history. For the Diaspora, Israel is no longer the critical safe haven, the potential escape route if things go murderously awry for them where they are now, as things did go for their parents' or grandparents' generation in central and eastern Europe sixty years ago. Since American Jews don't seriously anticipate having to pack their suitcases in a hurry and rush off to the Holy Land one step ahead of the Ku Klux Klan or Louis Farrakhan, they don't have to worry overmuch about what kind of Israel is developing several thousand miles away, about making sure it's the kind of place a refugee would want to call home.

But the growing American dislocation from Israel can't be ascribed solely to complacency. On my own lecture tours in the United States, on the panels and tours I participated in at the GA, in my conversations with visiting groups, in phone contact with family and friends in the United States, there is no mistaking a sense of, forgive me, distaste for Israel. It's a distaste that dates back to the 1982 invasion of Lebanon, where the world saw Israel as a would-be regional Big Brother, clomping in its muddy army boots over the heads of our hapless northern neighbors; distaste that was exacerbated by the Intifada—by the sight of our heavily protected soldiers firing live ammunition at stone-throwing Palestinian kids; distaste that became despair when one of our own people murdered our prime minister and not everybody here denounced the act; distaste that turned to embarrassment when the Jewish state, that purported Light Unto the Nations, fired the shells that killed a hundred Lebanese civilians at Kafr Kana.

Not all of this is fair. The Intifada, for example, was an object lesson in the potential for the electronic media to convey misleading images, a less-than-complete picture. For one thing, stones can and did kill. For another, the TV crews often arrived after the most intense moments of confrontation,

287

missing the opening volleys of Palestinian rock-throwing but catching the Israeli response. At Kafr Kana, to take another case in point, I refuse to believe for a second the U.N. contention that Israel's gunners deliberately targeted the base; I am convinced that the shells were misdirected. But the fact is that few outside observers—and by no means all Diaspora Jews—are prepared to give the benefit of the doubt to a country that is fighting to maintain a generation's occupation of another people or that is bombarding a neighboring state so heavily that hundreds of thousands of civilians are forced to flee their homes.

As if the distaste were not alienating enough, Israel has itself started to compound the problem in recent years, by capitulating increasingly to a coercive brand of Orthodoxy, while repudiating the Reform and Conservative Judaism with which most Diaspora Jews identify. No amount of the spin at which Benjamin Netanyahu was so adept could convince North American Jewry that Israel's ban on Reform and Conservative rabbis performing marriages or conversions was anything other than a slap in the face for their approach to the faith, a heavy hint that, as far as the Israeli establishment is concerned, Reform and Conservative Judaism are, sorry, just not Judaism. If Israeli leaders doubt how deeply that perceived insult has been felt, they need only attend any meeting of any group of non-Orthodox communal leaders anywhere in America—the very people who for decades have marched for Israel, written letters to their local papers about reporters' and columnists' perceived anti-Israel bias, raised money for Israel, joined missions to Israel.

There is a minority in the Diaspora whose frustration with Israel stems from opposite reasons. These are the people who, when I lectured in the United States soon after the Rabin assassination, walked out of my talks screaming abuse at me, phoned up the radio call-in shows I appeared on to harangue me—because I didn't regard Rabin as a traitor and peacemaking with Arafat as disgraceful. Especially at stops in New York, some Alexander from Albany or Phil from Brooklyn would misquote from articles I'd written, produce questionable statistics, invoke half-sentences from the Bible—all to deride the very notion of reconciliation with the Arab world. These people had nothing but praise for any and all of Israel's military adventures. But as for the relative Arab moderates Israel was working with, well, Arafat had been and remained a terrorist, Mubarak a thug, King Hussein an unstable despot.

Typically, these American Jewish critics had nothing to offer by way of alternative solutions—they had no need to look, of course, since they were quite content to have us continue to spill our blood on forever hostile frontiers. And while they had no intention whatsoever of participating in those battles themselves—by putting their bodies where their mouths were and actually moving to Israel—they engaged in a different kind of fighting. The more moderate contented themselves with distributing leaflets or mounting demonstrations lambasting the treacherous cabinet ministers of Jerusalem, but the fanatics, prior to the Rabin killing, went as far as punching one of Rabin's ministers (Shulamit Aloni, hit in the stomach by a local Jewish activist at a 1995 Salute to Israel gathering in New York) and throwing tomatoes at our ambassador to Washington (Itamar Rabinovitch, pelted during a 1993 appearance in a Queens, New York, Orthodox synagogue, of all places).

That these people—ready to shout and hurl tomatoes, but not to come and live here—feel themselves increasingly at odds with Israel is fine by me. Let the divide grow. Israelis who regard Arafat as duplicitous, the bus bombings as a consequence of a misguided peace process, West Bank shootings as an intolerable result of Israel giving guns to Palestinian policemen, feel that they are paying the direct price for government foolishness. No wonder they speak out with such heat. But the Alexanders and the Phils don't care as passionately as they would have you believe. For if they did, they would have relocated to Israel themselves, long ago.

But overall, is it a problem for the two main centers of international Jewry to be going increasingly separate ways? Most active Jews would say that it is, and I agree. After more than fifty years of Israeli statehood, most Jews have made their life choice about our country. The ones who had to, or wanted to, have made their homes here. The others have not. Although not all the would-be homecomers have been gathered from their exile—several thousand are still arriving every month from the former Soviet Union, along with a few hundred from this European country, a few dozen from that South American one, and a handful of generally Orthodox Americans—in general, the lines have been drawn. But that shouldn't mean farewell and goodnight. Israel is the historic heart of Judaism, and the modern state has got that heart pumping again. All Jews, wherever they are, should be able to feel a connection with it, for their sake and for Israel's.

Forty, thirty, even twenty years ago, a Diaspora-Israel get-together like the GA would have had the Israelis trying to convince the Americans to immigrate, arguing that the only valid Jewish life was the Jewish life lived in Israel, that here was the answer to parents' fears of their nice Jewish boys and girls "marrying out." Not any more. Israel's immigration emissaries have long since learned that only an unlikely upsurge in U.S. anti-Semitism will send their Jewish cousins scurrying to the airport, and that energetic proselytizing is a surefire turnoff. So there was little overt immigration-hyping at the Jerusalem GA.

What there was, though, was a great deal of very serious, very earnest debate about how to counter the Diaspora distaste with Israel: how to turn our country, once again, into a place American Jews will want to identify with, to get involved in, to give money to, to visit—the assumption being that a Diaspora Jew who gets enthused by a visit to Israel will come home feeling a deeper connection to his or her faith, and thence to his or her community, Israel thus acting as a catalyst for a richer communal life for Jews in America. The GA was structured as a series of roundtable discussions, panel debates, and tours around the country. On the tours, thousands of North American Jewish activists got to see the projects their communities were most involved in—a Montreal delegation that I met with, for example, visiting immigrant groups and child centers in the Negev to which they have channeled funding over the years. In the discussions and the debates, we and they tried to come up with ways to use their philanthropy to shape an Israel that could be closer to their hearts—by fostering women's groups, for instance, or environmental programs, or Arab-Jewish community projects, or Reform and Conservative kindergartens and schools. As things stand now, these Americans and Canadians are not about to come and live here, to give Israel the million-person-strong injection of Western-educated liberalism, tolerance, pluralism, and democracy that would transform it overnight into a country I, for one, would be much more comfortable living in. So, next best thing, we were examining how to effect change, albeit more incrementally, by using our visitors' financial and other influence. We were exploring how to help their values and priorities flourish over here, to render us less likely to lapse into political violence, less prone to breaking the bones of our enemies—to minimize that feeling of alienation and embarrassment, to strengthen the Diaspora-Israel bond, to heal the rifts.

Not all of this may be possible. But the will is clearly there, and the effort is certainly being made. And thousands of North American Jewish leaders defying the coincident

Persian Gulf flare-up to gather in Jerusalem served to underline how paltry is the effort being made within Israel to heal *our* rifts, to underline the lack of intensive, constructive interaction among *our* disparate groupings. Where are *our* multi-thousand-delegate conferences on religious interaction, *our* leadership forums seeking common ground, *our* across-the-spectrum constructive political debates? The nightly hysterical, spiteful television political-discussion shows, rivals and critics shouting and interrupting each other, are present-day gladiator contests. And the viewers lap them up. But if they are good for the ratings, they are not for the country—nothing productive comes out of them, and they are poisoning the wider culture of debate. Not much in the way of bridge-building, for that matter, comes out of the marginally more civilized proceedings in the Knesset either.

And what a pity that our leaders invest so much effort in scoring points off one another, and so little in scoring points for us all. Because it would not take all that much effort, all that much GA-style hardheaded direct addressing of our problems, to begin solving many of the most debilitating ones. If they could put their egos to one side for just a brief respite and take a sober look at the big picture, they might just realize that, while they've been bickering, their public has reached a consensus on many of our most divisive issues and would rather like them to implement it, please:

We would like to negotiate a permanent settlement with the Palestinians, with a permanent border that brings as many settlers as possible within Israel's sovereign orbit; provide fair compensation for settlers outside that orbit who relocate within sovereign Israel; and honestly acknowledge to those who choose to stay on inside Palestinian territory the risks that they are taking. Most of us would be prepared to give the Palestinians some say in the running of their neighborhoods in East Jerusalem, and the right to declare sovereignty in an area such as Abu Dis, on the edge of the city. Let's face it, as things stand, our "united" capital has long been redivided. The taxi drivers in the Jewish West won't take you to the Arab East. The wide new Road 1 cuts across the town like a knife, severing the ultra-Orthodox yeshivas that mark the end of Jewish West Jerusalem from the would-be Palestinian day laborers milling hopefully, just across the street, at the start of Arab East Jerusalem. Nobody shops in the other side's part of town. And the watermelon stands outside Damascus Gate where, pre-Intifada, we would munch juicy fruit in companionable Jewish-Arab harmony while watching appalling Kung Fu action movies on high-mounted TV screens, are a fond, fading memory.

We want to work toward normalizing relations with Syria, so that we can safely reach a compromise over the Golan Heights and withdraw our troops to the international border with Lebanon. (I'd love to go sightseeing in Damascus. As things stand, I can't even get anyone to dare write for the *Jerusalem Report* from there.)

We want to reform our electoral system properly, to give us politicians elected by geographical constituency, rather than proportional representation, so that they are genuinely accountable to their voters.

The non-ultra-Orthodox among us want to impose binding budgetary guidelines that ensure ultra-Orthodox schoolchildren get the identical per-capita allocation as the rest of Israel's young minds—no less and no more.

We need to legislate, as the Supreme Court has asked of the Knesset, some kind of community service for the thirty thousand ultra-Orthodox men currently avoiding conscription, service that leaves them plenty of time to study but alleviates the embittering grievance among army recruits who feel they are shouldering an unfairly heavy burden.

We also want to channel government funding to Israeli

Arab communities, and to outlying development towns populated chiefly by new immigrants and by Sephardim, to help alleviate those groups' grievances, too, and foster a greater spirit
of equal opportunity for all Israel's citizens. And by so doing
we want to prove to people, many of whom grew up in non-
democratic Arab nations, that democracy can work for them,
curb the rise of the political cynics who prey on them, and foster a pride in the state's institutions and ethos. To fund that
extra spending, we must impose higher taxes on the country's
most extravagant earners.

These are solutions the great majority of the Israeli public
would willingly endorse. But the consensus is time-limited. So
now I look to Ehud Barak—once our most decorated soldier,
now our overburdened prime minister, a man the generals of
his generation praise as their most talented colleague—to
implement them, and fast. I look to him to prove that the
Netanyahu years were a blip, best quickly forgotten, a bizarre
deviation from the path to peace. I expect him to prove that
the October 1998 Wye peace deal and his own subsequent
election victory were genuine turning points, the moments
when the moderates on the Israeli right effectively accepted
the land-for-peace strategy, the moments at which the entire
Greater Land of Israel ideology was shattered for all of Israel
save the settlers, and Rabin's vision, previously the preserve of
the left and the moderate center, became Israel's vision. I
expect Barak to steer us wisely to a Golan-for-peace treaty
with Syria. And I expect him to move Israel forward to a permanent agreement with the Palestinians, one we and they are
genuinely prepared to live with, one that would open the rest
of the region to us. It would be so futile for both our peoples
to have to endure another round of bloodshed to remind ourselves that our destiny is to share this land; that no matter how
many Palestinians there were here in 1948, or whether they
were Palestinians at all, there are millions of them here now,

and they are not about to go anywhere else. Painful though it may be, the Jews of modern Israel must accept that they are not going to be able to retain all of that land that God promised Abraham.

I look to Barak to stop the trend to ultra-Orthodox certainties becoming a flood, fueled by government funding extracted by disproportionately powerful rabbi-politicians, with the Israeli work force wilting under the strain of financing the yeshiva world. The ultra-Orthodox intransigence on religious and personal freedoms is leading us to internal disaster, to deepening social frictions and hatreds. Had they chosen to, the ultra-Orthodox leadership of Jerusalem could have successfully challenged for the mayoralty in 1998. Within a few years, and this is no extravagant nightmare, we could have ultra-Orthodox mayors throughout the country, an increasingly powerful ultra-Orthodox halachic legal system usurping the state's court network, and legislation leading us back to the Dark Ages. We non-Orthodox Israelis who today moan loudly when the summertime clocks are adjusted to suit dawn-linked Orthodox prayer schedules will moan louder still tomorrow when Jerusalem is declared a no-car zone on the Sabbath and Jewish holidays, when restaurants close down nationwide on the day of rest, and the airport and the radio and television fall silent. And we will want to do more than just moan the day after tomorrow, when the pressure builds for legislation setting public dress codes and outlawing homosexuality and abortion. Barak has to put a halt to all of that, by moving toward a formal separation of synagogue and state, and by addressing the very real frustrations that lead poor, hopeless Israelis toward blind faith.

It's so convenient to assure ourselves that we've all learned the lessons of the Rabin assassination, that another political murder in Israel is unthinkable; that, to quote complacent leaders from left and right, our democracy will prevail; that no Jew now could seriously attempt to blow up the Temple Mount mosques and replace them with a Third Jewish Temple, filled with the ritual objects being reconstructed by a right-wing Old City yeshiva; that because mainstream Israel is fundamentally decent, the extremists will wither away; that Israel isn't heading toward theocracy, we're just amending the "status quo"; that religious and personal freedoms will be guaranteed; that Russian and Ethiopian immigrants have settled in just fine; that the education system is okay; that there is no more Ashkenazi-Sephardi discrimination; that three murders a week isn't so terrible, that five hundred deaths a year on the roads is tolerable; that if our founding fathers could see us half a century on, they would marvel at how much we've achieved. A job well done—as a Tel Aviv police chief said to a colleague from the Shin Bet security service after the peace rally on the night of November 4, 1995, as Yitzhak Rabin headed down the steps to his car.

It's convenient, but it's an illusion. Israel needs to be healed. And if Barak, who started out as prime minister with a visit to the scene of his mentor's assassination *and* that prayer call at the Western Wall, invoking Rabin *and* Rashi, pledging to unify, to explain his policies, to woo the doubters, to be "the prime minister of all the people"—even those who hadn't voted for him—if he can't put us back together, I doubt that anybody can.

That Lisa and I have heart-wrenching discussions about our future here, as opposed to, say, Dallas or Westchester County, New York, is a luxury. In addition to our Israeli passports, I still have my English passport, Lisa her American one, and the kids the whole set. For us, America, Britain, Canada, or Australia is just a flight away, and not much hassle at immigration. My bona fide, genuine, born-here countryfolk, by contrast, are stuck. For them, Israel has to work.

Truth is, though, that for all my ambivalence and misgivings, I don't want to leave. I don't want to live in Dallas, Lisa's hometown, work on the *Dallas Morning News*, write pieces about carjacking and Seventh-Day Adventists, the Dallas Cowboys, and Houston's James A. Baker III Institute for Public Policy. I know that in America you really can feel part of a vibrant Jewish community and lead an openly enthusiastic Jewish life (unlike in England, where a well-known Orthodox rabbi noted accurately not long ago that "Jews feel like guests in their own country . . . trying to be more British than the British"). I know that in America you can rise high without having to play down your roots, and even a cabinet minister can talk proudly about his religion (as Agriculture Secretary Dan Glickman did when he came out of Clinton's Lewinsky apology meeting and cited the Jewish Day of Atonement principles of forgiveness). But the United States just does not pull me the way Israel does—not like infuriating, traffic-clogged, increasingly ultra-Orthodox Jerusalem. Here, I care about what's happening with a passion that simply doesn't apply anywhere else. So what if they give half of Texas back to Mexico in an exceptionally badly negotiated border remarcation accord. Who would notice? But here, well, my history and my soul are here. I scream at this country. It exasperates me. It is deep under my skin. I have invested so much of myself in it. And my heart still lifts when I stand on the pedestrian bridge leading to Jerusalem's Cinemathèque at night and gaze up to the Old City's sixteenth-century walls, bathed in soft golden illumination. I might forever be a slightly displaced former Brit in a slightly foreign land, but this is as close to home as it gets. I don't want to get off the roller coaster.

Lisa isn't quite so sure about all this. She has to drive more than I do. It is she who waits on line, second-hand-smoking, at the driver's-license renewal offices; she who gives the kids the what-to-do-if-a-bomb-goes-off briefings; she who spends more time in Josh's underfunded school; she who deals with the rudeness of everyday bureaucracy. The minor irritants never seriously got to her before the assassination. They were part of the crazy life here, and it was definitely worth living. And even more major traumas like the Gulf War didn't have her questioning whether this was the right country for us. Of course, we didn't have kids back then. Things got more difficult when the suicide attacks started, and Josh was asking her why they were happening. And now, the pros don't so easily outweigh the cons. Barak's victory notwithstanding, and, especially given the vertiginous rise of Shas, she is not entirely optimistic about where this country is heading. She wonders how any Israeli mother could possibly send her child to the kindergarten that Geula Amir, the assassin's mother, has happily continued running, with a healthy complement of kids, despite the grim evidence of the consequences of an Amir upbringing. Lisa, especially because of her father's experiences, used to believe that Israel was the only place for a Jew, the only place to raise her family. Part of that may have been idealized. But after Rabin's death, she feels that this is not the same country she came to, and with the boys getting older day by day, she is just not certain anymore that it's worth the most dreadful, unthinkable, unwriteable potential sacrifice.

Such fears notwithstanding, here we are. But we are wary, watching how Barak fares, and there is a certain tension between us because we do feel slightly differently, that tension rising and falling with our national fortunes. Two immigrant parents of three Israelis who already laugh at our appalling accents and, though we speak English to them at home, have begun speaking Hebrew to one another, and dressing up not as Superman and Hercules but *Soopehrrmun* and *Erkoolehz*. Maybe, hopefully, the pessimism will prove misplaced. Or maybe, if we don't move out of Jerusalem, we will get to see the tanks drive past—not utterly out of the question, given our proximity to the Bethlehem border crossing into Arafat territory. I always used to wonder, when I'd see the footage of snipers targeting civilians in Bosnia or wherever, when the camera would pan across the bullet-pocked apartment blocks, why the locals, or those who could afford to, hadn't moved out, fled the danger zone, gone to live somewhere else, anywhere else. Perhaps I'm beginning to understand.

Afterword

We drove out to Ofra a few weeks ago—Lisa's parents, with Natan, in his car; we, in our car, following right behind on the Ramallah bypass road. When we got there, the kids played computer basketball, read together, ate together. I borrowed a bike and cycled the few hundred meters to Ofra's newest neighborhood, another series of red-roofed homes—some already lived in—being built, naturally, by Palestinians. With Barak in power, peace talks intensifying, Palestinian prisoners being released, and "safe passage" corridors opening for Palestinians to travel across Israel to and from Gaza and the West Bank, there's concern at Ofra: initially, that the army will relinquish control to Arafat of the territory all around the settlement; ultimately, that Ofra's own future could be called into question—even though Barak has specified that Ofra will remain forever Israeli. Natan, who pointed out his biblical mountain to me, the army antennas standing tall at its summit, says he takes each day as it comes.

It's still early, but Barak does seem to have learned the most critical lesson about governing Israel in this generation: you can't do it with the support of only half the people. Rabin never publicly reached out to those on the right who objected to the West Bank–land-for-peace equation, and paid with his life. Netanyahu alienated the moderate sector of the electorate. Barak, though trying to revive Rabin's policies, is maintaining a very public dialogue with the settlers, and shows a far deeper understanding of the religious attachment to the West Bank than Rabin ever did. There are extremists, of course, who will never be mollified. The extremist rabbis, who have hardly played a central role in the defense of our historic land, are again issuing religious edicts forbidding any compromise over it—precisely the kind of edicts that Yigal Amir tried murderously to enforce. But if, as Natan says, it would have made a real difference had Rabin taken the settlers into his confidence, set out to them his reasons for compromise rather than deriding them, then maybe Barak is making that difference now.

Our fragile spirit of national unity, of course, is now being tested on another front: the northern border. For the first time ever, the leaders of Israel and Syria are assuring their peoples that the erstwhile enemy now appears to be serious about wanting peace. But having invested so deeply in the Golan over more than three decades, Israelis will find giving it up a dreadful wrench. Negotiating a fair, safe accord, and then persuading a majority of my countryfolk that the Golan is a price worth paying for peace—to a ruthless, ailing, obdurate dictator, heading a regime that could so easily turn hostile again—will be arguably the hardest battle Barak has yet had to fight. He needs a partnership with the opposition to ensure that the internal struggle does not turn violent, and a partnership with Assad and Arafat to prevent Iran from blowing up this final phase of Israeli-Arab reconciliation. Methodical and clear-headed, but curiously charmless, Barak has to convince a skeptical public that peace with Syria represents not the further shrinking of our tiny country, but the expansion of our frontiers: the longed-for opening of the gateway to Saudi Arabia and the Gulf principalities, Yemen, Algeria, Indonesia. Normality. Not a little Israel, but a big Middle East.

Time is precious. Barak and his multiparty coalition are always vulnerable to scandal and internal disputes. Who knows when Assad's health could bring him down. Arafat looks ever more frail. Mubarak is dodging assassins. Hassan of Morocco has followed Hussein of Jordan to the grave. But Hamas's leader, Sheikh Yassin, paraplegic, half-blind, and half-deaf, is still well enough to offer us charming assurances that "there is no cease-fire" and that "an Israeli bus could blow up tomorrow morning." As ever, we teeter on the brink of the unpredictable.

Netanyahu, having resigned as Likud party leader and given up his seat in Parliament, has reappeared in public life as a motivational speaker: he made his public bow at a mass seminar in Tampa, Florida, setting out his secrets of leadership excellence as part of an all-star cast including that other preeminent statesman and motivator, former president Gerald Ford. In his opening remarks, with a nice touch of self-deprecation, Netanyahu thanked Israel's voters for enabling him to pursue this new diversion. Our pleasure. Long may he flourish.

My mother and stepfather have moved into their new house, and it is magnificent—a three-story, golden-stone triumph of their optimism over my predictions of disaster.

The *Jerusalem Report* is being bought out by the owners of the *Jerusalem Post*. We're leaving our airy, elegant offices downtown, and moving into the *Post*'s strictly functional premises near the old bus station at the entrance to the city.

Josh, Adam, and Kayla are growing alarmingly fast. Josh is in second grade now, reading and writing Hebrew with increasing proficiency, just starting to learn English. Adam, who goes to first grade next year, speaks English like an Israeli, rolling his *r*'s and using "zis" for "this." Kayla, barely three, somehow knows to burble in English when she's with her grandparents, and in Hebrew in nursery school. At nighttime, just now, we're reading *Goodnight Moon* and Meir Shalev's *Aba Oseh Bushot* (Daddy Always Embarrasses Me) about a little boy and his demonstratively affectionate dad. They drift off to sleep to Hebrew songs about a group of men all improbably named "Mr. Chocolate," strolling back and forth across town to visit one another, or to the avuncular tones of Roald Dahl describing the extraordinary resourcefulness of Fantastic Mr. Fox.

Life is good. Fragile, but good. We, too, take each day as it comes.

—D.H., December 1999

Acknowledgments

I've lived in Israel for almost two decades, close to half my life. This book—which started out as a diary of my daily intensifying resentment at the havoc being wrought here by Benjamin Netanyahu—is the outgrowth of that half a lifetime, most of which I've shared with Lisa, my indescribably wonderful wife. It was she who encouraged and prodded me at critical moments in its writing, helped me shape the content, and took the strain as I rather neglected Josh, Adam, and Kayla to get it done. I love, and apologize to, them all. Several members of my wider family also bared parts of their souls for this project. I think we all had our eyes opened a little.

I've only ever had two real jobs in Israel—at the *Jerusalem Post* and at the *Jerusalem Report*. At the *Post*, N. David Gross turned me into a journalist, spotting something in me that I'd never known was there. In 1990, when an idyllic era ended there, Hirsh Goodman provided another at the *Report*. Many of the anecdotes here grew out of assignments for the *Report*, a magazine for which I take the deepest pride in working, and whose staff I am honored to count as my friends. Among the many of them who helped me with this book, I particularly want to thank Sharon Ashley, who offered innumerable insights and ideas, almost all of which found their way into the final text.

Thanks especially, too, to Jonathan Segal at Knopf, for having faith in this book, and for forcing me to break through my British reticence. And to Melvin Rosenthal, for fixing my more extravagantly nongrammatical constructions.

Thanks to Deborah Harris and Beth Elon.

And thanks, finally, to Skitz, who was late to meet me at Marble Arch, and so, unwittingly, set this whole enterprise moving. . . .

Index

Index

Index

Index

Index

Qatar, 64

Ra'anana, protest marches in, 151–2
rabbis, 25, 156, 192, 288; Netanyahu and, 156–7; Orthodox, 12, 244–5, 252–4, 256, 258, 266, 283, 297; Rabin and, 129, 132, 134–6; Reform, 251, 258, 288; ultra-Orthodox, 69, 242, 246, 253–4, 265, 273, 283–5; and West Bank withdrawal, 136
Rabin, Dalia, 139
Rabin, Leah, 122, 129, 131–2, 137, 140–2, 151, 176
Rabin, Yitzhak, 9–12, 55, 119–43, 210–12, 215–16; Arafat and, 19, 123, 126–8, 141–2, 184–5; assassination, 9, 11–12, 15, 17–20, 46, 63, 78, 103–4, 121–6, 129–31, 133–43, 149, 151, 159, 165, 168, 176, 184, 211, 249, 256, 283, 288–9, 295–6, 298, 300–1; and bombings, 128, 130, 141–2, 148; Diaspora Jews and, 288–9; election campaigns, 125–9, 131, 151–2, 216, 235–6, 245, 248–9; funeral, 131–3, 226; and Hamas, 112, 122, 126–7, 130; IDF and, 94–5, 100, 103–4, 122; integrity, 127–8, 130; memorial rally for, 151; military background, 10, 127–8, 131, 141; Netanyahu and, 127–9, 141, 148, 151–3, 159; Orthodox Jews and, 135–6, 245, 248–9; and peace process, 9, 11, 18–19, 115, 119–20, 123–31, 141–2, 182, 184–5, 191–2, 210–11, 216, 225–6, 235–7, 283, 289, 294, 300–1; public opinion on, 18–19, 121, 123, 128–9, 134, 142; and Temple Mount tunnel, 153–4; ultra-Orthodox and, 248–9, 265, 283; West Bank and, 1, 11, 19, 123–4, 127, 133
Rabin, Yuval, 139–41, 143
Rabinovitch, Itamar, 289
Rafah refugee camp, 55, 187–8
Ramallah, 40, 161, 203–4, 259, 300
Ramat Gan, 38, 141
Ras Burka, 209, 225–6
Reform Judaism, Reform Jews, 156, 198, 244, 249–52, 256–8, 266, 285, 291; marginalized, 250–2, 258, 288
Remembrance Day, 41–2, 247

Sadat, Anwar, 220, 226, 236–7
Saddam Hussein, 101, 187, 194–5;

Arafat and, 178; Scud attacks and, 85, 89; weakening of, 127
Samaria, 179, 199–200
Saving Private Ryan (film), 87–8
Schach, Eliezer, 283–4
Scud attacks, 85, 88–90, 99, 101, 187, 191
security, security concerns, 52, 86–7; politics of, 55–9, 159
Sephardim, 14–16, 294; Ashkenazim vs., 13, 28, 296; politics and, 16, 157, 253–4
Shamir, Yitzhak, 20, 125–7, 131, 156, 159
Sharansky, Natan, 175
Sharon, Ariel, 63, 117
Shas party, 15–16, 253–4, 272, 298
Shin Bet, 62, 114, 135, 145–6, 177, 296; bombings and, 166–9; decline of, 103–4; Netanyahu and, 147
Shinlung tribespeople, 74–5
"Shlav Bet," 105–10
Sidon, Ephraim, 174–5
Sinai, 10–11, 94, 210, 225–6, 237
Siren's Song, The (film), 88
Six-Day War, 10–11, 94, 127, 172, 234; territory captured in, 11, 21, 41
Solomon, Operation, 75–6
South Lebanon Army (SLA), 239
Soviet Union: anti-Semitism in, 22; demise of, 127; immigration from, 7, 15, 20, 22, 24, 27, 38, 48, 73, 105, 138, 175, 245, 247, 290, 296
Stern Group, 159
Suissa, Eli, 248
Supreme Court, Israeli, 47, 54, 132; challenges to authority of, 15–16, 254, 293; on Hamas deportations, 113; Hebron and, 164; Netanyahu and, 153
Syria, 46, 55, 99, 116, 158, 181, 214, 234; IDF and, 102–4, 110; Jews in, 237; and peace process, 8–9, 13, 34, 95, 118, 126, 131, 136, 147, 208, 210–11, 220, 235–40, 293–4, 301; in Yom Kippur War, 100

Tali Bayit V'Gan, 39–40, 53
Tea Packs (pop group), 3, 224
Tel Aviv, 13, 38–9, 44, 50, 57, 80, 125, 172, 180, 187, 201, 264–9, 296; bombings in, 59, 92–3, 141–2;

310